Are Our Descendants Doomed?

ARE OUR DESCENDANTS DOOMED?

Technological Change and
Population Growth

Edited by *Harrison Brown*
and *Edward Hutchings, Jr.*

NEW YORK | THE VIKING PRESS BRESCIA COLLEGE
LIBRARY
39182

Copyright © 1970, 1972 by California Institute of Technology
All rights reserved
First published in 1972 in a hardbound and
a paperbound edition by The Viking Press, Inc.
625 Madison Avenue, New York, N.Y. 10022
Published simultaneously in Canada by
The Macmillan Company of Canada Limited
SBN 670–13257–8 (hardbound)
    670–00341–7 (paperbound)
Library of Congress catalog card number: 74–161059
Printed in U.S.A. by The Colonial Press Inc.

BRESCIA COLLEGE
LIBRARY

Contents

Are Our Descendants Doomed?

Introduction:
The Growth and Distribution of
Human Population

H A R R I S O N   B R O W N

Harrison Brown is Professor of Geochemistry and of Science and Government at the California Institute of Technology.

Man emerged in the world of animals, and for the greater part of his existence he lived much as did the other animals about him. He preyed and was preyed upon. He ate whatever edible vegetation he could gather and whatever fish and game he could catch. Life was rugged, and life expectancy at birth was apparently quite short.

It is likely that even the earliest manlike creatures used tools, however crude, in their efforts to gather food and protect themselves. Gradually, technologies emerged that permitted human populations to expand. Clothing, fire, and crude habitations extended the range of climates that could be inhabited. Man learned how to make increasingly sophisticated tools and weapons, at first of wood and bone, then of stone, and eventually of metal. As the effectiveness of the tools and weapons increased, human populations increased and spread over the land areas of the world.

No matter how effective the tools, however, there is a limit to the number of persons who can inhabit a given area of land within the framework of a food-gathering culture. In natural surroundings, the maximum density of human population is basically determined by the populations of edible plants and animals. Overkill can drive species to extinction, and there is some evidence that the extinction of some animal species dur-

3

ing Paleolithic and Neolithic times resulted directly from human actions.

If humans had continued indefinitely to live as food-gatherers, they would have spread over the earth, and their number would have leveled off at about 10 million, no matter how effective their tools. This estimated maximum level of population is indicated by observations of food-gathering cultures that either still exist or that have existed until recently.

Life within a food-gathering culture can take many forms, but a number of constraints have resulted in the evolution of certain common characteristics. In the first place, men are basically gregarious, as are other primates, and prefer to live in close association with their fellow human beings—at least up to a point. The maximum number of persons who can live close together is strictly determined by the level of technology.

A group of food-gatherers living together in a nomad camp gather edible vegetation such as fruits, nuts, berries, and roots, and they hunt animals. The maximum number of persons who can live in the camp is determined by how effectively these two activities are carried out. For plants the radius of operations is limited by the desire of the plant-gatherer to return home by nightfall and by the density of edible plants. For game the radius of operations is limited by the distance a hunting party can travel, hunt, kill, and return to camp with the carcasses unspoiled. These constraints suggest that food-gathering camps have seldom supported more than one hundred to two hundred persons, who gather their food from an area of about 2000 square kilometers. Once the saturation level of population is reached, it must remain fairly constant over time. In man's history, numerous cultural patterns appear to have emerged that have given rise to the required degree of population stability. In some cases the natural death rate increased; in others the death rate was increased artificially by waging war or by the use of practices such as infanticide; and in still others cultural practices evolved that resulted in lowered birth rates. Certain sex taboos and rituals were practiced, for example, that appear to have affected fecundity.

For the greater part of man's existence as a species he has not been a very populous animal. Once the human population had spread over the earth it appears to have stabilized at a level somewhere between five and ten million persons, divided among perhaps fifty thousand widely scattered family or tribal units. But around ten thousand years ago a new technology began to appear that was to have a profound effect upon both the size and distribution of the human population. Man learned to protect and nurture those plants and animals that were useful to him and to destroy those that were less useful. The new techniques of agriculture and animal domestication spread most rapidly in those areas that could be cultivated readily, such as the great river valleys, which were endowed with ample water and naturally recurrent fertilization.

With a well-developed agricultural technology, several hundred times as much food can be produced from a fertile area of land than was collected by the food-gatherers. The new technology appears to have spread rapidly, and human population grew. There is good evidence that village-farming communities were functioning in the Middle East by about 6000 B.C.

Agricultural technology places its own restrictions upon ways of life. Wandering tribes began to decrease in number and were replaced by stationary farming settlements. The new technology and its limitations placed an upper limit on the size of a village. The distance from an individual's home to the soil that he tilled could not be excessive. With walking as the primary means of transport, the agricultural villages were limited to two or three hundred persons—not much larger than the nomadic camps they replaced. But the villages, of course, were much more closely spaced, often being separated from each other by only 2 or 3 kilometers. By contrast, camps of food-gatherers must have been separated from each other, on the average, by distances of at last 50 kilometers.

Another important effect of agricultural technology upon human culture and population derived from the fact that a man working in the fields could grow somewhat more food than was needed to feed himself and his family. This surplus was not large, amounting to something like 10 per cent, but it meant that 10 per cent of the people were able to engage in activities other than farming. Small family industries appeared, as did a variety of inventions and new technologies.

The small proportion of the population not engaged in farming did not have to live in the small villages, and they tended to congregate in considerably larger units. Gradually cities emerged, the maximum sizes of which were determined by the area of agricultural land that was accessible for food. This depended upon geography and the state of transportation technology. When men and beasts of burden were the only means of transporting agricultural and other raw materials to and from a center of population, a town of several thousand persons might be supported. By contrast, the use of water transport might permit the development of a city of a million or more inhabitants. It is partly for this reason that almost all of the early cities emerged in the great river valleys of the Tigris and the Euphrates, the Nile, and the Yellow River.

The emergence of cities resulted in the evolution of the great ancient urban civilizations, each of which developed its own characteristic culture, which was determined in part by geography and in part by the nature and the level of the local technology. By 2500 B.C. the Sumerians had developed a general system of irrigation in the Tigris-Euphrates valleys, and the Egyptians had developed a variety of elaborate technologies. Writing became well established, and various fields of learning such as medicine, astronomy, and mathematics were developed. However, one of the more significant developments for the future of human culture was the manufacture of tools made of metals, notably copper and bronze.

Copper is not an abundant element, but it is relatively easy to produce from its ores. The rarity of high-grade ore and the consequent high price of the metal prevented copper tools from being used on any major scale by farmers, but it was highly prized by the wealthier city dwellers who manufactured a variety of copper artifacts ranging from weapons to art objects. As local ore deposits were depleted, trade in copper became important, and the ancient traders ranged far in search of the metal, carrying the new techniques with them as they moved. As the technologies spread, populations spread also.

Iron is considerably more abundant than copper, but it is a much more difficult metal to obtain from its ores. The temperature required for reduction is quite high, and the technology of building furnaces that can achieve such temperatures is difficult. Satisfactory furnaces first appeared about 1100 B.C. in the Middle East, and from then on the use of metals became truly widespread. The availability of relatively inexpensive iron tools greatly accelerated the rate of spread of human population as huge forested areas were transformed into agricultural land.

The technology of the ancient world reached its peak at the height of the Roman Empire. So well designed were the engineering achievements of the Romans that many are still in use. Roman engineers went about as far as they could go without the help of an engine, such as the steam engine, that could concentrate large quantities of energy. In those days power was concentrated by mobilizing gangs of men and animals, and the Romans learned how to do this with great effectiveness. They even harnessed water and wind power on a modest scale, but throughout the years of imperial rise and decline, muscle remained the dominant prime mover.

Roman technology made possible the evolution of densely populated urban centers which were far larger than any that had existed previously. The city of Rome drew upon vast areas of the then-known world for its food and raw materials. New techniques of organization, coupled with those of engineering, permitted over a million persons to live together under crowded conditions and yet to function fairly effectively as a social organism. Nevertheless, life for the average inhabitant of the capital of the Empire appears to have been extremely harsh. Life expectancy at birth for city dwellers probably did not greatly exceed twenty years.

With the decline of Rome much of the technological and organizational knowledge which had made the Empire possible was either forgotten or rendered ineffectual. The changes had influenced the distribution of population markedly, but their effect upon the total level of population of human beings in the then-known world does not appear to have been substantial.

Following the Renaissance, new technologies, coupled with the old ones, permitted Europeans to circumnavigate the globe and to colonize newly discovered continents. They and their technology were transplanted to virtually all parts of the world that could be reached by sea. Varieties of wealth, including gold, exotic foodstuffs, novel forms of plant and animal life, and a diversity of minerals were returned to Europe from overseas.

Of all of the new imports, the potato had perhaps the most profound long-range effect. The plant was first brought to Spain and Portugal from South America, and because of its remarkable efficiency in converting solar energy into food calories, it was soon cultivated in Italy. Then its use spread northward to the rest of Europe, including Scandinavia. The evidence suggests that the spread of the potato was a major contributing factor to the rapid increase of population in Europe during the sixteenth and seventeenth centuries.

If new technological developments had not occurred after 1700, peasant-village culture would probably still have spread to all inhabitable parts of the earth. Eventually the population would probably have leveled off at about 5 billion persons, with 500 million in cities and towns. Long before the population had reached anything like that level, however, the emergence of new technologies dramatically changed the course of both population growth and movement.

In the late seventeenth and early eighteenth centuries, a series of technological innovations in England triggered the development of a practical steam engine. First, the technology was developed for treating coal so that it would be suitable for reducing iron ore to metal, thereby freeing the iron industry from its dependence on wood for charcoal and increasing considerably the general availability of metallic iron. The resulting increased demand for coal required that coal mining take place at considerable depth, and this created the need for effective pumps for the removal of ground water from the mines. The steam engine was first developed and applied as a source of power for the pumps.

The steam engine gave man for the first time a means of concentrating enormous quantities of inanimate mechanical energy, and it was quickly applied to a variety of tasks. By 1785 the new device was being used to drive spinning machines and power looms, and by 1813 some 2400 power looms were in operation in England. Soon the steam engine was applied to land and water transportation, to metalworking machines, and later to the generation of electricity. A process which we now call "feedback" came into full operation, and invention followed invention with accelerating speed.

The impact of the Industrial Revolution upon demographic history was enormous. Improvements in agriculture, transportation, and public health resulted in significant decreases in death rates. With birth rates little changed, the population of England increased rapidly.

During the nineteenth century in England and the greater part of Western Europe, the large variations in mortality that had been so characteristic of preindustrial society were virtually eliminated. In part this change was brought about by improved transportation and the introduction of scientific agriculture. Seed drills, better fertilization, crop rotation, introduction of roots and clovers, and better breeds of livestock—all contributed to dampening the fluctuations of crop yields and through them to dampening the fluctuations in mortality rates.

Another major contributing factor to the elimination of large variations in mortality, as well as to the generally decreasing level of mortality, appears to have been the over-all improvement in environment. An increasing proportion of the population was able to stay dry, warm, and clean; this change alone undoubtedly decreased the morbidity due to a number of infectious diseases. Improvements in health during this period were closely related to increases in wealth.

In addition to the elimination of major mortality fluctuations, the combination of improved food supply and environment resulted in a lessening of age-specific death rates, primarily among younger people (with the exception of infants). In all of the countries where the Industrial Revolution took root, life expectancy at birth increased—slowly at first, but with increasing speed during the last half of the nineteenth century. In these countries during the period 1850–1900, female life expectancy at birth rose from forty-three years to fifty-two.

Techniques of birth limitation were known long before the Industrial Revolution, but the conditions were seldom present that caused these methods to be practiced on any really wide scale. As industrialization spread, many elements in the changed environment lessened the desirability of large families. At first the fertility rates seem to have moved upward, but after about 1870 fertility decreased; at first slowly and then more rapidly. The number of live births per thousand women aged 15 to 44 in England and Wales fell from 154 per year in the decade 1871–80 to 109 in 1901–10 to 61 in 1931–40.

Advances in contraception technology also contributed to the rapid decline in birth rate. Development of the technology of rubber made possible the low-cost, mass production of reliable condoms and removable diaphragms. Advances in pharmaceuticals yielded a variety of solutions, jellies, and creams with the power of killing sperm or of decreasing sperm mobility.

When these changes in mortality, fertility, and population growth rates were taking place, other technological developments were bringing about the greatest mass migration of human beings in history. Scientific methods of agriculture and the development of labor-saving farm machines resulted in substantial increases in agricultural production per man-hour. As a result of these changes, the number of agricultural workers in the United States reached a maximum of about 11.5 million in the decade 1910–20, and the number has been declining ever since. By 1968 there were only 3.4 million.

Each year workers and their families moved by the hundreds of thousands from the country to the rapidly growing cities to find jobs in the new industries. In the thirty-year period 1910–40 when the total population of the United States increased by

43 per cent, the urban population increased by 77 per cent. By 1920 more people were living in towns and cities than in the countryside.

Since World War II, developments within the highly industrialized countries (including the U.S.S.R. and Japan, which began to industrialize at a relatively late date) suggest the emergence of a group of common situations and common critical problems. It is clear that we are rapidly approaching the time when virtually all persons will live in cities. It is also clear that the growing problems of most cities—having emerged as they did within the framework of an earlier technology—might be insoluble within the framework of the dislocations that have been brought about by our present technology.

In time scientific knowledge gave rise to relatively inexpensive means of controlling many epidemic and endemic diseases on a large scale, and many aspects of this knowledge spread to the poorer countries of Asia, Latin America, and Africa. Other elements of technological civilization, such as railroads and highways, were transplanted to these areas and also contributed to lowering average death rates. By making it possible to ship food from areas where agricultural production was normal to areas which were hit by crop failure, famine was virtually eliminated from the world scene.

During the nineteenth and early twentieth centuries, technology was transplanted to the poorer countries in a one-sided manner, which resulted in tremendous dislocations. Lifesaving technology reduced death rates, and with birth rates unchanged, populations increased rapidly. At the same time modern agricultural and industrial technologies were introduced to these areas much more slowly, with the result that the lot of the average inhabitant became increasingly miserable.

Today this situation is changing, but very slowly. Agricultural and industrial production are increasing in most of the poorer countries more rapidly than the population is growing, but very gradually. With each passing year the lot of the average individual is improving, but not so quickly that he notices it.

By contrast, in the richer countries technological change and agricultural and industrial production are increasing at rates that are much greater than the rates of population growth. As a result the average individual consumes noticeably more with each successive year. The rich are rapidly getting richer, while the poor are slowly getting less poor. Human society seems to be "fissioning" into two main groups, and the economic gap between the groups is widening rapidly.

It is difficult to foresee just where these developments are likely to lead mankind. Is the greater part of humanity, which is poor, likely to accept its lot? Or will it resort to rebellion on an unprecedented scale, with such violence that the earth will be thrown into upheaval? Will the poor drag the rich down with them? Or will the rich conclude that the status quo is basically unstable and make a substantial effort to secure total world development?

Dismal as the prospects for the poor countries may appear, the prospects for the rich countries are by no means bright. They must consume vast quantities of raw materials and energy of decreasing availability in order to produce the goods that people want, and in the process their factories excrete equally vast quantities of waste products into rivers, lakes, oceans, and the atmosphere. Technological man is changing his environment with unprecedented speed, and the ultimate effect of those changes can be only dimly perceived. As wastes are poured out, as cities become more congested, as wilderness is replaced by asphalt and concrete, and as man increasingly divorces himself from the world of nature from which he emerged, he enters an uncharted universe that offers few guidelines. Confronted on the one hand by the rebellion of poor countries which also want to be rich and on the other by a combination of the world's diminishing resources and deteriorating environment, technological man might well be a transitory phenomenon on the earth.

1

The Changing Balance
of Births and Deaths

KINGSLEY DAVIS

Kingsley Davis is Director of International Population and Urban Research, Ford Professor of Sociology and Comparative Studies, and Lecturer in the Department of Demography at the University of California, Berkeley.

Since world population growth is simply the balance between births and deaths, they are the central topics of population study. In treating them I shall first describe the crucial turning points in the entire history of human population growth. This will put the latest turning point—our main object of study—in proper perspective.

As Table I shows, a major shift occurred sometime around 8000 B.C. Up to then *Homo sapiens* had multiplied very slowly —about one-tenth of I per cent per century (assuming that the species had about 50,000 members some 400,000 years ago). The next jump in the rate did not come until around A.D. 1750. From 1750 to the present the average rate of growth has been approximately eighteen times that of 8000 B.C. to 1750.

Although subject to a wide margin of error and somewhat exaggerated by the use of long-run averages, the two changes in rate are so pronounced that they are unlikely to be due solely

Research for this paper was supported partly by Ford Foundation funds, made available to International Population and Urban Research through the Institute of International Studies, and partly by a training grant from the National Institute of General Medical Sciences to the Department of Demography, University of California, Berkeley (5 To1 GM01240).

Table 1. Population history of the human species

	Estimated population (*thousands*)	Average increase per century in prior period (*per cent*)
400,000 B.C.	50	
8000 B.C.	5,000	0.1
A.D. 1	300,000	5.3
A.D. 1750	791,000	5.7
A.D. 1970	3,620,000	99.8

Sources: The first figure is speculative. The next three estimates are from Durand (1). The last estimate is made by the present author on the basis of trends up to 1967 and later; it is subject to revision as returns from censuses taken in or near 1970 come in. The rate is $(1 - e^r)$.

to error. They suggest that the two big events in the expansion of the human population were the Neolithic revolution, which gradually added agriculture and animal husbandry to the quest for food, and the Industrial Revolution, which harnessed inanimate energy. Of the two, the second was the more abrupt and influential. The last 220 years represent less than a thousandth of human history; yet they account for more than a fifth of the total population increase. In those 220 years the earth's inhabitants multiplied 4.5 times.

Apparently man's sociocultural envelope has given him a unique niche in the animal kingdom. It is an extraorganic adaptive mechanism that keeps ahead of his organic adaptation. The long early evolution was a slow process of adaptation to living in a sociocultural system, which itself took ages to perfect. The development of agriculture relieved the pressure of selection, but before this relaxation could result in compensatory loss of genetic capacity to resist hardship, a second cultural achievement, the Industrial Revolution, came along to release the pressure even more. The result is an organism built for rugged existence, which lives in a pampering hothouse.

The story has still another chapter. Within the modern period since 1750 an accelerating trend has developed that, as Table 2 demonstrates, winds up with a rate five to ten times the

Table 2. Growth of world population, 1750–1970,
with and without mainland China

	World as a whole		World without China	
	Population (millions)	Increase per decade in prior period (per cent)	Population (millions)	Increase per decade in prior period (per cent)
1750	791		591	
1800	978	4.3	655	2.1
1850	1262	5.2	832	4.9
1900	1650	5.5	1214	7.8
1950	2517	8.8	1957	10.0
1970	3614	19.8	2863	21.0

Sources: Estimates from 1750 to 1900 are from Durand (1). The 1950 estimate is from United Nations (2, p. 97), and the one for 1970 is by the author.

rate at the beginning of the period, depending on whether mainland China is included. In the final tenth of the last 220 years, four-tenths of the total increase took place. The big change came after World War II; the period from 1946 to 1970 is the climax of a long process of human multiplication. The time has been too short for much organic evolution to have occurred after the release from the pressure of selection. The divergence between the conditions the human body is built for and the conditions under which it lives is rapidly becoming wider. However, although the changing envelope keeps ahead of the genetic erosion that it leaves, the erosion is there nonetheless, and turning back becomes increasingly difficult. If the sociocultural envelope proves unstable, the inevitable rise in mortality will not be due solely to man's old bacterial and viral enemies; it will also be due to his weakened genetic capacity to fight these enemies.

The Contemporary Paradox of Demographic Strength and Economic Weakness

When we leave the longer history and look in more detail at the last few decades, we come upon a paradox. Within the present century, as Table 3 shows, the balance of growth has shifted in favor of those peoples whose sociocultural apparatus, at least from an economic point of view, is less efficient. The table also shows this switch is new—occurring after 1920—and

Table 3. Population growth in developed and
less developed regions, 1900–70

Regions[a]	At start of period (millions)	At end of period (millions)	World population at start of period (per cent)	Population growth per decade during period (per cent)
1900–20:				
Developed	251	309	15.2	11.0
Less developed	1399	1551	84.8	5.3
1920–30:				
Developed	317	349	17.0	10.1
Less developed	1543	1721	83.0	11.5
1930–40:				
Developed	528	565	25.5	7.0
Less developed	1542	1730	74.5	12.2
1940–50:				
Developed	649	674	28.3	3.9
Less developed	1646	1843	71.7	12.0
1950–60:				
Developed	741	845	29.4	14.0
Less developed	1776	2160	70.6	21.6
1960–70:				
Developed	959	1078	31.9	12.4
Less developed	2046	2536	68.1	23.9

[a] For each period shown, the countries in each category are the same at the beginning and the end; but between one period and the next they are switched from the "less developed" to the "developed" category if their economies justify it. In 1900–20 "developed" included Canada and the United States, Australia and New Zealand, northwest Europe (with Germany). In 1920–30 Hungary was added; in 1930–40 the Soviet Union; in 1940–50 Czechoslovakia and Japan; in 1950–60 Argentina, Israel, Italy, and Uruguay; and in 1960–70 Chile, Poland, South Africa, Spain, Venezuela, and Yugoslavia.

Sources: Data for 1900 are chiefly from Durand (1); also for 1900 and for later dates from United Nations (3–5); for late figures, United Nations (7).

became more pronounced at the very time that world population growth took its greatest leap forward, from 1946 to the present. This development suggests that the same conditions that caused the balance of growth to shift to the less developed countries also caused the acceleration of world population growth.

In any case the shift was not due to a slowing down of population growth in the industrial nations. On the contrary these nations as a group experienced their *fastest* population increase from 1950 to 1970. They experienced a postwar baby boom that brought their fertility levels up to approximately those of the 1910s and 1920s, and in the meantime their death rates declined substantially. Since the base population had become larger, the absolute natural increase from 1946 to 1970 showed a much greater contrast with the past than did the *rate* of increase. Whereas from 1920 to 1930 the developed countries gained 22 million, from 1960 to 1970 the *same* countries gained 52 million. Clearly, the widening gap in population growth between developed and less developed countries is due to a rise in the agrarian countries, not to a decline in the industrial nations. It is this rise, plus the maintenance of growth in advanced countries, that explains the worldwide postwar acceleration of population growth.

Is World Population Growth Slowing Down?

Faced by the staggering gain in population during the last twenty-five years, people wonder how much longer the upsurge will continue. The answer depends, of course, both on the facts and on the theory of causation used to put the facts together.

A candid look at this growth gives small comfort to those who hope that a worldwide slackening is imminent. If the estimate for 1970 is accurate, the *percentage* gain in world population in the last decade was greater than in the previous decade, and the absolute gain was substantially greater. Here are the figures for world population increase.

	Absolute (*millions*)	Relative (*per cent*)
1940–50	222	9.7
1950–60	488	19.4
1960–70	609	20.3

The fact that the rate rose very little in the last decade suggests that possibly the rate has reached its peak and is about to start down. However, the same could erroneously have been said (in fact, was said) in 1940 because the 1930–40 rate had fallen below that of 1920–30. Another hint that the relative gain may start tapering off is that the proportion of the world's people living in developed areas is rising, but as Table 3 shows, it is rising with agonizing slowness. Also, the growth rate in the developed areas is stubbornly high; in fact, these areas grew more rapidly between 1950 and 1970 than the less developed areas did before that!

A "decline" seems remote when we look at the absolute figures. The rate of increase could drop substantially without altering the enormous increments the world will have to accommodate. For instance, during the 1970s the rate of increase could drop by one-seventh and still bring the same absolute increase (615 million) to the earth's population. Observers who think the less developed countries will "go through the demographic transition" as the industrial countries have done may find it disconcerting that the industrial countries had a more rapid population growth from 1950 to 1970 than the less developed countries did before 1950. If "going through the demographic transition" means finishing population growth, even the industrial nations have not gone through it.

If the current history of the nonindustrial countries were analogous to the past history of the now advanced countries (which it is not), it would not portend a speedy decline in population growth, because the spread of modernization is painfully slow. According to my allocation of countries in Table 3, the *proportion* of the world's population in less developed countries dropped from 85 to 68 per cent in sixty years, but their absolute population rose from 1399 to 2046 million.*

Is the Decline in Mortality Continuing?

If indications of a drop-off in population growth exist, they must be found in the mortality and fertility data. It would not be surprising if the extremely swift decline in mortality in the nonindustrial regions slows down in the future. I refer, however, to measures of mortality, such as life expectancy, which are independent of the age structure, rather than to the crude death rate. If a slowing down of the decline in mortality does occur, it could take two forms: temporary but sharp rises in the death rate due to catastrophes, or gradual reduction in the rate that could be represented by some sort of smooth curve. By its very nature catastrophic mortality—due to war, famine, epidemics, and other disasters—is hard to predict. This does not make it any less probable, but the fact that we cannot calculate the probability within a specified time forces us back to the smooth-curve assumption. There is also a different attitude toward the two possibilities. People are willing to tolerate a slowing down of mortality decline, but they recoil from a rise in mortality. Over the long run, of course, a jagged line might yield the same result—the same average rate—as a smooth line, but a possible rise in mortality tends to be viewed as one

* Perhaps the less developed countries are less "underdeveloped" today than they were yesterday. However, an indication that poverty characterizes more people today than formerly is that the world's rural and agricultural population is growing. According to our data, the rural population of the earth grew by 11 per cent per decade between 1950 and 1970; in the less developed countries alone, it grew by 16 per cent per decade. In the poorest countries of the world, according to data compiled by Joginder Kumar at International Population and Urban Research, University of California, Berkeley, agricultural density (the farm population or farm labor force in relation to land used for agriculture) is rising. This is happening even in countries in which land for expansion is abundant. In seven Central American countries, for instance, the combined number of males in the agricultural labor force was 22.8 per square kilometer of arable land in 1950 and 23.8 in 1960. The agricultural land in the region expanded by 21 per cent during the decade, but the agricultural labor force increased by 26 per cent.

of the problems caused by rapid population growth, not a means of solving the problem. On the other hand, if the mortality improvement *gradually* ceased, most people would reluctantly accept it on the grounds that the length of life cannot go on increasing forever.

There is convincing evidence that gains in longevity are slowing down in both the richer and in the poorer countries. In eight of the European nations with the most advanced longevity, the gain in average length of life reached its peak in 1920–30, and after that it declined to about half that rate of improvement in 1950–60 (8, pp. 26, 28). (See Table 4.) In the United States

Table 4. Changes in life expectancy in
developed countries, 1860–1966

	Northwest Europe[a]		United States (whites) [b]	
Year	Life expectancy (years)	Gain in prior decade (per cent)	Life expectancy (years)	Gain in prior decade (per cent)
1860	40.7			
1870	41.5	2.0		
1880	43.3	4.3		
1890	45.4	4.8		
1900	47.8	5.3	47.6	
1910	50.8	6.3	50.3	5.7
1920	55.0	8.3	54.9	9.1
1930	59.9	8.9	61.4	11.8
1940	64.8	8.2	64.2	4.6
1950	68.8	6.2	69.1	7.6
1960	71.8	4.4	70.6	2.2
1966	72.4	1.2[c]	71.3[d]	1.4[c]

[a] Denmark, England and Wales, France, Holland, Norway, Scotland, Sweden, and Switzerland combined. Sources: (8, p. 26; 2, Table 29; 6, Tables 4, 21).
[b] Source: (10, p. 12).
[c] Computed on a decade basis.
[d] Relates to 1967.

the white population showed a similar peak in 1920–30 and after that an even more drastic drop-off in improvement. The pattern is similar in Australia and New Zealand. It can be argued that such a drop-off is inevitable and that the species has, as a part of its genetic heritage, a maximum life span that can be approached but not exceeded. Such reasoning, however, is not compelling. Why did the gain in longevity reach a peak around 1920–30? What specific causes are slowing it now? Whatever the causes, science may find a way to overcome them. Even genetic determinants are subject to modification or rectification by man. The present slowdown in mortality improvement in the industrial nations may prove to be only a temporary lull.

The less developed countries have had a far more rapid improvement in mortality rates than the industrial nations ever had, and it has carried them almost to the levels of the industrial nations. We would expect, then, that they would be showing—or will soon show—an even more drastic drop in the rate of improvement. We do find evidence of a slowdown, but whether it will prove more or less drastic than that shown in the industrial nations is too early to determine. The more advanced the country is, the higher its life expectancy and the greater the evidence of its slowing down in rate of improvement. In a group of fairly advanced Latin American countries the rate of improvement began to drop after a life expectancy of approximately fifty years had been reached. In a less advanced group, where such a life expectancy had not been reached at the time of calculation, no slowdown in the acceleration of life expectancy improvement had occurred (8, pp. 21, 26). In the industrial countries the fastest improvement came when life expectancy had reached about fifty-five, and it tapered off after sixty. All told, then, mortality decline will probably contribute less to future acceleration in population growth than it has in the past. However, we are only speaking of *acceleration*. There is nothing in the smooth trend of the last few decades to suggest a *rise* in mortality, only a deceleration in its decline.

Furthermore, the effect of mortality on population growth is not simply a function of life expectancy; it is also a function of the age structure. As a result of the recent rapid drop in mortality, the age structure in the less developed countries is increasingly favorable to a low crude death rate. For this reason, a drop in death rates is contributing more to rapid population growth in the less developed countries than the life-expectancy data suggest.

A rapid fall in mortality has the effect of making the age structure younger because the greatest saving of lives occurs in the young ages. In twenty-three less developed countries with reasonably good data at two points in time—in 1950–55 and in 1960–66—the change in the age structure was toward a younger population in all but two cases. On the average the percentage in each age group was as follows:*

	Under 15	15–39	40 and over	Total
Beginning date	38.4	40.1	21.5	100.0
Ending date	42.0	37.4	20.7	100.0

The degree to which such age structures can yield low death rates is generally not realized. As the less developed countries rapidly approach a life expectancy equal to that of the highly developed countries, they reach a condition in which almost nobody dies under age 40. Yet, because of high fertility and rapid mortality decline, they have a high and rising proportion of their population under that age. The result is extremely low crude death rates. The point is illustrated in Tables 5 and 6, which compare Denmark and Costa Rica. In Denmark, according to the mortality conditions of 1963–64, over 95 per cent of those born survive to age 40. With 58.8 per cent of its population under age 40, Denmark had at that time a crude death rate of 9.8 per thousand. Costa Rica, on the other hand, had 82.4 per cent of its population under age 40 in 1963. If it had had exactly the same age-specific death rates as Denmark (which would mean, of course, the same life expectancy at birth —72.5 years), its crude death rate would have been only 4.2 instead of 9.8 as in Denmark. In other words, since under modern public-health conditions almost nobody dies under

* These are weighted averages with each country weighted according to its total population. Of the twenty-three countries, seven were in Africa, eleven in Latin America, and four in Asia. Totals do not always add to 100.0 per cent because of rounding.

Table 5. Age structure of Costa Rica and Denmark

	Percentage of population		
	Under 15	15–39	40 and over
Costa Rica:			
1950	42.9	39.3	17.8
1963	47.7	34.7	17.6
Denmark:			
1963	24.0	34.8	41.3

Sources: United Nations (3, Table 5; 5, Table 6).

Table 6. Relation of life expectancy to crude death rates

	Life expectancy at birth (years)	Death rate (per thousand)
Costa Rica, 1963:		
Actual	63.4	8.5
With Danish age-specific mortality	72.5	4.2
Denmark, 1963:		
Actual	72.5	9.8

Sources: United Nations (2, Table 24; 6, Table 13; 19, Table 19).

age 40, and since in less developed countries today almost everybody is under age 40, the annual death rate in these countries is—and will be—lower than it has ever been in the past history of the now-industrialized nations. This will more than overcome the tendency of mortality decline to taper off; thus the contribution of declining mortality to natural increase may accelerate population growth in these countries for the next thirty years.

Fiction and Fact in Fertility Analysis

There is currently a strong movement for government policies to curb population growth by reducing birth rates. Since such movements require organization, loyalty, sloganized ideologies, and wishful thinking, it is not surprising that analyses of reproductive behavior have been obscured by propaganda. The predominant view in population-policy circles has been that birth rates can be reduced by providing family-planning services—that is, furnishing couples with effective contraceptives. I have criticized this view elsewhere on the grounds that either its statement of the problem or its theory of what is causing the problem is wrong (11–13). If the problem is that population growth is having unfortunate consequences, then it is a problem of the society as a whole, not of individuals, and it is a problem of industrial, as well as nonindustrial, societies. The solution to this problem cannot lie in furnishing couples with contraceptive devices because this would give individuals, and not society, control of fertility. Furthermore, the rapid population growth of the last twenty-five years is not due solely, or even mainly, to births parents do *not* want, but to births they *do* want. To be effective a policy must do more than furnish technological devices and services; it must make social and economic changes that affect individual reproductive decisions. Analysis of reproductive behavior confirms this.

As is well known, the industrial nations all had a long decline in fertility. In the West the decline became noticeable after the middle of the nineteenth century, and in Japan, a half-century later. Most of these countries reached such a low point in the 1930s that a continuance of the age-specific fertility and mortality rates, once the age structure had normalized itself in terms of those rates, would have caused the population to decline each generation. Instead of bringing relief this situation brought alarm, and pronatalist policies were initiated. No population decline was actually in store, but the authorities *thought* it was, because they misinterpreted the meaning of the net reproduction rate by overlooking its unreal assumptions. Swedish, French, German, and Italian authorities thought that the total number of children couples wanted had diminished, whereas only the number they desired *at the moment* was low.

After the war, instead of a population decline, the industrial countries had a baby boom. It was explicable neither by the reasoning behind the pronatalist policies of the 1930s and early 1940s nor by the reasoning behind the family-planning policies of today. It occurred even when a country had no program to encourage births and in spite of the fact that contraceptive technology and birth-control services were improving rather than deteriorating. The baby boom came because postwar economic and social conditions encouraged couples to have the number of children they wanted, which in the majority of cases was two, three, or four.*

The term "boom" suggests that the rise in fertility was temporary, but it was the low fertility of the Depression, from 1929 to 1941 inclusive, that was temporary. After that—for some twenty-nine years now—most industrial countries, including the United States, have never gone back to a point as low as any year in that thirteen-year period. From a similar beginning point around 1946–47 the level fluctuates, with different wave lengths in different countries, but the low points are higher than those of the Depression. Nearly all the industrial nations had a second baby boom in the late 1950s. Significantly this second one was, on the average, higher than the first. The generally high level of fertility and reduced mortality have given the industrial nations their most rapid rate of population growth during this century. The main difference, however, is not in the rate of increase but in the absolute numbers added. In the United States, for instance, during seventeen years of high fertility, from 1946 to 1962, the average birth rate was slightly less than it was during an equal period from 1909 to 1925, but the death rate was sufficiently lower to give the country a higher rate of natural increase in the later period. (See Table 7.) The difference in the rate of increase, however, is slight in comparison to the difference in absolute gain—41.4 million in the later period against 26.0 million in the earlier. From the stand-

* At no time since 1936, when a national opinion poll in the United States first inquired about ideal family size, has the desired number of children been low enough to be even close to yielding zero population growth. In 1936 the proportion considering *three or more* children ideal was 59 per cent; it was never that low again (in 1966 it was 70 per cent!). See Blake (14, 15).

Table 7. Natural increase and population growth in
two seventeen-year periods in the United States

	1909–25	*1946–62*
Average annual rates (per thousand):		
Birth rate	28.2	24.6
Death rate	13.4	9.6
Natural increase rate	14.9	15.0
Absolute numbers (thousands):		
Births	49,225	67,799
Deaths	23,255	26,360
Natural increase	25,970	41,438

Sources: (9, p. 2; 10, pp. 1–2). The death rate for the registration area was
assumed to apply to the entire population of the United States.

point of demands on the environment, it is the absolute population increment that counts, not the rate.

Since the fertility rise in industrial nations does not come
from a deterioration in contraceptive technology or services, it
is strange that the main population-control policy being advocated in the United States is an extension of government-spon-
sored family-planning services. Perhaps the policy will soon
change. Informed leaders are rapidly beginning to see that our
high fertility is made up of "wanted" babies.

The Demography of Fertility in Less Developed Countries

A recent phenomenon that has attracted little attention but
is likely to be much discussed in the near future is the widespread decline in crude birth rates in the less industrialized
countries. The trend is most evident in those countries that are
on the verge of rising, or have just risen, into the urban-
industrial category. Among the poorer nations, these countries
by and large have the most reliable birth registration. Therefore,
they will be much cited as evidence that the birth rate in the less
developed world is coming down, and since several of them
have either public or private family-planning programs, they will
be hailed as proving that family planning effectively reduces the

rate of population growth. But crude birth rates are not reliable indicators of fertility (which is better measured on the basis of age-specific rates), and inferences about less developed regions that are based on countries for which "fairly reliable data are obtainable" inevitably reflect a sampling bias of unknown magnitude.

I have compiled crude birth rates for twenty-five countries ordinarily classed as "developing" with birth registration at least reliable enough to suggest trends. They are not a large, and certainly not a representative, sample of the less developed countries of the world, but they comprise a larger list than is often used.* They exclude such "city countries" as Hong Kong and Singapore and some of the more developed countries such as Puerto Rico, Greece, and Poland.

On the average, the twenty-five countries showed a *rise* in the crude birth rate between 1953 and 1960 and a decline between 1960 and 1967.

	Average crude birth rate (*per thousand*)
1953	38.3
1960	38.7
1967	34.7
	Change (*per cent*)
1953–60	+1.2
1960–67	−10.4

Two things are worth noting about these figures—first, the sheer level of the crude birth rate; second, the recency of the decline. Even though four European countries—three with modest birth rates—are included in the list and even though registration is incomplete, the *average* crude rate as recently as 1960 was higher than any crude birth rate estimated for the

* The following countries are included: Africa—Algeria, Madagascar, Mauritius, Tunisia, Réunion; Latin America—Chile, Colombia, Costa Rica, Dominican Republic, El Salvador, Honduras, Jamaica, Mexico, Nicaragua, Peru, Trinidad-Tobago; Asia—Ceylon, Iran, Taiwan; Europe —Albania, Bulgaria, Rumania, Cyprus; Oceania—Fiji.

white population of the United States in any year after 1861 (16). The rate was high enough in 1960 to multiply the population about ten times in eighty years. This seems to suggest that the rate began to decline because it was creating an intolerable situation; however, the extremely rapid mortality decline that characterized these countries after 1930 and particularly after 1940 tended to affect crude birth rates in various and somewhat contradictory ways. First, it tended to *increase* them by raising the fertility of women in general, because women now spent more of their reproductive lives in a married state. Fewer wives were widowed within the reproductive span. Arriaga has found that for eleven Latin American countries combined, females lived *in marital unions* "6.3 years longer on the average under the mortality conditions of the 1960s than under conditions of the 1930s" (8, p. 155). A ten-year decline in mortality such as occurred in Costa Rica after 1927 would cause a 4.1 per cent rise in the gross reproduction rate (17) with *no increase in marital fertility*. Second, lowered mortality and better health conditions may have exercised an upward effect on crude birth rates by raising marital fertility—through lowering the age of menarche, increasing the chance of conception, and reducing fetal mortality; but this effect is balanced by an opposite tendency of mortality decline to lower marital fertility by reducing infant mortality and thereby lengthening the interval between births (18).

The net direct effect of the rapid drop in mortality may be favorable to raising crude birth rates, but the indirect effect through the age structure (like the effect shown earlier for crude death rates) is unfavorable. In Ceylon, for example, the change in the age structure between 1953 and 1963 was slight. (It had been mainly accomplished during the prior decade.) The percentage under 15 moved only from 39.7 to 41.5; yet the effect on the crude birth rate was substantial. If the 1963 age-specific fertility rates are applied to the 1953 age structure, the crude birth rate for 1963 increased from 34.5 births per thousand inhabitants to 37.0. A similar calculation for Mauritius shows that the 1966 crude birth rate would have been 39.0, instead of the actual 34.9, if the population had still had the 1955 age structure.

The tentative conclusion I draw is that the effect of rapid mortality decline in changing the age structure and thus pushing the crude birth rate down has recently been more powerful than its effect in raising age-specific fertility and thus pushing the crude rate up. If so, only a portion of the recent drop in crude birth rates in less developed countries can be attributed to lowered marital fertility or to marital postponement and greater celibacy.

That some of the drop *is* due to such voluntary factors is indicated not only by the magnitude of the crude birth rate changes—which from 1960 to 1967 amounted to a 10.4 per cent drop for the twenty-five developing countries—but also by the timing. That the change was not observed from 1953 to 1960 but was observed after that suggests that the countries in our list (which are more advanced than all less developed countries as a class) are reaching the point in urban-industrial growth at which reduction in fertility comes by postponing marriage and limiting births within marriage by contraception, abstinence, and abortion. This impression is strengthened by taking a group of ten marginal countries—marginal because they can be classified as either developed or less developed.* In these countries the average crude birth rate declined in both periods.

Average crude birth rate
(*per thousand*)

1953	35.4
1960	33.4
1968	25.2

The drop in the period 1960–68 was *faster* than in the larger group of twenty-five countries. It was sizable, 32.6 per cent,

* The countries in this list are Chile, Costa Rica, Hong Kong, Greece, Poland, Portugal, Puerto Rico, Singapore, Taiwan, and Trinidad-Tobago. Four of these appear in the list of twenty-five less developed countries, and six do not.

and could hardly have been due to the younger age structure. It looks as though modernization is beginning to have some effect on voluntary fertility in less developed countries, at least among the more advanced of them.

Family Planning Programs and Fertility Decline

If the family planners take credit for the fall in crude birth rates in less developed countries, they will be confusing the public. To postpone or abjure marriage or to limit the number of offspring within marriage, people do not need a government program. They do not need clinics or a 100 per cent effective or medically supervised contraceptive. They need some means, to be sure, but these can be simple things like *coitus interruptus,* douches, condoms, extravaginal coitus, or induced abortion. What is needed is a desire to limit births, and this is created by altered social conditions that increase the opportunity costs of children, as well as by a larger ratio of living children to births. Age-specific fertility is going down in the most advanced of the less developed countries whether or not these countries have a family-planning program. Where such programs exist, the fertility decline always started well before the program got started. In Japan fertility declined more rapidly before there was a subsidized family-planning program than after. The notion that an official family-planning program speeds up the change from a nonindustrial to an industrial level of fertility seems plausible, a priori, but there is as yet no firm evidence for it. The idea that a family-planning program can bring fertility decline to a country without social and economic modernization (as has been the case with mortality) is not even plausible, much less proven.

Conclusion

The conclusion I draw from this analysis is that for the next thirty or so years the world will be largely bound by its recent population splurge. The spectacular fall of mortality in two-thirds of the world has left us with populations heavily weighted toward the younger ages. As these swollen cohorts move into young adulthood—if no catastrophes occur—the death rate will descend to unparalleled low levels: 4 or 5 per thousand. At the same time, *even if age-specific fertility falls,* there will be so many of these young adults in the population, proportionately speaking, that the birth rate will remain high. Rates of population increase of 2 to 3 per cent per year in the less developed regions of the world therefore seem inevitable—even assuming that the rate of mortality *decline* slows down and that age-specific fertility falls substantially. The age structure hangs like a cloud over the future. The prospect of doubling the world's people thirty years from now must be faced.

As yet no policies adequate to get out of this bind are being put into effect. Human societies have always had difficulty in motivating people to pursue goals that benefited them collectively rather than individually. In the past they ingeniously solved the reproductive problem by building into institutional structures powerful incentive systems that yielded high birth rates in the face of calamities, hardships, and perpetual poverty. Now—suddenly, in terms of biological history—societies must do an about-face. The past response to good conditions has been sizable families and population growth. Human beings are now being asked to respond differently. But they are only being *asked.* The incentive systems are not being altered. As a consequence, no change of behavior adequate to meet the collective situation is being made.

The question is not simply one of the individual against society. The incentive system for reproduction and population growth is social and economic, not instinctive. What is required, therefore, is *social* change, not repression of some biological instinct. By the same token I am not anxious to present the devotion of people to collective goals as an easy prescription for limiting population. On the contrary there is no evading the fact that collective goals can set the population aim high as well as low. The cry of genocide, the revival of claims for *Lebensraum* by certain countries, the persistence of the belief that economic growth and military might depend on manpower—these straws in the wind do not indicate that population control in behalf of collective goals will necessarily mean population limitations in behalf of humanity as a whole.

References

1. John D. Durand. "The Modern Expansion of World Population," *Proceedings of the American Philosophical Society,* Vol. III, June 1967, p. 137.
2. United Nations, *Demographic Yearbook, 1967.* New York, 1968.
3. United Nations, *Demographic Yearbook, 1960.* New York, 1961.
4. United Nations, *Demographic Yearbook, 1962.* New York, 1963.
5. United Nations, *Demographic Yearbook, 1965.* New York, 1966.
6. United Nations, *Demographic Yearbook, 1968.* New York, 1969.
7. United Nations, *Population and Vital Statistics Report.* New York, January 1, 1970.
8. Eduardo E. Arriaga. *Mortality Decline and Its Demographic Effects in Latin America.* Berkeley, Calif.: Institute of International Studies, 1970.
9. National Center for Health Statistics, *Natality Statistics Analysis.* Washington, D.C., February, 1967.
10. National Center for Health Statistics, *Vital Statistics of the United States, 1967.* Vol. 2, *Mortality,* Part A. Washington, D.C.
11. Kingsley Davis. "The World's Population Crisis," *Contemporary Social Problems,* 2nd. ed., rev., Robert K. Merton and Robert A. Nisbet, eds. New York: Harcourt Brace Jovanovich, 1966. Pp. 374–408.
12. Kingsley Davis. "Population Policy: Will Current Programs Succeed?" *Science,* Vol. 158 (November 10, 1967), 730–40.

13. Kingsley Davis. "Will Family Planning Solve the Population Problem?" *The Victor-Bostrum Fund for the International Planned Parenthood Federation, Report No. 10.* Washington, D.C., 1968. Pp. 16, 30.
14. Judith Blake. "Ideal Family Size among White Americans," *Demography,* Vol. 3, No. 1 (1966), 164–65.
15. Judith Blake. "Family Size in the 1960's—A Baffling Fad?" *Eugenics Quarterly,* Vol. 14 (March 1967), 67.
16. Ansley J. Coale and Melvin Zelnik. *New Estimates of Fertility and Population in the United States.* Princeton, N.J.: Princeton University Press, 1963. Pp. 21–23.
17. Eduardo E. Arriaga. "The Effect of a Decline in Mortality on the Gross Reproduction Rate," *Milbank Memorial Fund Quarterly,* Vol. 45 (July 1967), 336–39.
18. Jeanne Clare Ridley, Mindel C. Sheps, Joan W. Lingner, and Jane A. Menken, "The Effects of Changing Mortality on Natality," *Milbank Memorial Fund Quarterly,* Vol. 45 (January 1967), 77–93.
19. United Nations, *Demographic Yearbook, 1966.* New York, 1967.

Discussion of Professor Davis's Paper

T. Paul Schultz is Director of Research on Population Behavior for The Rand Corporation.

Professor Davis has alluded to one of the frustrating facts of life in international demographic research: In low-income countries, where rapid population growth appears to constitute the greatest hardship, we know the least about the magnitude of the problem and know all too little about its causes and its consequences. We are therefore indebted to Professor Davis for a thoughtful survey of historical evidence of demographic trends, a detailed discussion of developments in the twentieth century, and his own judgments of what is occurring today and what is in store for us in the future.

In general, I am in relatively close agreement with his interpretation of the past, and in any case I have neither the demographer's credentials nor the experience to quibble about detail. I would prefer, therefore, to accept Professor Davis's description of the past and present and instead raise a further topic for discussion here: What are the uneasy solutions? And more basic for many of us who are committed to research in this area: What demographic information or knowledge do we need to improve our policy response to the evident problem of rapid population growth in the low-income countries?

Aside from emotional appeal, and there is much of that today, of what practical use is the fact that populations double in twenty-one rather than twenty-three years or that the rate of population growth in country X is 3.3 rather than 3 per cent per year? I wonder if this type of information about substantial changes in the magnitudes of population growth really elicits different policy responses. I suspect not. What the policymaker needs to know, rather, is *why* birth rates are high, *how* effective various policies at his disposal might be in reducing the level of birth rates, and what is the cost to other social objectives.

Trends over time at the national level do not provide us with evidence to infer that one policy or one program has affected the birth rate. Professor Davis himself, in his famous *Science* article three years ago (I), challenged the advocates of family planning, contending that the decline of birth rates in Taiwan—the most famous example of a successful family-planning program —had preceded the program and consequently one could not infer that the program had contributed to this decline in fertility. I should like to take his argument one step further and suggest that any single time-series of a vital rate, or more appropriately age-standardized birth rates, cannot provide us with the statistical evidence to infer with confidence that any particular policy has influenced fertility. Many other factors change over time, and they change with the glacial speed that demographic variables do. Our interpretations and analyses must dig deeper. We must get beyond these aggregate levels of vital rates and population growth. Regional trends in birth rates may provide us with stronger evidence of which factors in particular regions accelerated the decline in birth rates or which factors are, on the other hand, supporting high levels of fertility observed elsewhere in low-income countries.

Let me argue that the most promising research strategy we have today is to focus on the family or small community and observe fertility from survey or census data—hopefully from reliable data—in order to trace variations in reproductive behavior among individuals and communities to the constraints and opportunities of the environment that would be expected to influence desired and achieved fertility. We must try to understand at the local level what contribution the environment is making to the observed reproductive behavior of women. Perhaps then we shall also be able to isolate what additional contribution local policies, such as a family-planning program, are making to the decline of fertility.

This research strategy may not allow us to conclude that the birth rate is 44 per thousand rather than 42 per thousand in the country as a whole, but it may permit us to infer what factors are likely to influence the birth rate, which way the birth rate is likely to go in the future, and how much the birth rate is likely to change. Evidence accumulated in this fashion on the local determinants (correlates for those who are skeptical) of birth rates will provide the basis for selecting among alternative policies those that will be most effective, or least costly in resources, in accomplishing a desired decline in birth rates.

One example will perhaps show how this research strategy can bring into focus somewhat different policy implications from those that have been widely publicized. In my own work, first in Puerto Rico, then in Taiwan, and several other countries, I have tried to analyse fertility at the lowest administrative unit or at the family level in order to understand cross-sectional variation in terms of environmental factors (2, 3).

A widely held belief, which is rarely tested with statistical rigor, presumes that the decline in child death rates contributes to the decline in birth rates because parents frame their family goals in terms of wanting a particular number of *surviving* children. This hypothesis led me to expect that I might explain some of the variation in fertility by the variation in child mortality. The positive partial correlation between these two variables was, for example, very strong in Taiwan in the 1960s. If one compares death rates there two to four years ago with current birth rates, the relationship becomes statistically much stronger and more significant. This two to four years is about the time it takes for a woman to replace a child if she has lost one. Some of this lag may be biological in nature because when an infant dies and lactation stops, conception can proceed more promptly. But this lagged relationship is most strongly evident among older women—women who often have completed their ideal family size and are, perhaps, deciding whether to have another child on the basis of the survival of earlier offspring.

Similar results have come out of other studies in the Philippines and Pakistan, environments with much lower income and higher mortality (4, 5). These results suggest, then, that the decline in mortality elaborated by Professor Davis is not independent of fertility; indeed, the decline in mortality puts pressures on parents when the increasing size of their surviving families forces older women to try to find means to restrict their fertility. This does not indicate that population growth is self-equilibrating. Not only are there more children surviving because of the improved regime of mortality, but there are also many more adults. Probably less than half the decline in crude death rates is accounted for by more children surviving in families with still-fertile parents. Consequently, the "population explosion" will still follow from the increased life expectancy for adults, but to the extent that it is related to improved child survival it will create compensating pressures for a subsequent decline in fertility.

To demonstrate this and put in perspective some of the other issues Professor Davis has brought out in his paper, Table 1 simulates the consequences of the changes in mortality that are noted in the developing world. I postulate initially a world in which the population is growing 1.5 per cent annually and both birth and death rates are very high. As a parallel to the decline in mortality witnessed in most low-income countries since World War II, I assume the death rates decline abruptly from this high level. More precisely, mortality conditions are assumed initially to be those characterized by Coale and Demeny's (6) model life tables, West level 8, declining in ten years to level 15 and in the second decade stabilizing at level 17.

If we assume no change in fertility by age, Case I unfolds as a mechanical deduction from our assumptions. The consequences are what we have observed taking place in the last ten to twenty years. The rate of population growth increases to 2.65 per cent per year, and if fertility does not fall, population growth rises eventually to 3 per cent. But the surviving number of children that parents have also rises, and rises very sharply; within twenty years it has increased by more than 25 per cent. The question is: Are parents indifferent to having four surviving children rather than the traditional three? I judge not. Using the empirical research I have reported as a basis for conjecturing behavioral patterns, I assume in Case II that once parents reach

Table 1. Population simulations

Time (years)	Crude birth rate	Crude death rate	Infant death rate	Population growth rate	Percentage of population under age 15	Average number of surviving children per woman by age						
						15–19	20–24	25–29	30–34	35–39	40–44	45–49
	(per thousand)			(per cent)								
CASE I[a]												
0	40.5	25.5	195	15.0	38.5	0.36	1.21	2.14	2.81	3.15	3.18	3.08
10	38.7	12.7	98	26.5	40.5	0.40	1.34	2.37	3.06	3.36	3.33	3.18
20	37.5	10.1	73	28.1	41.9	0.40	1.41	2.59	3.45	3.83	3.76	3.52
30	38.5	10.1	72	29.0	42.2	0.40	1.41	2.61	3.56	4.08	4.18	4.00
40	38.9	10.0	72	29.6	42.9	0.40	1.41	2.62	3.56	4.12	4.29	4.25
Increase in size of surviving family (per cent)						11	17	22	27	31	35	38
CASE II[b]												
0	40.5	25.5	195	15.0	38.5	0.36	1.21	2.14	2.81	3.15	3.18	3.08
10	37.5	12.6	98	25.3	40.2	0.40	1.33	2.34	3.01	3.32	3.32	3.18
20	35.1	10.0	73	25.6	40.5	0.40	1.40	2.50	3.23	3.57	3.59	3.44
30	35.8	10.2	72	26.1	40.1	0.40	1.40	2.51	3.28	3.66	3.75	3.67
40	35.6	10.1	72	26.0	40.5	0.40	1.40	2.52	3.28	3.67	3.78	3.75
Increase in size of surviving family (per cent)						11	16	18	17	17	19	22

[a] Constant age-specific fertility ($m = 27$). Source: Coale and Demeny (6, Table XIII, p. 30).
[b] Birth control that is 85 per cent reliable is used when parents reach traditional desired surviving-family size of 3.08 children and surviving-family size is distributed normally about the mean with a standard deviation of half a child.

their traditional surviving-family size goal, they exercise birth control that is 85 per cent effective. A good family-planning program might increase the effectiveness of birth control, however.

Given this assumption, we see that the birth rate does not continue to rise but begins to decline after ten or fifteen years. The rate of population growth does not continue to rise after a decade but stabilizes at about 2.6 per cent. The size of the surviving family continues to rise because parents are using unreliable means of birth control; family size increases by 17 to 22 per cent after forty years. Clearly, better birth control, more birth spacing, and a reduction in the number of surviving children that parents actually want would all contribute to a more substantial and rapid reduction in fertility and population growth.

This simple simulation exercise has suggested how information derived from microanalysis of family and aggregate data can be used to interpret the aggregate phenomena described by Professor Davis. This simple model predicts declines in age-specific fertility that are very similar to those now occurring in the more rapidly developing countries such as Taiwan. This interpretation of the "changing balance of births and deaths" does not treat births and deaths as independent of one another, nor does it imply that income or urbanization are particularly useful indices for the social and economic systems that determine desired fertility.

Professor Davis adopts the profoundly pessimistic viewpoint in his paper that there is little basis for anticipating a decline in crude birth rates in low-income countries until economic development, industrialization, and urbanization in these countries reaches the advanced levels achieved in Taiwan and Puerto Rico. But beneath the national vital rates discussed by Davis, variation in reproductive behavior among individuals and groups in low-income societies appears to be responding to changing environmental incentive patterns. Diversity and change are already present, although estimated national crude birth rates are in many cases seemingly stationary.

A growing body of evidence indicates that improvements in child nutrition and local health facilities, for example in India, might reduce infant and child mortality, with a secondary effect of reducing birth rates substantially within a decade. Modification of education, employment, and welfare policies might further change elements in the family setting that would accelerate the short-run shift in parental demands toward a goal of a smaller surviving-family size. Finally, a program that reduces the search and use costs to all individuals, particularly the poor and disadvantaged, of reliable modern birth control may markedly hasten the spread of this new technological innovation and, in the short run, reduce the rate of population growth.

Economic development measured in terms of increasing per capita income is a frustratingly slow process. But with the current structure of development, partial solutions to the imbalance of births and deaths are in prospect in the short run. Additional solutions to the population problem will be illuminated by research aimed at understanding why reproductive behavior differs among families. I am hopeful that some of these suggested solutions will require only a modest and socially acceptable reordering of existing social and economic development objectives in low-income countries.

References

1. Kingsley Davis. "Population Policy: Will Current Programs Succeed?" *Science,* Vol. 158 (November 10, 1967), 730–40.
2. T. Paul Schultz, with Marc Nerlove. *A Model of Family Decisionmaking in Puerto Rico: Love and Life between the Censuses.* RM-6385. Santa Monica, Calif.: The Rand Corporation, September 1970. Presented at Econometrics Meetings, New York, December 1969 and at the Population Association of America Meetings, Atlanta, April 1970.
3. T. Paul Schultz. *Evaluation of Policies: A Framework for Analysis and Its Application to Taiwan's Family Planning Program.*

R-643. Santa Monica, Calif.: The Rand Corporation, December 1970.

4. T. Paul Schultz and Julie DaVanzo. *Analysis of Demographic Change in East Pakistan: A Study of Retrospective Survey Data.* R-564. Santa Monica, Calif.: The Rand Corporation, October 1970.

5. Alvin J. Harman. *Fertility and Economic Behavior of Families in the Philippines.* RM-6385-AID. Santa Monica, Calif.: The Rand Corporation, September 1970.

6. Ansley J. Coale and Paul Demeny. *Regional Model Life Tables and Stable Populations.* Princeton, N.J.: Princeton University Press, 1966.

2

Some Consequences
of Rapid Population Growth

ROGER REVELLE

Roger Revelle is Richard Saltonstall Professor of Population Policy, Center for Population Studies, Harvard University.

In this chapter I shall not discuss the possibly apocalyptic effects of a continuation of present rates of population growth into the far future. Instead, I shall confine myself to some consequences of rapid growth for societies and individuals in the less developed countries over the next few decades.

In thinking about these consequences, it is useful to consider both the kinds of effects and the nature of the causes—whether these be the speed of growth itself, the underlying high birth rates, or population size and density. We are also concerned with the time horizon over which the effects occur and the scale —that is, whether we are dealing with a country or a region or with the family, village, community, or other small social unit.

Economic Consequences

Rates of population growth in less developed countries are at least half, and in some cases equal to, the rates of economic

This chapter is in part a summary of certain portions of *Rapid Population Growth, Consequences and Policy Implications* (Baltimore: The Johns Hopkins Press, 1971, Vol. I, pp. i–xi, 1–105; Vol. II, pp. i–xii, 1–696), prepared by a Study Committee of the Office of the Foreign Secretary, National Academy of Sciences. Professor Revelle served as Chairman of the Study Committee.

growth. Chiefly because of the high fertility of these countries, the ratios of children to adults are also very high when compared to those of developed countries, and the number of children and young people entering the age of labor force participation is rapidly increasing. Both of these factors produce serious economic consequences; planners and political leaders, therefore, need to take population growth into account in all long-range planning.

The classical mode of the economic consequences of rapid population growth focuses on these factors (4, 5)—the high dependency burden resulting from the high proportion of children and the rapid growth in the labor force. During the next fifteen years the size of the labor force will not be affected by changes in fertility. But with continuing high fertility the total economic output must be divided among a much larger number of persons, and hence, per capita incomes will be smaller than would be the case with lower fertility. Because of the lower dependency burden results, a rapid decline in fertility will result in an increase in per capita incomes relative to those that would exist if fertility remained constant. This advantage will persist even after a new equilibrium has been reached because the proportion of adults who could participate in the labor force would be higher and the proportion of dependent children smaller in the low-fertility population.

The rapid growth of the labor force that results from a rapid rate of population growth means there must be a much higher level of total capital investment if the capital stock per worker is to remain constant. If savings and investment are a relatively constant fraction of the gross national product (GNP), the capital stock per worker will be greater when population and labor force growth are slow relative to that for a high rate of growth. If fertility declines, the savings required to keep the capital stock per head constant will decrease. The effect will be felt to some extent soon after fertility starts to decline because it will be possible to allocate more investments to the physical means of production and less to education, welfare, and other investments in human resources. But the full effect will be evident only when the arrival of the smaller cohorts, or age groups, resulting from fertility decline starts to slow down the rate of growth of the labor force.

The classical mode also subsumes certain additional advantages of low fertility that amplify and reinforce the two main effects just cited. With a higher income per capita, savings per head will be larger. In countries suffering from unemployment or underemployment, a higher per capita rate of capital accumulation will make it possible to employ a larger proportion of the available manpower, and in particular, it will be possible to expand employment in the modern industrial sector. Finally, a higher income per capita may have a feedback effect on labor productivity through better nutrition, health, education, and housing (5).

Although some economic arguments can be made in opposition to these deductions—chiefly that the rapid growth of the labor force means the rapid replacement of older workers by younger and presumably more flexible ones (12) and that economics of scale and specialization will arise with a larger population(3)—the principal difficulty is the relatively small magnitude of the effects.

A widely quoted estimate (4, 5) shows the relative gains in income per capita (adjusted for age distribution) that would result in India from a 50-per-cent linear reduction of fertility occurring over a period of twenty-five years. Twenty years after the beginning of fertility decline, per capita incomes would be 15 per cent higher, and 40 per cent higher after thirty years, the difference increasing rapidly afterwards. Thus the short-term gains, although appreciable, are far from spectacular. It can be effectively argued that the gains attributed to declining fertility could be achieved by a number of alternative means, such as a slightly higher savings-investment rate or by slight improvements in labor productivity or in the efficiency of using capital (9).

If instead of focusing on an economic model we examine what is actually happening in the less developed countries, it is evident that rapid population growth is having serious interacting effects in several economic areas. Three examples are: food and agriculture, unemployment and underemployment, and savings and investment.

Food and Agricultural Production

During the 1950s development strategies in many less developed nations were concentrated on attempts at industrialization, in part based on the example of such recently developed countries as the Soviet Union. But these strategies did not anticipate the unexpected and unprecedentedly high rates of population growth which appeared after World War II and accelerated throughout the next fifteen years. Though industrialization sometimes proceeded at a rapid pace, industrial employment usually increased more slowly; and the absolute number of people supported by the industrial sector lagged behind the growth of population, with the result that the number of people tied to the land in agriculture greatly increased. At the same time population growth has brought about a vast increase in food requirements. Consequently, agriculture continues to be the base of the economy in most of the less developed world. In recent years it has been widely recognized that much greater emphasis on agricultural improvement is essential for over-all economic and social growth, and more balanced development strategies have been undertaken (15, p. 73).

In Asia, where nearly all arable land is already farmed and most of the world's people live, a revolution in agricultural technology must occur if rapidly growing populations are to be fed even at present levels, let alone improved levels. For both economic and physiological reasons the rate of growth of food supplies should be substantially greater than the rate of population growth. An agricultural revolution has already begun with the introduction of new high-yielding, fertilizer-responsive "dwarf" varieties of wheat, rice, and other cereals. If it is to continue, large expenditures for development of irrigation, transportation, storage, food processing, and fertilizers must be made. Large amounts of imports that require foreign currency will be necessary. This situation will require over-all economic development at a higher rate than has recently prevailed, and these demands must be taken into account in planning resource allocations and priorities and in raising capital funds (16).

The new agricultural technology is much better suited to some regions than to others. In India irrigation development is easy to accomplish in the Gangetic plain of Uttar Pradesh and Bihar, but it is difficult and expensive in most of the Deccan plateau, which covers central India (17). In East Pakistan existing new cereal varieties cannot be grown and chemical fertilizers cannot be used in the 30 per cent of the country that is flooded for five months each year, except for one crop during the dry season. National farm prices will almost certainly fall because of greatly expanded production in the regions where the new technology can be successfully applied. The farmers in the less favored regions may then be unable to sell their crops at prices sufficient to pay for the water, chemical fertilizers, and other inputs needed for high-productivity agriculture. They will be forced back on subsistence farming, which will be insufficient to feed the growing populations of their own villages. Large numbers of poverty-stricken and unskilled countrymen will be driven out, either to cities and towns or to the more favored agricultural regions, where most of them will become landless laborers. The challenge to policymakers, either to develop new agricultural technologies for nonirrigated land or to provide employment and a new way of life for these people, is very great, especially because of the difficulties of raising employment in the industrial sector as fast as the labor force grows.

In the regions where the new agricultural technology can be successfully applied, capital and land give greater returns than labor, so it can be expected that the larger landowning farmers will gradually take over from small farmers and tenants, increasing still further the proportion of landless laborers and aggravating inequities in income distribution. New land-tenure policies or other means of protecting small-farm owners and tenants are called for. Problems of unemployment and underemployment may be increased as a result of unchecked agricultural mechanization unless governments strongly encourage labor-intensive agriculture combined with selective mechanization that increases the demand for labor (e.g., tube wells to provide irrigation water and cultivating machinery for rapid seed-bed preparation that will facilitate growing an extra crop during the year).

Rapid population growth in rural areas where the supply of arable land is limited results in either a fragmentation of farms from one generation to the next or in the migration of younger sons and their families to towns and cities. The average size of farms in the Punjab of West Pakistan has decreased by about 50 per cent in one generation. The effects of farm fragmentation can be overcome by the formation of agricultural cooperatives among the small farmers, but experience in less developed countries shows that this usually occurs only under the impetus of strong government or other outside encouragement (15, p. 75).

Unemployment and Underemployment

The existence of large and rapidly growing supplies of cheap labor in many less developed countries tends to hold back the adoption of capital-intensive, labor-saving technology in industry and thereby slows down increases in productivity and in standards of living (15, p. 76). Even labor-intensive industries are unable to provide useful employment for all jobseekers.

Policies to reduce the growth of the labor force by fertility control can have little effect during the next fifteen or twenty years because the cohorts who will be entering the labor force and seeking employment during that period have already been born. For the near future emphasis needs to be placed on (a) retaining as many workers as possible in agriculture by government policies that favor hand labor and the kinds of mechanization, such as tube wells, small tillers, and grain dryers, that raise the demand for labor by fostering multiple crops; (b) service occupations; and (c) relatively small scale consumer-goods industries, which in the aggregate can employ large numbers of workers. At the same time efforts to increase the productivity of workers should be accelerated as rapidly as available resources allow because only in this way can standards of living be raised. The productivity of labor in many less developed countries is now so low that industries often cannot compete with similar industries in the advanced countries even when wages are held at a subsistence level (15, p. 76).

Saving and Investment in Human versus Material Resources

The high rate of educational expansion in the less developed countries means that parents and governments have been spending more to improve the education and skills of children, even though this has become more difficult as the number of children in each family increases. These investments in the "quality" of children may be taking place at the expense of savings by households and corresponding capital investment in the physical means of production. Statistical analysis (11) of a large number of less developed countries indicates that the level of "physical savings, measured in terms of national income in any particular country over a period of time, remains a relatively constant fraction of per capita incomes. This fraction does not increase as per capita incomes rise, but from country to country it shows a strong inverse correlation with child dependency ratios; that is, the proportion of children less than 15 years old to adults 15 to 65. Total savings, including that invested in human capital through education and better nutrition and child care—though still low in absolute terms because of low per capita incomes—are considerably higher than physical savings and may be rising more rapidly than per capita incomes (18).

Public investments in education and welfare services reduce the amount that can be spent by governments on capital investments for short-term increases in production. In low-income countries the proportion of the GNP that can be drained off in taxes by all levels of government is limited by the necessities of human survival. For example, 60 to 90 per cent of the national income in India must be used to meet the physiological needs of the people for calories, protein and other nutrients, clothing, and shelter (16). Governments also face many other difficulties in raising sufficient direct and indirect taxes to provide the revenue that must be shared among education, health and welfare services, and capital expenditures for development. Such difficulties include the need to maintain a swollen bureaucracy to help provide employment for the rapidly growing labor force, and the low levels of imports *and* exports available for customs revenue, and to handle the problems of tax collection, either from millions of small-farm owners or from large landowners who are skilled in tax evasion.

The situation of average households in low-income countries is similar to that of governments. The proportion of total savings to income cannot be increased very rapidly as per capita incomes grow—even if strong incentives exist—simply because the necessities of life require that a high proportion of income be used for food, clothing, and shelter. The increasing number of children in the average family keeps this proportion high even when total family income rises. In economists' terms, the "elasticity" of savings to rising incomes tends to be close to one because consumption needs are not adequately met at present income levels and a major share of increases must be used for increasing consumption (15, p. 49).

Political and Social Consequences

Many of the ills of our modern world—urban violence, political instability, crime, aggressive behavior, revolution, and hypernationalism—are popularly ascribed to rapid population growth. But empirical attempts to show a relationship between population and these political and social pathologies have been unsuccessful. It is claimed nevertheless that because rapid population growth helps to perpetuate poverty, disease, and economic inequalities in the less developed countries, the "ultimate" consequence will be "revolutionary upheaval," political "disintegration," massive "breakdown," or some other cataclysmic political and social upheaval. Against this view is the observed fact that unrest grows with industrial and economic development because improved living conditions bring a higher level of expectations (22).

One reason for the popular belief that population growth and political pathology are closely related is that population change is nearly always associated with socioeconomic change, and change carries with it a high likelihood of social disruption. We perceive the results of interdependent stimuli. Demographic change is the most readily quantifiable of all the changes that are actually occurring, and therefore it is the most easily blamed for unpleasant consequences.

Population growth does increase strains upon administrative systems and governmental resources in the less developed countries where the governments have assumed major responsibility for development and are attempting to meet rapidly increasing demands for education, housing, agricultural and industrial development, transportation, and employment. With high rates of population growth it becomes more difficult for governments to meet these demands; administrative leadership, which is usually the scarcest of all resources in developing countries, must be spread very thin. At the same time a rapid expansion of the governmental bureaucracy, often simply to make more jobs, places a further strain on scarce administrative resources.

In some less developed countries political problems may actually be somewhat ameliorated as the population increases. Countries with large territories and small, dispersed populations, such as many African countries, must maintain a high ratio of bureaucrats to ordinary citizens in order to extend the government's writ throughout the countryside. Increasing population density may reduce the per capita costs of government and make possible a more coordinated and effective political organization. On the other hand, in countries with high population density the quality of political participation and governmental effectiveness tends to diminish with further population growth. Organizational structures necessarily become more elaborate and the people more regimented. These observations, taken together, suggest that from a political viewpoint there is an optimum population size for any particular country. We do not know enough, however, to be able to state what this optimum size should be in the different circumstances of different countries (22).

Intergroup Conflicts

In countries without a homogenous population, rapid population growth creates or aggravates political and economic conflicts between racial, cultural, religious, and linguistic groups. Numbers are an important element of political power, especially in countries that are attempting to introduce or to maintain democratic institutions and processes. Ethnic groups tend to differ from each other in birth and death rates, and therefore their relative numbers tend to change with time. Conflicting groups usually perceive these changes to be much larger than they really are. Conflicts are worsened by the inability of many less developed countries to provide education and other services for all their people. It is generally the lowest socioeconomic groups, the poor or the politically disadvantaged, who are left behind. Since income and occupation often coincide with differences in religion, caste, tribe, or language, a half-developed system of primary- and secondary-school education may sharpen both class and ethnic differences. It is striking that in most multiethnic states (including the United States) the struggle between social groups over educational opportunities is one of the most bitterly contested issues.

Intergroup relations may be further exacerbated by another result of rapid population growth in most less developed countries—large-scale migration from the country to the city or from one region to another. Often people of one group move into a region where other groups have previously predominated (22).

The problem of ameliorating these conflicts has not been solved, and they represent a serious threat to the existence of many states. In some cases far-reaching measures such as mass migration or fragmentation of states into autonomous or semi-autonomous smaller units may be the only feasible policy options. But governments can do much by a more even-handed treatment of different groups—providing not only equal but increased educational and employment opportunities and services for all—and by political and legal devices that protect minorities without jeopardizing the basic interests of the majority. These policies may require rather drastic but pragmatic departures from normal democratic procedures (15, p. 70).

Intergenerational Stresses

The recent decline in mortality has not in fact increased average family size very much. Many large families existed even in the old days of high mortality. The outstanding change has occurred between generations; there has been an explosion in the number of families from one generation to the next. This has created two kinds of stress: *inter*generational because the children must wait longer before they inherit family farms or other assets; and *intra*generational, between siblings, because there are more children to share the inheritance from the parents. Young people entering adulthood are most subject to these stresses, but they may also be best able to recognize their cause and to modify their fertility behavior accordingly.

Urbanization

Two thousand years from now our century may be thought of as that time in history in which man's way of life changed from a primarily rural to a primarily urban one. In 1900 no more than a quarter of the world's population lived in cities and towns; by the year 2000 probably more than 50 per cent will be city dwellers. No comparable period of history has witnessed such a profound transformation. Just as populations are now growing more rapidly in the poor countries than they ever grew by natural increase in the currently rich ones, so the rate of growth of cities is now faster in the poor countries than it was during the period of most rapid urbanization in Europe, North America, and Japan.

In rich countries cities are growing largely by migration from the countryside, and rural populations are declining. In poor countries both rural and urban populations are growing rapidly because of the excess of births over deaths, but the cities and towns are also absorbing large numbers of rural migrants and are therefore growing much faster than the populations of the countries as a whole. For example, between 1950 and 1960 in twenty-four countries with per capita incomes of less than $250 per year, cities of more than 100,000 inhabitants grew 60 per cent more rapidly than the total population. The average rate of growth of these large cities was over 4 per cent per year; they were thus doubling in population every seventeen years, whereas the doubling time for the entire population was nearly thirty years (164), and even longer for the countryside. The migration from the country to the city was at least partly due to the lack of satisfactory jobs for the fast growing numbers of young people in the villages.

Consequences of Large Family Size

The primary cause of the high proportion of children in the less developed countries (usually from 40 to 50 per cent of the entire population less than 15 years old) is not their rapid population growth but their high birth rates, which existed even when these populations were growing very slowly. Even before the postwar decline in mortality these high-fertility countries had young populations. When their populations began to grow rapidly as a result of the mortality decline, they became markedly younger, the more so the higher the rate of population growth. This is because human populations tend to increase or decrease from the bottom up. The younger age groups grow or decrease in number earlier and more rapidly than older ones. If and when fertility rates decline in the future, the populations of the less developed countries will become older, reaching a maximum average age when the populations become stationary at a low mortality level and the proportion of children will decline to less than 30 per cent. There will then be between two and three adults for every child under 15 years of age instead of the present nearly one-to-one ratio. The average size of families will sharply decrease, and the proportion of families with five or more children under 15 will become small.

Today this proportion is probably 20 to 25 per cent of all child-rearing families in the less developed countries. The exact proportion is not known and can be determined only by further demographic measurement and analysis.

Many studies have been made of the effects of family size on the well-being of children within the family. Children in large families suffer more from malnutrition and illness than do children in small families. There are higher mortality rates among younger children, slower physical growth, and less intellectual development. Family size is not the only cause of these effects, but it is an important element in the interacting network of causes (21).

Mortality, Health, and Physical Development

That infant and child mortality is much higher in large families than in small ones is illustrated by a study of eleven villages of the Indian Punjab during 1955–58 (23). Out of 1000 children, 206 died during the first year of life in families in which the mother had given birth to seven or more living children. In families of only two children the infant mortality was 116 out of 1000. The differences in mortality rates were even larger for children between 1 and 2 years old—95 per thousand for the children in families of seven or more live births and 16 per thousand for two-child families. The same proportionate differences in mortality rates between children of small and large families are found in New York City, though the levels of mortality are very much smaller (3A).

The effects of short intervals between births are about the same as those of large numbers of children. Data from the Punjabi study show that for 1955–58, 310 out of 1000 children who were born less than a year after a preceding child died during the first two years of life. This mortality rate was 59 per cent greater than that of children born between three and four years after a previous birth and more than twice as high as the mortality rate among children born after an interval of more than four years. The proportional differences in deaths during the second year of life between the three groups of children were about twice as large as the differences during the first year, though the mortality rates were considerably lower (23).

Malnutrition and Family Size

In poor countries the high mortality rates among children in large families and in families with close birth intervals may be largely due to malnutrition. The greater the sibling number, the greater is the likelihood of malnutrition in low-income families. Studies of preschool children in Colombia, for example, show that more than 47 per cent of the children in families in which there were four or more preschool children were seriously malnourished, but only 34 per cent of children in families with only one preschool child were malnourished (21). In Thailand 70 per cent of the children whose next youngest sibling was born within twenty-four months were malnourished, in contrast to 37 per cent of those in families without a younger sibling (21).

Physical Growth and Family Size

Since growth is related to nutrition, it would be expected that the height and weight of children in large families would be smaller on the average than in small families. Even in high-income countries the children of poor families are larger at any given age when the number of children in the family is small. For example, in a sample of 2000 London day-school students 11.25 years old, children from one-child families were about 4 per cent taller and 15 to 18 per cent heavier than children from families with five or more children (19). These differences showed up, however, only among the poorer social classes (6).

Intelligence and Educational Performance

Large numbers of children in the family diminish not only physical size but also linguistic skills, intelligence as measured by intelligence tests, and educational performance. These elements are to some extent interrelated; for example, heavier children mature earlier and early maturers do better in school than late maturers. Experiments show that the apathy that is a major consequence of malnutrition is highly correlated with such psychological elements as lack of ambition, low self-discipline, low mental alertness, and inability to concentrate (12).

Both physical growth and the greater cultural nurture associated with small families appear to be related to intelligence. In the sample of 2000 British day-school children, intelligence increased with height and decreased with family size. The average verbal reasoning scores of children over 135 centimeters tall in families of one or two children were about 8 per cent higher than those of equally tall children in families of four or more. The difference for children of the same age less than 135 centimeters tall between large and small families averaged about 6 per cent. Tall children from both large and small families scored about 8 per cent higher than short children.

In studies of Scottish children the average IQ of only children was 113; that of children with five or more siblings was 91. In France only children between the ages of 6 and 12 had an average mental age one to two years higher than children with eight or more siblings (1, 7).

Unlike the case with physical growth, the differences in educational performance between children in small and large families were present in all social classes. Data from the British National Survey of Health and Development show the performance of children in families of different sizes in educational tests at 8 and 11 years of age. In the upper manual working class only children and those in two-child families scored about 10 per cent higher than children in families of six and about 20 per cent higher than children in families of seven or more children. The difference in the lower manual working class between only children and children in large families was about 17 per cent. In the upper middle class the difference in educational performance between children in large and small families was somewhat less than 10 per cent. The difference in educational performance in all classes was slightly larger at 11 years of age than at 8 (6).

That the difference in children of large and small families persists in adult life is indicated by the average scores of army recruits on tests of different types in Great Britain. In the tests, which measured general, verbal, and special mechanical intelligence, the recruits from small families scored 10 to 13 per cent higher than those from families of five or more children, and the difference increased with increasing family size. On the other hand, the difference in tests of physical ability was much smaller; recruits from small families performed only about 4 per cent better than recruits from large families (20). In the United States 47 per cent of all young men rejected for military service on mental grounds came from families with six or more children (16A).

Intelligence and Family Size

It is likely that the ability to think abstractly, which underlies most kinds of human problem-solving, develops at an earlier age and to a greater degree if children learn the necessary verbal skills either from adults or from siblings considerably older than themselves. The smaller the family size, the easier it will be for children to develop such skills. These concepts receive support from psychological evidence that suggests that a young child's intelligence level can be raised by the environment in which he is brought up, including the cultural stimuli provided by the family or by an urban setting. A high proportion of persons of outstanding intellectual achievement were either only children or came from families in which there was a large age gap between siblings (1).

Children in large families may suffer more deprivation of maternal care because of greater maternal illness and the stress of large numbers of children on the mother. The effects of extreme maternal deprivation are drastic and impressive. They result in lower linguistic skills and IQ scores and less success in later life. In one study about 50 per cent of children deprived of maternal care were in a state of dazed stupor; they were apathetic, silent, and sad, made no attempt at contact with others, often suffered from insomnia, were prone to infection, and dropped behind other children in development. The effect is also well illustrated by a study comparing children brought up in institutions with those brought up in foster homes from early infancy. At the age of 3 the IQs of the institutionalized children were 28 points lower than those of the children who had been cared for by foster parents (12).

There is evidence that most parents in the less developed countries would like to control their family size. Many of them have more living children than they wanted to have. If these parents could have had only the number of children they wanted, those children would probably have been better cared for. If effective means were made available for all parents who want to control their family size, a considerable proportion might use these means and be better parents as a consequence (21).

Intelligence and Economic Development

Intellectual capacity and the ability to manipulate abstractions that typify educated intelligence are important to economic development not only through the contribution of skilled specialists to the society (e.g., engineers, lawyers, physicians, architects, and teachers) but also because of the broad category of managerial skills—from farm budgeting to central administration—that rest on intellectual capacity. The greater ability of intelligent workers to adapt to change and innovation is also important (12).

Education and Population Growth

Economic development requires much more than an accumulation of capital and an increase in the number of workers. New types of productive instruments have to be created, and new occupations have to be generated and learned in new contexts and locations. New types of risks have to be assumed, and new social and economic relationships have to be forged. Consequently, four of the most important needs for development are: (a) improvements in the quality of labor through education and other means of skill acquisition, as well as better health and welfare; (b) more favorable conditions for the introduction of innovation and technical change; (c) institutional changes leading to more effective organization and management at both governmental and private levels; and (d) a better environment for entrepreneurs. All these factors are interrelated, and to an extent all depend on improvements in education (15, p. 47).

Recent Educational Expansion

The number of children enrolled in the primary schools of the less developed countries taken as a whole rose 150 per cent during the fifteen years from 1950 to 1965, and the percentage of all children 6 to 12 years old who were in school rose from less than 40 per cent to more than 60 per cent. This marked increase in enrollment ratios (the fraction of the total age group who are in school) reflected in large measure the value placed on education by the people of all classes and income groups in the developing countries (8).

Public pressure for more education probably came partly from increasing returns to skill and education as industrialization proceeded and partly from the widening disparity between the incomes of people who had some formal education and those who were illiterate. This disparity in turn came from the growing demand for skilled labor and the slackening in demand for uneducated and unskilled workers (whose numbers were rapidly increasing because of high rates of population growth). Studies in four Latin American countries and in India show that the earnings of people with five to six years of schooling are double or triple those of persons who have spent less than two years in school. Persons with eleven years of education earn three to six times as much as functional illiterates (12).

Educational Costs per Child in
Developed and Less Developed Countries

On the average, the developed countries, with their high per capita incomes, are able to spend both a greater percentage of national income and far greater amounts of money on public education than the poor countries.

Even if the poor countries maintained the same over-all level of educational expenditure as the rich countries, expenditures per child would be much less because of their larger proportion of children, than is the case with low-fertility countries. For example, in 1965 the United Kingdom used 6 per cent of its GNP for education, and Ghana used 5 per cent. But the school-age population (5–19 years) was about 37 per cent of the total population in Ghana and 22 per cent in the United Kingdom. Thus Britain used nearly twice as large a percentage of its GNP per head of the school-age population as did Ghana. In absolute terms, the United Kingdom, with a GNP per capita of $1800, spent about $500 per child for education, and Ghana, out of a total GNP per capita of $300, spent about $40 per child (15, p. 50).

Education in the developing countries is further handicapped by the fact that educational costs per child in school in terms of per capita incomes tend to be relatively high. The differential in incomes between educated and uneducated people is much larger than in the developed countries, and consequently the ratio of teachers' salaries (which constitute 60 to 80 per cent of educational costs) to per capita incomes in developing countries is commonly two or three times the ratio in developed countries (13).

Future Increases in Enrollment Ratios

In spite of the rapid expansion of education in the less developed countries, the absolute number of illiterates increased from 1950 to 1965 because the number of children in the primary-school age group rose more rapidly than the number being educated. Educational planners are aiming at a reversal of this situation in the future by raising enrollment ratios to above 90 per cent as rapidly as possible (8).

Such an increase in enrollment ratios will be extremely difficult to accomplish in less than twenty to thirty years. One reason is that accelerating rates of population growth and the low number of people who have received secondary and higher education during the past twenty years have resulted in a small proportion of potential teachers relative to the numbers of potential students. Teachers must be recruited from the smaller and more poorly educated cohorts of these past years, in the face of competition from industry and other sectors. Moreover, the increase in the percentage of GNP used for education that is required to raise enrollment ratios cannot be achieved quickly because it requires a reorganization of fiscal and tax procedures that may not be possible until the GNP becomes much larger (15, p. 51).

Effects of Fertility Decline on Education

If the desired rise in enrollment ratios takes place over twenty years or more, the rate of growth of the school-age population will greatly affect the total number of children in school. Calculation for a typical less developed country shows that if enrollment ratios rise from 40 per cent to 95 per cent in thirty years and fertility rates are not reduced, there will be a 517 per cent increase in enrollment at the end of this period; whereas if fertility declines by 50 per cent during the next fifteen years, the increase in enrollment in thirty years will be only 200 per cent. A 50 per cent saving in enrollment would thus be attained at the end of thirty years by the assumed rapid reduction in fertility. Fertility reduction would give a saving of only 3 per cent at the end of the first ten years, but the saving would be 30 per cent at the end of twenty years (8).

A calculation of future educational costs for Pakistan assumes a growth in GNP of 6 per cent per year or about 350 per cent by 1995. Even with this very high rate of growth more than 8 per cent of national income, in contrast to less than 2 per cent in 1965, would have to be devoted to education in order to accomplish the planned increase in enrollment and teacher/pupil ratios unless there is a marked decline in fertility. Almost no country today allocates such a high percentage of resources to education. If the economy grows at a slower rate, the increase in enrollment ratios would probably be impossible to attain without a sharp reduction in fertility (8).

Increases in the quality and skills of the labor force and in other individual and social characteristics related to education are probably the most important elements in economic and social development. At the same time there is evidence that a certain level (or rate) and character of development are necessary conditions for a marked decline in fertility. Although both these propositions rest largely on statistical grounds and are difficult to quantify or state in any rigorous fashion, the empirical relationships seem clear. We may say with some conviction that an increase in the quantity, an improvement in the quality, and a raising of the average level of education in most developing countries would promote economic development and thereby a slowing down of population growth. Wider educational opportunities, particularly for girls, also lead to lower fertility in at least three direct ways. The age of marriage of women tends to rise, thus shortening the effective reproductive age span; educated women have fewer children after they are married; and educational costs to parents lead to a smaller desired family size (15, p. 54).

Time Lags in Educational and Economic Development

Both high rates of population growth in the poor countries and the poverty that is synonymous with underdevelopment severely impede a rapid expansion of education. The time lags of interaction between population and economic change and educational improvement are long. A reduction in fertility would significantly improve educational prospects only after about ten years, and there is also a lag of about ten years in the effects of education on economic development. Thus the less developed countries cannot afford to relax their efforts to bring about a reduction in fertility by all acceptable means and must take advantage of every opportunity for capital investment and institutional change that offers a possibility of speeding up the development process.

References

1. Anastasi, Anne. "Intelligence and Family Size," *Psychol. Bul.,* May, 1956.
2. Browning, Harley L. "Migrant Selectivity and the Growth of Large Cities in Developing Societies," *Rapid Population Growth: Consequences and Policy Implications,* Vol. II. Na-

tional Academy of Sciences, Baltimore: The Johns Hopkins Press, 1971. Pp. 273–314.

3. Clark, Colin. *Population Growth and Land Use.* New York: Macmillan, 1967.

3A. Chase, Helen C. *The Relationship of Certain Biologic and Socio-Economic Factors to Fetal, Infant, and Early Childhood Mortality and Father's Occupation, Parental Age and Infant's Birth Rank.* Albany, N.Y.: New York State Department of Health, 1961, mimeograph.

4. Coale, Ansley J., and Edgar M. Hoover. *Population Growth and Economic Development in Low-Income Countries.* Princeton, N.J.: Princeton University Press, 1958.

4A. Davis, Kingsley. *World Urbanization 1950–1970, Volume I: Basic Data for Cities, Countries and Regions.* Population Monograph Series No. 4, Berkeley: Institute of International Studies, 1969.

5. Demeny, Paul. "The Economics of Population Control," *Rapid Population Growth: Consequences and Policy Implications,* Vol. II. National Academy of Sciences, Baltimore: The Johns Hopkins Press, 1971. Pp. 199–221.

6. Douglas, J. W. B., J. M. Ross, and H. R. Simpson. *All Our Future.* London: Peter Davies, 1968.

7. Hunt, J. McV. *Intelligence and Experience.* New York: The Ronald Press, 1961.

8. Jones, Gavin W. "Effect of Population Change on the Attainment of Educational Goals in the Developing Countries," *Rapid Population Growth: Consequences and Policy Implications,* Vol. II. National Academy of Sciences, Baltimore: The Johns Hopkins Press, 1971. Pp. 315–367.

9. Kuznets, Simon. "Population and Economic Growth," *Proceedings of the American Philosophical Society,* Vol. III, No. 3 (June 1967). See also E. Kleiman, "A Standardized Dependency Ratio," *Demography,* Vol. 4, No. 2 (1967).

10. Ladejinsky, Wolf. "Ironies of India's Green Revolution," *Foreign Affairs,* Vol. 48, No. 4 (July 1970), 758–768.

11. Leff, Nathaniel H. "Dependency Rates and Savings Rates," *American Economic Review,* Vol. 59, No. 5 (December 1969).

12. Leibenstein, Harvey. "The Impact of Population Growth on Economic Welfare—Nontraditional Elements," *Rapid Population Growth: Consequences and Policy Implications,* Vol. II.

National Academy of Sciences, Baltimore: The Johns Hopkins Press, 1971. Pp. 175–198.

13. Lewis, W. Arthur. "Education and Economic Development," *Readings in the Economics of Education.* Paris: UNESCO, 1968.

14. Myrdal, Gunnar. *Asian Drama,* Vol. III. New York: Random House, 1968, Appendix 7.

15. National Academy of Sciences, Study Committee of the Office of the Foreign Secretary, *Rapid Population Growth: Consequences and Policy Implications,* Vol. I. Baltimore: The Johns Hopkins Press: 1971. Pp. xii, 105.

16. President's Science Advisory Committee, *The World Food Problem,* Vol. II. The White House (May, 1967), pp. 641–672.

16A. President's Task Force on Manpower Conservation, *One-Third of a Nation: A Report on Young Men Found Unqualified for Military Service.* Washington: Government Printing Office, 1964.

17. Schultz, Theodore W. "The Food Supply—Population Growth Quandary," *Rapid Population Growth: Consequences and Policy Implications,* Vol. II. National Academy of Sciences, Baltimore: The Johns Hopkins Press, 1971. Pp. 245–272.

18. Schultz, T. Paul. "An Economic Perspective on Population Growth," *Rapid Population Growth: Consequences and Policy Implications,* Vol. II. National Academy of Sciences, Baltimore: The Johns Hopkins Press, 1971. Pp. 148–174.

19. Scott, J. A., "Intelligence, Physique and Family Size," *Brit. J. Prev. Soc. Med.,* October, 1962.

20. Vernon, P. E. "Recent Investigations of Intelligence and Its Measurements," *Eugen. Rev.,* 43, 1951.

21. Wray, Joe D. "Population Pressures on Families: Family Size and Child Spacing," *Rapid Population Growth: Consequences and Policy Implications,* Vol. II. National Academy of Sciences, Baltimore: The Johns Hopkins Press, 1971. Pp. 403–461.

22. Weiner, Myron. "Political Demography: An Inquiry into the Political Consequences of Population Change," *Rapid Population Growth: Consequences and Policy Implications,* Vol. II. National Academy of Sciences, Baltimore: The Johns Hopkins Press, 1971. Pp. 567–617.

23. Wyon, John B., and John E. Gordon. *The Khanna Study: Population Problems in the Rural Punjab.* Cambridge: Harvard University Press, 1971.

Discussion of Professor Revelle's Paper

John P. Holdren is a physicist in controlled thermonuclear
fusion at the Lawrence Livermore Laboratory of the University
of California.

Dr. Revelle has offered a wide variety of instructive arguments, most of which are difficult to fault. I shall focus, therefore, on issues that I believe deserve more emphasis than his paper gave them and on those on which a technologist's perspective may be useful.

First, in discussing food and agricultural production I would stress the problem of malnutrition. I think that the degree to which lower death rates are due to improvements in nutrition is perhaps less than Dr. Revelle has implied. For example, much of the lowering of death rates in the less developed world has been due to environmental engineering—the widespread use of DDT, the filling of swamps, and so forth—that has reduced the incidence of malaria and certain other diseases in much of the world. An additional substantial contribution to lowered death rates has been made by the import of Western medical technology. These factors notwithstanding, child mortality in the age class from 1 to 4 is still often 10 per thousand per year as compared to about 1 per thousand per year in the same age class in the United States. In some less developed countries this rate is as high as about 35 per thousand per year. This situation is in large measure a result of the particularly severe consequences of malnutrition to children as opposed to adults. An adult receiving his caloric requirement is usually receiving his protein requirement as well, but this is not true for children because, proportionately, they require more protein. Substantial work has been reported recently correlating mental retardation with malnutrition in the early years.

Unfortunately much of the increase of per capita food production that has occurred in recent history has occurred not in the less developed countries but in the developed ones. In particular the change in per capita food production between 1939 and 1968 expressed as a percentage was as follows: in Latin America, per capita food production went down by 5.7 per cent; Africa, down by 4 per cent; the Far East, excluding mainland China, down by 2.8 per cent. Increases were reported in North America (up 18.3 per cent), in eastern Europe (up 33.9 per cent), and so on throughout the developed parts of the world. The popular assumption that improvements in global agricultural productivity always mean better diets for the hungry nations is not warranted.

Although some improvement in the standard of living is taking place in many parts of the world, it should be emphasized that the gap between the developed and the less developed countries is actually *widening* at this time. From 1960 to 1968 in the developed countries, GNP was increasing on the average at 5 per cent per year. With a mean population-growth rate in those countries of 1.2 per cent per year, *per capita* gross national product was increasing at 3.8 per cent per year. In the less developed countries during the same period, GNP was increasing 5.2 per cent per year, actually somewhat higher than in the developed countries. But with their mean population-growth rate of 2.4 per cent, their *per capita* increase was substantially less, only 2.7 per cent per year. Thus the less developed countries are experiencing just enough improvement to cause the so-called revolution of rising expectations; they are getting a sufficient taste of improvement to want a lot more, sufficient to understand what the "haves" have and, as "have-nots," to want it too. At the same time the gap is widening between the developed and developing countries in spite of the improvements that have been made, and combined with the rising expectations this contributes to a highly unstable situation.

Prospects for the Future

The technical potential may exist to provide both improved diets and a raised standard of living for the 6.5 to 7 billion people that demographers tell us will be here by the year 2000; but I would emphasize the difference between what is theoretically feasible and what is operationally practical. Most importantly we are faced with a problem of competing rates, and we are starting out behind. The rate of application of technology and the rate at which other aspects of development can proceed must compete with the rate of population growth. Yet nutrition and standards of living are so far from adequate in much of the world today that it would be difficult for technology to provide even a *stationary* population with a decent existence within a reasonably short time. In the perspective of population growth, if one examines the costs of and the lead time required for massive technological development, the picture is somewhat less optimistic than would be appropriate to the simple technological-feasibility argument—namely, what we could do in theory if we did everything right, if we had plenty of time, and if we were willing to spend the requisite amount.

There are some textbook examples of this sort of problem. One of them is the Aswân High Dam in the United Arab Republic (U.A.R.), where the gains in newly irrigated land from the project will feed less than the U.A.R.'s population growth during the period of construction. This is an example of the lead-time problem with large-scale technology. A second difficulty with the Aswân High Dam and with many other massive technologies is the unforeseen or ill-considered environmental consequences that increase with the haste with which technology is applied. And the haste with which we apply technology is proportional to how far behind we are when we start and to the magnitude of the population-growth rate we are trying to keep up with.

In the case of the Aswân High Dam the fertility of the Nile Delta has been threatened because the silt once carried down the Nile in its annual flood is now caught behind the Aswân

High Dam. This silt sediment will in the long run—perhaps one to two hundred years—fill up the reservoir and eliminate the irrigation potential that was the original purpose of the dam. For a similar reason (the loss of nutrients flowing down the Nile) the sardine fishery in the Mediterranean in that vicinity has suffered considerably. In this case a trade has been made between calorie production on the newly irrigated land and high quality protein production in the form of the sardine fishery. In the present world situation, characterized more by a deficiency of protein than by a deficiency of calories, this seems a very poor trade. An additional (and predicted) ecological consequence of the Aswân High Dam project is the enormous increase in the prevalence of schistosomiasis in the U.A.R. This disaster has occurred because an intermediate stage of the blood fluke that is associated with this parasitic disease is carried in snails that live and spread in irrigation canals. These examples illustrate the kinds of side effects that can be anticipated from massive, hastily applied technology. We are going to be seeing more of them in the future, and it cannot be emphasized too much that their number and seriousness will be proportional to the haste with which we apply new technology.

In the same connection Dr. Revelle mentioned some of the difficulties of extending the Green Revolution. The problems of the Green Revolution really boil down to the problems of development itself: the enormous increases in capital needed to buy fertilizers, the heavy use of pesticides, the provision of irrigation, the education of farmers for mechanized agriculture, and the other subtleties of transforming the subsistence system into the market agricultural system. I am sure that Dr. Revelle agrees that all this requires, or will require, a great deal more technical aid from the developed countries than we are providing now or are considering for the future. The United States today falls substantially short of the United Nations' recommendation that the developed countries should contribute 1 per cent of their GNP to foreign aid of this sort. The United States is now putting a small fraction of that, perhaps 0.3 per cent, into foreign aid. I suspect that what would be required in the way of very carefully considered technical aid is perhaps 10 to 15 per cent of the GNP of the developed nations over the next thirty years.

Environmental Problems

I would also like to comment on the question of what percentage of environmental problems in developed nations (such as the United States) can be attributed to population and to what degree we can alleviate these problems by direct assaults on the problems themselves. It is undoubtedly true that none of these problems would vanish even if we had a zero rate of population growth, and I am not sure there is anyone who disputes this. I think the emphasis that has been placed on population growth in many quarters is an entirely warranted response to total neglect of that component in many previous analyses. Certainly direct attacks on pollution, waste, planned obsolescence, and overconsumption based upon gadgetry are required. In addition we must replace environmental absurdities, such as the present use of biocides, with ecologically sound practices. All these things must be done independently of trying to come to grips with population growth. But those who think that successes in these areas will permit continuing population growth with impunity do so under misconceptions about biology, about technology, or about both.

To give some examples, I would like to consider some of the arguments that have been advanced, such as: "We can clean up the mess without tampering with population growth, and if we do so, we can accept population growth for some time to come." One of the main thrusts of the "clean-up" argument has been the switch to biodegradable sorts of wastes. Actually *most* pollutants are biodegradable, but we are simply overwhelming the natural buffers that exist to degrade these things. It does not matter if one's wastes are biodegradable if there are not enough biota to handle the degradables. This, incidentally, is one of many environmental problems related to population size but largely unrelated to population distribution. That is, the amount of waste we produce per capita multiplied by the number of *capita* is the amount of waste that we have to do away with, and there are indications that some of the associated problems are global in nature rather than local. One such indication is the ubiquity of chlorinated hydrocarbon pesticides—which have shown up in the fat of penguins in the Antarctic and in the ice cap on Greenland. Another ominous indicator is the global increase of turbidity, or dirtiness, in the atmosphere, which some authorities say is increasing by as much as 30 per cent per decade. In all these areas the problem boils down to the fact that we are in some danger of overwhelming the natural buffers that permit our continued existence on this planet.

The technological solutions to many kinds of pollution generally tend to shift the impact rather than to remove it. There are obvious examples. Incinerating garbage pollutes the air. A switch from fossil fuel to uranium or plutonium as the heat source for generating electrical power leaves radioactive wastes rather than more conventional air pollutants. To carry it a step further, abolishing paper plates might lead to the consumption of more detergents. The point is that, in every case, our situation seems to illustrate what has been called a basic rule of ecology: There is no such thing as a free lunch. It is critical that we understand this; we have to realize that man will always have an impact on the environment and that the impact under any set of assumptions about economics and technology will always be proportional to population size.

Finally, we must understand that increases in the carrying capacity of this planet have been, and presumably will continue to be, achieved at the expense of biological diversity. Man replaces complicated ecological communities with simpler ones, such as our enormous monocultures of wheat, rice, and corn. Even among the agricultural crops themselves, such as cereals, the tendency of the Green Revolution has been to replace a wide variety of locally adapted strains with single new strains because of their obvious advantages of high yield, fertilizer sensitivity, insensitivity to day length, and so forth. The disadvantage of this sort of behavior is that monocultures are exceptionally vulnerable to various kinds of pests. For example, the "miracle" rice IR8 developed by the International Rice Institute has, as one of its principal attributes, a short stalk so that the higher yields of grain do not cause the stalk to break or bend over. Unfortunately the shorter stalk makes the grain more accessible to rats, and now in the Philippines and elsewhere there are "miracle" rats in "miracle" rice fields. Again, there is no such thing as a free lunch (except perhaps for the rats).

The recurrent theme that population policy can have little short-term effect either on the food situation, on the employment situation, or on the environment situation should not be misunderstood. It is certainly true that population programs will be slow to take effect because of the inertia in human attitudes and in the age structure, but the suggestion often seems implicit (and I do not believe Dr. Revelle is guilty of this) that we should assign low priority to population programs for this reason. I suggest that this is suicidal because ultimate success in any of our great problem areas is contingent on leveling off population. For anything we manage to do in the way of improving our technological behavior, improving the operation of our economic system, and diminishing our waste will ultimately be diluted and wiped out by population growth. If, on the grounds that changes in population policy will not have any short-term effect, we *do* assign low priority to population programs, we shall find twenty years hence that we are still committed to an enormous increase in population—as we are today—because of the age structure. Such a situation will hopelessly aggravate the problems I have mentioned, as well as those that Dr. Revelle discussed more thoroughly in his paper.

3

Unemployment and Underemployment

BRUCE F. JOHNSTON

Bruce F. Johnston is Professor of Economics, Food Research Institute, Stanford University.

In dealing with this very large topic, I propose to concentrate on the problems of unemployment and underemployment in the late-developing low-income nations that contain well over half of the world's population. Specifically, I shall focus on economies in which so little structural change has taken place that some 70 to 80 per cent of the labor force is engaged in agriculture—a situation in which employment problems are liable to be acute and intractable.

These late-developing countries are confronted by unique problems and opportunities. In a sense all of mankind's stock of scientific knowledge and technology is at their disposal. However, because they are underdeveloped, their efforts to modernize their economies are limited by an acute shortage of capital in all its forms—human skills and knowledge, as well as physical capital—and this severely limits the rate at which they can use new technologies. I shall be emphasizing that these countries face especially important problems in the timing and sequences in which innovations are introduced and in adapting existing knowledge and technologies to fit their conditions and their aspirations. Inappropriate sequences and a lopsided pattern of economic growth can easily give rise to difficult, explosive problems of unemployment and intensified underemployment.

Unemployment problems are important in developed countries and semi-industrial economies too. In the United States automation causes problems because the effects are concentrated on disadvantaged groups who face shrinking job opportunities for the unskilled. Observers who have studied the introduction of the mechanized cotton picker in the Delta region of Mississippi are convinced that the rapid displacement of unskilled farm laborers accelerated migration to urban areas and thus accentuated the problems that we face in our urban ghettos.

I shall say nothing more about problems of population and technology in the high-income countries except to note a superficial similarity that actually sharpens the contrast between the two sets of problems. In both poor and affluent societies a large percentage of the population is engaged in the service sector. In affluent scocieties such as the United States, service occupations range from teaching at institutions like Caltech to separating middle-aged men and women from their excess pounds—and dollars—in elegant reducing parlors. In poor countries the service sector includes petty traders, street hawkers, shoeshine boys, and domestic servants and other household retainers. In the high-income countries the proliferation of services may indicate that people do not have anything better to do with their money. In poor countries a lot of people do not have anything better to do with their time.

The Nature of Employment in Agrarian Societies

First, I want to say a few words about the economic structure of low-income societies and the special nature of their problems of unemployment and underemployment.* The basic

* A recent monograph by Turnham (1) of the Organisation for Economic Co-operation and Development, Development Centre, presents a particularly useful review of problems of unemployment and underemployment in the less developed countries and summarizes much of the empirical evidence that is available.

point is so obvious that it is easily overlooked: Their very different stage of development and economic structure has a fundamental influence on the character of the problems they face and conditions the kinds of policies that are appropriate. I also want to stress that these structural features will exist for a number of years or even decades. As a matter of simple arithmetic the process of structural transformation is bound to be rather slow when the labor force in agriculture bulks large and the total labor force is growing at 2.5, 3, or 3.5 per cent per year. Because of the constraints imposed by the limited stocks of capital—human as well as physical—there is no rapid or easy way that the present occupational composition of the labor force can be altered. We are conditioned by our past experience to emphasize the importance of increasing agricultural productivity in order to "release" labor from agriculture for industry and other nonfarm employment. But for most of the contemporary developing countries the problem is not how to release labor from agriculture but how to devise strategies for agricultural development that will make it possible to absorb a growing farm labor force into productive agricultural employment while facilitating the growth of the nonfarm sectors that will *eventually* permit a reduction in the absolute size of the agricultural work force.

The predominance of agriculture in most of the less-developed regions of the world is an "initial condition" of great importance that stems from the primacy of man's need for food. That 70 or even 80 per cent of the households in such countries are engaged in agricultural production to feed their own family members and the relatively small percentage of the population living in cities is an eloquent indication of the low level of agricultural productivity. By contrast, in the United States only 5 per cent of the nation's working population is engaged in agricultural production. It would be an error however to ignore the fact that there is a complex interrelationship between the low level of agricultural productivity and the economic structure of the low-income countries. Low agricultural productivity is in part a reflection of the fact that the commercial market for farm products and the level of cash income received by farmers are often very limited. In some cases there is the possibility of exporting agricultural products to foreign markets. That may be a very important possibility for a country that can enlarge its share of world exports; but for the developing countries as a group the possibility of expanding agricultural exports modifies but does not eliminate this constraint.

In examining the problems of unemployment and underemployment in the context of rapid population growth, it is important first to note the dualism that characterizes low-income economies—most people are involved in traditional agriculture and only a few are absorbed by a coexisting modern sector. In countries such as India, Pakistan, and Nigeria, farming is done by primitive techniques and very little capital equipment is used. Furthermore, as a result of institutional arrangements such as the family farm or "communal" systems of land tenure, agriculture has a special character as the "self-employment sector." Like the shoeshine boy or the self-appointed guardian of parked cars who hopes to collect a tip for his surveillance, members of farm households do not have to find an employer willing to offer them a job in order to earn a livelihood, meager as it may be. India and Pakistan, however, are important examples of low-income nations where a sizable fraction of the rural households do not own land and are dependent on wages received as agricultural laborers.

In contrast, employment opportunities in manufacturing and other modern sectors are distinctly limited. Additional workers are hired only up to the point where the additional cost is matched by additional returns. Shortages of capital and, frequently, demand constraints slow the pace at which output and employment in these modern sectors can be expanded.

One consequence of this dualism is that in the traditional sectors underemployment is a more pervasive problem than open unemployment. Meaningful progress toward eliminating poverty—and probably toward reducing the present rapid rates of population growth—depends on a broad process of modernization. And a necessary condition for the process of modernization is the structural change that is indicated when a rising proportion of the working population becomes engaged in producing the wide array of nonfarm goods and services that dominate consumption patterns in societies with high per capita incomes.

Population Growth and Employment

The most obvious implication of the very high rates of population growth in the developing countries is that even with a modest rate of increase in per capita incomes the growth of demand for food is very rapid. The "awesome power of compound interest" also has disturbing implications for the growth of a country's labor force and the process of structural transformation. The rate of change in the occupational composition of the labor force will inevitably be slow in countries where most of the labor force is still in agriculture and where total population and labor force are growing at 2 or 3 per cent annually.

The growth paths in Figures 1 and 2 compare the changes in total, farm, and nonfarm labor force in two hypothetical countries over a fifty-year period on the basis of alternative assumptions about the rate of growth of the total labor force and of nonfarm employment. Projections were made starting with a total labor force of 10 million in each of the countries. For Earlyphasia it was assumed that the initial farm labor force accounted for 80 per cent of the total and for Middlephasia that the labor force was divided equally between agriculture and nonagriculture. Figure 1 is based on the assumption that the total labor force is growing at a "moderate" rate of 1 per cent per year; Figure 2 on a "very rapid" rate of 3 per cent. For each assumption the growth path of the farm labor force was computed by iteration on the basis of three different rates of growth of employment in the nonfarm sector—"moderate," "rapid," and "very rapid," defined as 1.5, 3, and 4.5 per cent respectively.

In this computation procedure it was assumed that the size

of the farm labor force is determined as a residual on the basis of exogenously determined rates of change in the total labor force and in nonfarm employment. Although this assumption is fairly reasonable during the early phase of growth, the hypothetical projections shown in Figures 1 and 2 are obviously not to be taken too seriously. Hopefully, careful projections of this nature will strengthen the will to implement policies and programs to insure that birth rates will begin to fall soon and with sufficient speed so that rapid growth of the labor force will be a problem of twenty or thirty years rather than fifty or more.

In order to support a rising percentage of the population in the nonfarm sectors there must be an increase in output per farm worker (or an increased reliance on food imports). But when the farm labor force continues to bulk large in the total, the "required" rate of increase in farm productivity is fairly slow; hence it seems reasonable to assume that the change in the size of the farm labor force is determined essentially as a residual in a country at an early phase of development.

Another qualification to be noted is even more important. Although agriculture is the "self-employment" sector *par excellence,* a part of the residual labor force will be found in urban areas eking out an existence in family workshops, in the "service sector," or as casual laborers. Many countries have the problem of a "floating population" or unemployed "school-leavers" queuing up for the limited number of jobs that become available. This problem is aggravated by the "excessive" wage differentials characteristic of jobs in the modern sector in which employment by government or by foreign firms bulks large and wage rates have little relation to the supply of and demand for labor. It is also aggravated by factors that keep farm incomes at a very low level, such as limited access to land and to technical knowledge, and by the limited ability of farmers to purchase farm inputs because cash income is low. Whatever the reasons, if income-earning opportunities in agriculture are meager, it may be quite rational to chance being one of those

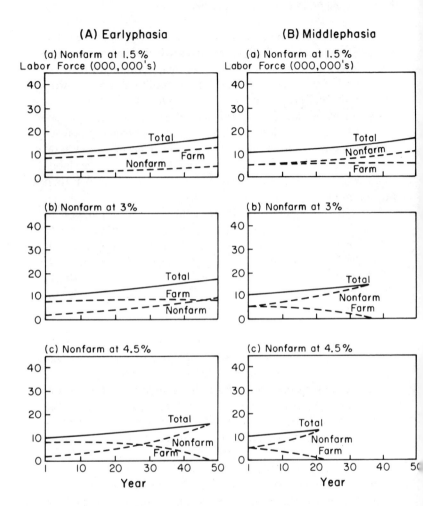

Figure 1. Hypothetical growth paths for total, farm, and non-farm labor force over a fifty-year period in the imaginary under-developed countries of Earlyphasia and Middlephasia, from an initial labor force of 10 million. Assumption: moderate growth of the total labor force of 1 per cent per year. Source: Author's calculations.

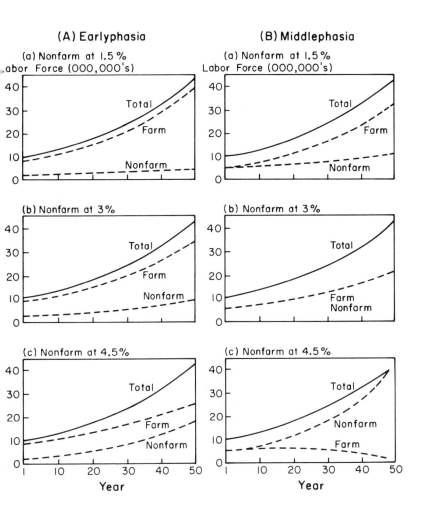

Figure 2. Hypothetical growth paths for total, farm, and non-farm labor force over a fifty-year period in Earlyphasia and Middlephasia, from an initial labor force of 10 million. Assumption: very rapid growth of the total labor force of 3 per cent per year. Source: Author's calculations.

fortunate enough to land a job in the modern sector while living a catch-as-catch-can existence in an urban shanty town.

Triple-pronged Revolution: Policy Issues

I turn now to some of the policy issues relating to development and employment. The crucial problem the developing countries face is to bridge an enormous technological gap. Much more is involved, however, than a straightforward process of "catching up." Economic growth requires and induces a broader process of social change that involves educational, scientific, and governmental institutions—as well as the changes in technology, skill, and organization that affect economic performance directly. The paths to be followed will be unique in important respects, and they must be traveled at a much more rapid pace than occurred in the developed countries.

Hunter. (2) has emphasized that late-developing countries face especially difficult problems of choice because they are "bedeviled by inheriting or adopting ideas and standards developed from the quite different experience, circumstances and needs" of the industrialized nations. The technologies available often do not suit their needs. Institutions and standards of welfare evolved from the experience and needs of the richest countries have been introduced without sufficient critical re-evaluation and adaptation to local conditions. Premature introduction of minimum wage legislation is a case in point. Against those disadvantages must be set the potential advantages that contemporary developing countries have in the accumulated knowledge of modern science and technology. There is a vast range of technologies and a variety of institutional inventions and organizational devices to choose from, and much of this can be adapted to the needs of the less developed countries. A fundamental difficulty derives from the multiplicity of the options available combined with the constraints imposed by shortages of capital in all forms. Hence, the problems of choice, timing, and sequences are of critical importance.

The unique features and special complexity of contemporary development problems are epitomized by the fact that in devising a rational approach to developing the agricultural sector and promoting over-all economic growth, developing countries need to take into account what amounts to a "three-pronged revolution"—a demographic revolution, an agricultural revolution, and (for lack of a better term) a manufacturing revolution.

The *demographic revolution* is manifest in the unprecedentedly high rates of population growth that have created problems of a magnitude unique in history. As I said earlier, the problems of absorbing a rapidly growing labor force into productive employment may prove to be a more difficult problem than supplying food.

The *agricultural revolution* is epitomized by the high-yielding, fertilizer-responsive varieties of rice, wheat, and maize. Although its impact is very recent and uneven, it is now transforming production possibilities in an increasing number of less developed countries. Widespread introduction of new varieties and greatly increased use of chemical fertilizers offer the hope of rapid and relatively low-cost increases in agricultural production. Moreover, it is possible to achieve these increases in farm output by an intensification of agricultural production that will permit the absorption of a sizable fraction of the growing labor force into productive employment. The extent to which increased farm output is accompanied by greater opportunities for productive employment in agriculture will be determined, however, by the means employed to realize the potential of the new varieties of crops. And the pressures that lead to a capital-intensive rather than a labor-intensive approach to agricultural development are strong.

By *manufacturing revolution* I mean the advances in industrial technologies that have made possible low-cost production of manufactured products, including many critical farm inputs. Such production is usually based on capital-intensive methods that are often characterized by substantial economies of scale. The advances in the manufacture of chemical fertilizers and in the mining of potash and phosphate rock are important examples. The substantial and continuing decline in the real price of chemical fertilizers is a vital component of the Green Revolution. Most of the new processes, especially those used in producing nitrogen fertilizers from natural gas and atmospheric nitrogen, require very large-scale plants entailing heavy capital investment and employing only a handful of workers. This general tendency in manufacturing and mining industries means that even a rapid rate of capital formation and expansion of output may lead to only a small increase in employment. The difficulties faced by late-developing countries because of the demographic situation are accentuated by those economic characteristics of modern technologies that make for relatively slow growth of employment opportunities in the nonfarm sectors.

The triple-pronged revolution presents three interrelated problems. First, there is the problem of reducing birth rates so that population and labor-force growth rates will decline to more manageable levels. Second, there is the problem of devising and implementing strategies for developing the agricultural sector that are appropriate to the problems that confront low-income agrarian societies today. The approach adopted to achieve expanded agricultural production to meet the increased demand associated with population growth and rising per capita incomes should be designed to minimize the problems of rural unemployment and underemployment. These problems can easily be aggravated if the spread of mechanization displaces farm labor more rapidly than the nonfarm sectors can create alternative employment opportunities. Third, there is the problem of pursuing policies in the manufacturing and other nonfarm sectors that will foster rapid growth of both output and employment.

It would be splendid if I could offer convincing answers to these problems of agricultural strategy and policies for industrial development—or if *someone* could offer such answers! The unhappy fact is that economists have only belatedly begun to pay serious heed to these issues. However, I should like to sketch three sets of ideas which, I believe, suggest some of the elements that will be important in arriving at answers to those problems—answers that can differ considerably depending upon the unique institutional, historical, and resource characteristics of particular countries.

Agricultural and Industrial Development

The first set of ideas derives from a study of the Industrial Revolution in England and France by the Belgian economic historian Bairoch (3). Bairoch gives explicit attention to the relevance of the Industrial Revolution to the problems facing developing countries today and to the implications of new features, such as the rapid rate of population growth. One of the major conclusions of his study is that an increase in agricultural productivity and the growth in demand for agricultural inputs supplied by industry were major forces that gave impetus to the process of cumulative economic growth in England and France. The distinctive features of the problems confronting developing countries lead him to argue that there is particular need today to pursue policies that will maximize the positive, growth-promoting interactions between agricultural and industrial development. Such policies need special attention because of factors that weaken the "diffusion mechanisms" that were so important to the West and Japan in translating an initial impulse—notably the increase in agricultural productivity and farm demand for industrial products—into a process of cumulative growth. The six factors that he considers are: (a) an increase in the disparity between traditional and modern technologies; (b) the increase in the amount of investment per worker; (c) the predominance of large-scale, centralized factories and the increased difficulty in recruiting and training technical workers and entrepreneurs; (d) reduced natural protection due to the lowering of transportation costs; (e) an excessive bias toward reliance on agricultural exports; and (f) excessive income differentials between the traditional and modern sectors.*

I turn next to the analytical framework presented by Johnson (5) in the 1968 Wicksell Lectures, which represents a dynamic

---

* Bairoch's propositions are examined in more detail along with Schultz's "industrial impact hypothesis" in Johnston (4).

theory of the process of economic growth that is especially relevant to understanding the interactions between agricultural and industrial development. It is also relevant to the problems involved in bridging the technological gap between high- and low-income countries in such a way as to minimize the explosive problems of unemployment. Johnson, along with many other economists, has rejected the narrow view that the concept of capital should be confined to physical capital in the form of factories and equipment. He argues for a broad conception of capital to include human skills, social capital, and the technical and organizational knowledge by which the human and material factors of production are combined in the production process. Within that conceptual framework he characterizes the process of economic growth as:

> . . . a general process of capital accumulation, that is, of investment in the acquisition of larger stocks of the various forms of capital; and the condition of being "developed" consists of having accumulated, and having established efficient social and economic mechanisms for maintaining and increasing large stocks of capital per head in the various forms. Similarly, the condition of being "under-developed" is characterized by the possession of relatively small stocks of the various kinds of capital, and the existence of relatively weak and inefficient mechanisms for maintaining and increasing those stocks, particularly of inefficient mechanisms for coordinating the growth of the various forms of capital so as to keep the rates of return on them roughly in alignment, and high enough to encourage accumulation. (5)

That the "mechanisms for coordinating the growth of the various forms of capital" are generally inefficient is not surprising. There are inherent problems and special shortcomings within developing countries that make it difficult to coordinate the growth of physical capital and investments in "knowledge production" and in the creation of human capital "so as to keep the rates of return on them in alignment, and high enough to encourage accumulation." Although a competitive market system can be a valuable mechanism for guiding many allocation and investment decisions, Johnson rightly emphasizes that "improvement of the degree of integration of the [market] system and of the quality of the information it generates and disseminates is itself part of the process of economic development."

Beyond the problems of achieving efficient market mechanisms, "the process of growth will be strongly conditioned by the nature and quality of political decisions in the relevant areas." Investment decisions about public utilities and other types of infrastructure are either taken by the government or are strongly influenced by government policy. Furthermore, investments in "knowledge production" and in the creation of human capital also depend heavily on government decision-making processes, and because of their special features, the likelihood of underinvestment and misallocation of resources is considerable.

Viewing growth as a process of capital accumulation in this broader sense also underscores the importance of two propositions that Rosenberg (6) has stressed. Since economic growth is in many respects a learning process where the human factor acquires new skills, aptitudes, and aspirations, it is important to consider the effects of a number of feedback mechanisms on the productivity of the human agent. And there may be important differences between agriculture and manufacturing, or the different types of manufacturing or agricultural activities, in the kinds of qualitative changes in the human agent that are generated and in the impact of different patterns of using resources on productivity changes over time.

Also pertinent to questions relating to agricultural strategy and the process of structural transformation is Rosenberg's emphasis on the special importance of the sector producing capital goods and "its role as a source of new technology appropriate to a country's factor endowment . . ." (6). He suggests that the degree of development of this sector is a critical factor accounting for differences in the growth performance of industrial economies and "primary producing countries" where little structural transformation has taken place.

> It is probable that one of the most important factors contributing to the viability and flexibility of industrial economies is the exist-

ence of a well-developed capital goods sector possessing the technical knowledge, skills and facilities for producing machinery to accommodate the changing requirements of productive activity *plus* the ability and the incentive for raising productivity of machinery production itself—thereby reducing its cost and encouraging its further adoption. Herein may lie the most important feedback of all which is central to explaining the differences in behaviour between industrial and primary producing economies. Industrial societies, through the role of their highly developed capital goods producing industries, have, in effect, internalized in their industrial structure a technological capacity which undertakes technological change and adaptation almost as a matter of course and routine. Underdeveloped economies, of course, import much of their capital goods from abroad, but this expedient deprives them of a learning experience in the production, improvement and adaptation of machinery which may be vital to economic growth. (6)

Strategy for Agriculture

The approach to agricultural development that is adopted will have both *direct* and *indirect* effects on the ability of a developing economy to absorb a growing labor force into productive employment.

Although economists commonly stress a trade-off between output and employment objectives, there do not appear to be inherent reasons for serious conflict between those objectives within agriculture. Admittedly there are strong pressures that tend toward premature tractor mechanization, which aggravates problems of unemployment and underemployment. But there is strong evidence that supports the view that in the agricultural sector there are no *inherent* reasons for serious conflict between output and employment objectives. With a broad-thrust approach to increasing the output and productivity of the great majority of a nation's farmers by labor-intensive, capital-saving techniques, a growing labor force can be absorbed into productive employment in agriculture even though the underlying man-to-land ratio is unfavorable.

The tremendously important yield-increasing innovations

represented by the new varieties of wheat, rice, and maize accompanied by heavier application of fertilizer enhance the prospects for achieving increases in farm output by a labor-using, capital-saving expansion path because these innovations can be used efficiently by both small and large farm owners. The substantial substitutability of the factors of production in the agricultural sector and the potential for increasing factor productivity are, however, dependent upon the broad strategy adopted for sector-wide programs. For example, government policies and programs affecting the quantity and quality of resources devoted to agricultural research and extension will be of major importance. The extent to which research, extension, and credit arrangements are geared to the needs of small-scale farmers with limited capacity to purchase inputs will have a particularly strong influence on the factor proportions that characterize the agricultural sector's expansion path.

The indirect effects of a country's approach to agricultural development on the process of structural change and on the growth of nonfarm output and employment are related to the pattern of income distribution and the composition of rural demand. It is important to emphasize that comprehensive programs to redistribute incomes are not feasible in low-income countries. Hence, the pattern of income distribution is determined almost entirely by the distribution of income-earning opportunities. Although the aggregate demand of rural households for nonfarm products is constrained by the growth of farm cash income, the type of rural demand for inputs and consumer goods will differ according to the type of agricultural strategy adopted. Logic and history suggest that the nature of this rural demand will, through its effects on the level and composition of investment in the nonfarm sectors, influence the magnitude of the effects of agricultural expansion on the growth of nonfarm employment and output.

Given the great importance of agriculture to the economies of many developing countries, it is almost certain that these indirect effects will be important. The experiences of Japan and Taiwan suggest that a broadly based approach to agricultural development has important advantages because of such indirect effects and because of the direct benefits from the expansion of farm production using labor-intensive, capital-saving technologies that provide productive employment for a large and growing labor force. The agricultural expansion associated with a broad-thrust approach generates a wide demand for relatively simple types of farm equipment. It reduces the foreign-exchange requirements of expanded farm output and maximizes the positive interactions between agricultural and industrial development. Improved but inexpensive equipment, such as bullock-drawn plows and cultivators, seed drills with fertilizer attachments, and stationary threshers, is generally produced by a large number of small firms that make maximum use of domestic resources (including otherwise untapped sources of capital). This type of manufacturing growth leads to a broad diffusion process that maximizes the opportunities for "learning by doing" and thus promotes the development of entrepreneurial and technical skills in metalworking firms. And metalworking firms have a critical role to play in the assimilation of increasingly complex technologies and in adapting them to local conditions.

An important and highly relevant feature of the growth of manufacturing in Japan and Taiwan has been the parallel development of a "semimodern" sector of small-scale firms using labor-intensive, capital-saving techniques alongside the growth of a modern sector of large, capital-intensive firms in those lines of production in which economies of scale are of decisive importance. This dual pattern of industrial development and the labor-intensive, capital-saving strategy for agriculture have undoubtedly been major factors in avoiding serious problems of unemployment in Japan and Taiwan and in enabling those countries to make strides toward substantially reducing underemployment in agriculture despite the small size of their farm units.

Taiwan's experience is especially interesting in this regard because it was the first country to experience the sort of explosive growth of population that has now become commonplace. Taiwan has already experienced a large increase in the absolute size of its farm population and a reduction in the size of the average farm unit, but as a result of the combined effect of higher yields, improved irrigation and expanded multiple cropping, and enlarged production of higher-valued crops it has been possible to reduce underemployment in agriculture significantly and to raise incomes per farm worker in spite of the reduction in the size of the average farm. Now, as a result of the rapid growth of nonfarm output and employment Taiwan seems to have reached that critical turning point where the absolute size of the farm population begins to decline.

The vigorous growth of small-scale, fairly labor-intensive firms in the semimodern industrial sectors in Taiwan and Japan has been facilitated by factors other than the stimulus of a broadly based rural demand for inputs and consumer goods. Organizational arrangements, such as subcontracting by large-scale enterprises to small factories or household workshops, made it possible for the smaller ventures to expand as efficient and viable units utilizing techniques appropriate to the distribution of factors in a labor-surplus economy. The spread of transport facilities and the availability of electric power in rural areas also facilitated this dual pattern of industrial development.

There is a serious lack of statistical information about the semimodern sector of industry in most of the contemporary less developed countries, but it appears that small-scale firms using labor-intensive, capital-saving techniques have not experienced anything like the vigorous growth that has characterized the economic development of Japan and Taiwan. (The growth of the semimodern sector in Japan was sluggish during the 1920s and early 1930s apparently because of unfortunate economic policies that were partly based on an ill-advised and persistent determination to return to the gold standard at the prewar parity.)

In concluding my discussion, I want to stress the complexity of the problems and the lack of consensus that prevails. The difficulties stem in part from the extraordinarily rapid growth of population and labor force in the contemporary developing countries. The problems are compounded, however, by the multiplicity of the options that are potentially available and by the imperfect understanding on the part of economists, foreign advisers, and indigenous leaders of the complex problems of choice, timing, and sequences that are faced by late-developing countries. The options include an enormous range of production technologies, but the limited resources of capital, foreign exchange, and entrepreneurial and technical capability in these countries curtail their capacity to absorb new technologies. They have an acute need to adapt the technologies available to their drastically different factors of production—a scarcity of capital and skilled manpower and an abundance of unskilled labor. But their sector producing capital goods has limited capacity to reduce their dependence on imported equipment and to adapt the new technologies to local conditions. They have a wealth of models from which to choose, but there are major difficulties in arriving at a consensus concerning a consistent, coherent strategy for development. This last problem is almost inevitable, given the appeal of competing ideologies, the conflicting recommendations proffered by foreign experts, the complex and novel character of the problems, and the different ways in which various social and political groups perceive their interests.

There are other important elements to the problem. For example, there is a growing conviction among some students of development problems that the import-restriction policies that many countries have adopted to promote industrialization have had the effect of impeding the type of structural change required for sustained growth. An important Organization for Economic Co-operation and Development study of industrialization (7) emphasizes that these policies have resulted in the underpricing of capital and overpricing of labor in a way that aggravates problems of unemployment and underemployment.*

* Sicat (8) has posed the issues forcefully in a fable that contrasts the economic policies of the Philippines and Taiwan.

Tractor Mechanization

The particular policy question that I pose is whether developing countries that have experienced little structural transformation should seek ways to encourage a broad-thrust approach to agricultural development similar to the pattern pursued in Japan and Taiwan. Although I am persuaded that the advantages of this labor-intensive, capital-saving approach to agricultural development are great, many persons—foreign advisers, technical specialists, and leaders within the developing countries—are convinced that the Green Revolution must be accompanied by the rapid spread of tractors and other types of labor-saving equipment.

My concern about rapid tractor mechanization in countries such as India, Pakistan, the Philippines, or Nigeria is with timing. I believe that at this stage of their development returns will be greater if resources are invested more widely—in chemical fertilizers, extending water-control facilities, strengthening extension programs, and other components of a broad-thrust approach. There is no question about the impressive technical efficiency of tractors and tractor-drawn equipment, although it is worth noting that the gap in technical efficiency between imported items such as tractors and inexpensive equipment of local manufacture could be narrowed considerably. If research and development activities geared to equipment suited to small-scale agriculture were to receive a fraction of the support that has been devoted to research and development activities on farm equipment in developed countries, it could foster much wider use of simple equipment of improved design. This would increase labor productivity substantially by easing labor bottlenecks rather than by massive displacement of farm labor.

One of a number of special advantages that Taiwan has enjoyed has been the possibility of drawing upon research and development activities in Japan where environmental conditions are fairly similar. Because of soil, climatic, and other differences much of the equipment developed in Japan is not directly transferrable to the Indian subcontinent, tropical Africa, and other developing regions.

Given their economic structure, if the late-developing countries follow a policy of trying to introduce simultaneously the full range of both yield-increasing and mechanical innovations, it follows that development will be concentrated in the subsector made up of large-scale, capital-intensive farm units while the mass of the farm population will be bypassed. For example, in India with 70 per cent of the population and labor force in agriculture the level of commercial demand and the total cash income accruing to the agricultural sector could support a few islands of fully modern agriculture—one or two "Iowas" of large farms employing the full gamut of modern technologies and purchased inputs. But all of Indian agriculture cannot become like Iowa's until the country's economic structure has been transformed and the whole economy moves into the twentieth century.

There are often strong pressures to emphasize the most rapid possible development of a subsector made up of highly commercialized, capital-intensive farm units. In addition to the technical efficiency of tractors and their prestige as a symbol of modern agriculture, concentration on a relatively small number of large units offers an alternative to the more difficult task of reaching hundreds of thousands, or millions, of farm households. It is a formidable task to organize agricultural-extension programs and the other supporting services required to enable small-scale farm units to reach progressively higher levels of efficiency by a cumulative process of change. Rapid tractor mechanization also receives support because investment of scarce resources of capital and foreign exchange in labor-displacing equipment is often profitable to the larger farmers who are able to mechanize, even though it is uneconomic from society's point of view.*

* Certain types of farm mechanization may, of course, be very profitable from society's point of view. For example, the diesel- and electric-powered tubewells that have spread so rapidly in West Pakistan and the Indian Punjab have provided supplementary irrigation, which has facilitated fuller utilization of labor and bullocks as well as land. Al-

Such a discrepancy between private and social profitability may exist because: (a) market wage rates for farm labor overstate the opportunity cost of labor; (b) there is frequent underpricing of capital as a result of overvalued exchange rates and subsidized credit programs; and (c) individual farm operators cannot be expected to take into account the social costs of exacerbating problems of unemployment and underemployment.

The experiences of Japan, Taiwan, and the countries in which the Green Revolution is now spreading demonstrate that the approach I have suggested is not an impossible task if profitable yield-increasing innovations are available. It is at least a plausible hypothesis that an approach that leads to wide involvement of the farm population in technical and economic change will facilitate the spread of family planning in rural areas.

Even if one is persuaded that the structural characteristics of economies that are still predominantly agrarian make it desirable for them to imitate Japan or Taiwan in their agricultural strategies, difficult problems remain as to the choice of policies and programs that will achieve that pattern of development. And the problems are urgent. The new crop varieties have given important breathing space; for a time, food supplies can keep pace with rapid population growth. But once the new production possibilities have been exploited, additional opportunities for relatively low-cost increases in food production will be much more limited. Therefore, it is imperative for the developing countries to exploit these opportunities in ways that will have a maximum positive impact on over-all economic growth and modernization—including the most rapid possible reduction of birth rates.

---

though it is impossible to quantify the discrepancy between social and private profitability with any precision, there is no reason why government policies on taxes (and subsidies) should not be based on a judgment of the negative effects associated with labor displacement and the positive benefits because of feedback effects in the same way that tax decisions have been guided traditionally by judgments relating to equity and ability to pay.

References

1. David Turnham (with the assistance of I. Jaeger). *The Employment Problem in Less Developed Countries.* Paris: Organisation for Economic Co-operation and Development Centre, June 1970.
2. Guy Hunter. *Modernizing Peasant Societies: A Comparative Study in Asia and Africa.* London and New York: Oxford University Press, 1969.
3. Paul Bairoch. *Révolution Industrielle et Sous-Developpement.* Paris: Société d'Edition d'Enseignement Supérieur, 1964.
4. B. F. Johnston. "Agriculture and Structural Transformation: A Survey of Research," *Journal of Economic Literature,* Vol. VIII, No. 2 (June 1970), 369–404.
5. H. G. Johnson. "Comparative Cost and Commercial Policy Theory in a Developing World Economy," *The Pakistan Development Review* (Karachi), Supplement, Vol. IV, No. 1 (Spring 1969), 1–33.
6. Nathan Rosenberg. "Neglected Dimensions in the Analysis of Economic Change," *Bulletin of the Oxford University Institute of Economics and Statistics,* Vol. 26, No. 1 (February 1964), 59–77.
7. Ian Little, Tibor Scitovsky, and Maurice Scott. *Industry and Trade in Seven Developing Countries.* London: Oxford University Press, on behalf of the Organisation for Economic Co-operation and Development, 1970.
8. G. P. Sicat. "A Fable for Our Times: A Tale of Two Countries." Mimeograph. School of Economics, University of the Philippines, Quezon City, 1970.

Discussion of Professor Johnston's Paper

KENNETH D. FREDERICK

Kenneth D. Frederick is Assistant Professor of Economics at the California Institute of Technology.*

Professor Johnston's paper brings us to the heart of a vast and extremely complex topic: the unemployment and underemployment implications of rapid population growth. I agree with him that the role of agriculture is central to the employment problem in the less developed countries. Previous fertility rates guarantee a rapidly growing labor force for the next fifteen years. The view that significant increases in unemployment and underemployment can only be avoided by a labor-intensive agricultural development is supported by the sheer size of the rural sector in most areas of the world, the limited potential for absorbing additional labor in industry without massive infusions of capital and skilled labor, and the low marginal productivity of—and the social costs generated by— the rapidly expanding and already underemployed urban service sector.

Fortunately, as Professor Johnston indicates, adoption of the high-yielding grain varieties in the less developed countries can be compatible with an increase in agricultural employment. However, it should be emphasized that a labor-intensive agricultural development pattern is by no means assured. Professor Johnston states that the extent to which increased farm output is accompanied by greater opportunities for productive employment in agriculture will be determined by the means employed to realize the potential of the new crop varieties and by government policies and programs affecting research, extension, and credit for small farmers. Over-all, however, I feel that his paper understates the immediacy of the need for pro-

* Currently with Resources for the Future, Inc.

grams designed to ensure such development and the obstacles to designing and implementing them. In the absence of such programs it is likely that existing forces would have just the opposite effect on agricultural employment.

Although the shape of agricultural production functions with high-yielding varieties is unknown, experience to date indicates that the advantages of mechanization may be considerable. This view was summarized by Landsberg. He stated that "the new technology has very exacting requirements that are largely unattainable without mechanization, especially as multiple cropping is involved, seeding at precise depths, water control, etc. . . ." (1). Although the evidence is not all one-sided, recent experience provides considerable evidence for this statement. Machinery played a key role in the phenomenal increase in wheat yields in Morocco where proper seedbed preparation is one of the most important inputs—if not the most important. Deep plowing instead of traditional shallow stick-plowing may double short-run yields under Moroccan conditions. In general, the semidwarf wheats are much more sensitive to the depth of planting than the traditional varieties. Experience also indicates that machinery to place and space seed properly is important in order to attain substantial increases in corn yields (2).

In West Pakistan the high-yield varieties of wheat and new production techniques were introduced without significant additions of equipment. The wheat program resulted in a substantial increase in production that initially generated a significant increase in the demand for labor. In fact, labor scarcities developed during some critical periods—especially harvest—causing serious crop losses. This factor and government policies that overvalue labor relative to capital in the rural sector have apparently made the use of combines and threshers economically feasible.

Mechanization resulting from normal labor scarcities is certainly desirable—and in many cases essential—for higher per capita incomes. However, to the extent that the high-yield varieties create production bottlenecks by enhancing the peak (although not necessarily the over-all) demand for labor, mechanization might result despite the presence of tremendous seasonal unemployment and underemployment. Farm machinery would alleviate the peak labor pressures, but it would also greatly aggravate the seasonal unemployment problems.

The substantial increases in income that sometimes can be derived from multiple cropping might prompt mechanization even in the presence of unemployed and underemployed labor. "Timeliness" in harvesting and land preparation become particularly important with multiple cropping and can often only be achieved through mechanization. Introducing the new grain varieties is apt to increase multiple cropping in some areas because the success of both multiple cropping and the new varieties is highly dependent on a common input—i.e., an adequate and predictable supply of water. The new varieties are very responsive to water, and irrigation greatly enhances the possibilities for multiple cropping. Consequently, the attraction of multiple high-yield crops may prompt rapid mechanization on irrigated lands regardless of the abundance of low-priced labor.

Even in the absence of any economic advantages to mechanization, it is likely that the new techniques would be adopted first, and perhaps exclusively, on large-scale farms in many regions. Professor Johnston makes several references to the experiences in Japan and Taiwan where agricultural development has proceeded rapidly on the basis of small-scale family farms. I question the relevance of these models to the great majority of the world's low-income, rural areas. In Brazil, for example, farmers of Japanese origin have been quicker to novate and generally more successful in all aspects of farming than other family farmers. Experiences in other developing areas, such as India and West Pakistan, indicate that owners of large farms are much more apt to adopt new techniques. Mansfield summarized the results of research on innovators in the farm sector as follows:

> . . . the technical leaders seem to have relatively advanced formal education, higher social status, more cosmopolitan inter-

ests and social contacts, larger farms, higher gross farm incomes, greater farm efficiency, more specialized enterprises, and greater farm ownership than their slower competitors. (3)

The much higher capital costs and the more exacting production requirements of the new varieties will certainly hinder and may prevent many, often illiterate small-farm owners from ever adopting the new varieties. Economies of scale in the supply of production inputs place the small farmer at a substantial disadvantage in many regions. In an effort to minimize both administrative costs and risk, banks prefer to lend to the wealthy farm. Salesmen of farm inputs such as fertilizer find it unprofitable to visit small farms, and even extension agents frequently avoid the smaller farms. In addition, the high capital requirements and greater sensitivity to water of the high-yield varieties increase the farmer's risk with the new varieties—a risk farmers with small farms are less able and likely to assume.

Although large-scale farming does not necessarily alter the relative utilization of capital and labor, it is generally a prerequisite for mechanization. Two factors make it very likely that the spread of large-scale farming would lead to a premature mechanization of agriculture. First, farmers with large farms tend to favor mechanization, either associating it with social status or fearing labor-management difficulties. Second, government policies frequently undervalue capital and overvalue labor relative to their social costs.

The sequence in which the high-yield varieties of crops are introduced is also very important. Economic theory suggests that in a perfectly competitive industry such as agriculture excess profits resulting from a reduction in costs are temporary. As competition brings the benefits of the new technology to the consumer in the form of lower prices, farmers who failed to modernize are worse off than before. For those farmers who are slow to respond to the new techniques because of such problems as lack of credit, irrigation, knowledge, declining prices and their deteriorating competitive position could cause additional problems that might result in forced land sales and an increase in urban migration and unemployment.

In one sense, Professor Johnston's conclusion that there is no rapid or easy way to alter the present occupational composition of the labor force (characterized by the overwhelming importance of the farm labor force) may be too optimistic. In the absence of well-designed programs that stimulate innovation among farmers with small farms, the most likely result of existing pressures and the impetus of the high-yield varieties may be an increased dichotomy between wealthy and poor farmers. Most farmers may be left with a choice between attempting to eke out an existence in farming with even less chance of becoming commercial producers and migrating to the already overpopulated cities in the hope of being one of the lucky few to land a job. The net result could be a substantial increase in the inefficient, underemployed urban service sector.

In the longer run, population growth rates will have to be curbed if the unprecedented opportunities for increasing per capita incomes through labor-intensive agricultural development are not to be lost in an increasing crush of humanity on a fixed amount of land.

References

1. Alan Sweezy. "Woods Hole Population Conference." Social Science Discussion Paper Series, California Institute of Technology, October 20, 1969. Mimeograph. P. 7.
2. United States Agency for International Development, Spring Review of the New Cereal Varieties, "Major Physical Inputs," May 13–15, 1969. Mimeograph. Pp. 21–22.
3. Edwin Mansfield. *The Economics of Technological Change.* New York: W. W. Norton & Co., Inc., 1968. P. 133.

4

Population, GNP,
and the Environment

ALAN R. SWEEZY

*Alan R. Sweezy is Professor of Economics at the California
Institute of Technology.*

The average American consumes far more gasoline and electricity, discards more beer cans, Coke bottles, and automobile
bodies, and occupies more space than the average Indian,
African, or Latin American. The average American today generates more air and water pollution, disposes of more solid
waste, and occupies more space than his predecessors did fifty
or even twenty years ago. Some people have concluded from
this that population growth is not an important cause of environmental problems. The standard of living and the state of
technology so predominate, they say, that for all practical purposes one can forget about population growth when dealing
with the environmental problems of the future.

Others draw the opposite conclusion. They point out that
although today's affluent American may do more damage than
today's Indian or yesterday's American, two of today's affluent
Americans would do still more damage than one. It's like the
old riddle: What makes more noise than a pig stuck under a
gate? The answer: two pigs stuck under a gate.

Who is right? Is population important, or isn't it? The answer depends on two things: First, what effect does the size
of the population have on the degree of its affluence? If we
have twice as many Americans fifty years from now will they

be twice as wealthy and do twice as much damage? Second, what is the relative magnitude of the contributions of population growth and of technological progress to environmental deterioration? Does the latter completely dwarf the former?

In exploring these questions it will be useful to distinguish between two different sets of environmental problems: pollution and congestion. Population growth affects pollution primarily through its influence on the size and composition of the gross national product (GNP). It has a direct effect on congestion.

Population and GNP

To understand the size of the GNP, we naturally turn to growth theory. The standard treatment classifies the determinants of growth under three headings: the labor force; the capital stock; and the state of technology and organization or, more broadly, the "residual." The relation between population growth and each of these factors is too complex for a detailed examination here, so I shall mention only a few of the most general influences. In the long run, assuming the maintenance of full employment, the size of the labor force varies directly with the size of the population. The GNP tends to be larger with a larger labor force—though how much larger depends on certain key parameters.

What influence population growth has on technological and organizational progress has been widely debated. For instance, it is argued that with a growing population the number of talented people will also be increasing and this should mean more bright ideas about how to improve organization and technology. Leibenstein's "replacement effect" would mean a more rapid increase in the average level of education and skills when the population is growing than when it is not (1). On the other hand, population growth places an extra burden on the educational system, which in the poorer countries may act as a serious brake on progress. I am inclined to think that population growth, especially rapid growth, reduces the size of the residual in the less developed countries but that it is likely to have little effect one way or the other in the United States.

The amount of capital per worker is likely to grow faster as the rate of population growth slows, assuming that fiscal and monetary policies are used to keep the economy from slipping into a depression. For one thing, smaller families may save a larger proportion of their income, though this is by no means certain. More importantly, the net saving that is done can be used for concentrating capital for the existing labor force rather than spreading capital out for an increasing labor force. How important this will be depends on how sharply returns diminish as the amount of capital per worker increases. I suspect that they diminish rather gently in the less developed countries, especially if the necessary investment in human capital is included, but rather sharply in a highly developed country like the United States.

To pull these various strands together, let me give some numbers based on analyses of past growth in the United States.* They are in no sense predictions but are designed merely to show what the relative magnitudes might be.

If population remained constant but technical progress and capital accumulation† continued at the same rate as in the past, the GNP fifty years from now might be three and a half to four times its present size. If in addition the population doubled— which could easily happen—the GNP might be something like one and three-quarters times as large as *that,* or six to seven

---

* Using Solow's methods of analysis (2), Nelson (3) finds that the residual accounted for three-fifths of the growth of the potential GNP from 1954 to 1960, i.e., 2.1 per cent of a total, 3.5 per cent annual growth rate (assuming b, the exponent of L, is 0.75). If the size of the residual is independent of the rate of growth of the labor force, as I have assumed it to be, this gives a doubling time of the GNP due to technological progress alone of approximately thirty-five years. In his original paper Solow attributed an even larger proportion of growth to the residual, but that was because a large part of the period covered by his statistics was subject to the distorting influence of depression and war.

† This assumes, as above, that the size of the residual is independent of the growth of the labor force but that the amount of capital per worker is not. If capital per worker remained constant, doubling the labor force would also double the GNP.

times its present size. Thus, in a sense both sides are right. Technological progress has been a bigger factor in accounting for past growth of the economy than population growth. But population growth is far from negligible. A return to the fertility rates of the late 1950s and early 1960s—really rather moderate by world, or its own earlier, standards—would give the United States a population of over 500 million fifty years from now. That is twice as many as it would have if it managed to bring the net reproduction rate down to one in the course of the next decade. Twice the population would mean not a great deal less than twice the GNP, with its associated pollution and other environmental problems.

Direct Effects of Population Growth

Population growth also has direct effects. Pollution depends on the composition, as well as on the size, of the GNP. If people spend more money seeing psychiatrists and less money driving cars, there will clearly be less air pollution. If I am right in thinking that slower population growth would mean more rapidly rising per capita income, it is relevant to ask what effect this would have on the composition of the demand for goods and services that make up a GNP and hence on the amount of pollution associated with a GNP. It seems likely that of two equal GNPs the one with higher but fewer incomes would generate less pollution. Unfortunately, this is difficult to prove. Almon estimates the income elasticities of demand for major categories of consumption in *The American Economy to 1975* (4). Rejecting the use of time-series regression as incapable of separating "the effects of variables so closely collinear," he is forced to turn to data on the consumption expenditures of different income groups at the same point in time. The results would be very interesting if we could be reasonably sure they would hold over time rather than only for the period in which the data were collected. His estimate for gasoline, for instance, is 0.7, meaning that the increase in consumption of gasoline is less than proportional to the increase in per capita—actually in this case per family—income. In other words, the air pollution content of a GNP in which per capita income was increasing rapidly but the number of people slowly or not at all, would be significantly smaller than that of a GNP characterized by the opposite combination of factors. It is hard to know, however, how much reliance to put on this finding. For one thing, people's consumption patterns may be influenced by their position in the income scale as well as by the actual amount of their income. Almon himself discards the result he gets from the cross-sectional data for one important category of consumer expenditure —or nonexpenditure—personal saving.

In spite of the theoretical difficulties, I think an examination of all the different types of evidence might throw considerable light on this subject. We are planning to do further research along these lines at Caltech.

Congestion

Pollution depends on the size of the GNP and what might be called its pollution coefficient, which in turn depends on the composition of demand and the state of technology. Population is important only as it affects either of these variables. In the case of congestion, population has a more direct effect. Rising per capita income generates a demand for more space. But beyond a certain point the consequences of an increase in the demand for space will differ radically, depending on whether the source of the demand is higher incomes or more people. For example, if people are so poor that most cannot get to the beach on weekends, those few who are able to get there can enjoy relative peace and quiet. But as the standard of living rises, more and more people will be able to go to the beach, and the amount of space they will have once they get there depends on how many people are there. A further rise in per capita incomes will, at worst, mean that the desire for additional space will be unfulfilled. An increase in the number of people, on the other hand, will mean an actual decrease in the space available to each person or family. In the first case, the problem arises because per capita real income is growing. The second case causes per capita real income to decline. It is the inverse of Alice's problem at the mad tea party; in the case of space, you can never have more, but you can always have less.

But what has this to do with the situation in the United States? Haven't we lots of space, not only for our present population, but for any increase that is likely to occur in the next fifty to a hundred years? * In answering this question we must first ask: Enough space for what? The traditional view is that a society needs enough space for its dwellings, its factories, offices, roads and streets, and enough land to grow its food and fiber on. Perhaps it also needs a few parks, race tracks, and sports stadiums. Beyond that, space is superfluous, and there is no reason population should not go on increasing until it is all occupied.

This narrow view is rapidly changing. We are coming increasingly to admit the validity of other demands for space. These demands, moreover, are for particular kinds of space rather than for space in general: for beach areas in southern California or northern New Jersey, vacation areas in New England or New York State, actual and potential Yosemites and Yellowstones. As people's horizons widen, even more expansive demands are gaining recognition. An increasing number of people think it is important to preserve unspoiled wildlife habitats, natural forests, and wilderness areas. They are reluctant to see encroachment on areas of unusual natural beauty and grandeur.

Several years ago Murray Gell-Mann was asked what he thought of a scheme for bringing water from Alaska to irrigate land in the Southwest. His reply was, "Why ruin two beautiful and distinctive landscapes to make more ordinary farmland when the same thing can be accomplished through birth control?" † This must have seemed idiosyncratic in the extreme at the time. I am sure it would seem less so now.

Needless to say, we may run out of these special kinds of

* See Coale (5) and Eversley (6). Eversley's views are much more extreme than Coale's since he thinks even Britain could comfortably absorb double or more its present population.
† In a private communication.

space long before we run out of space in general. The example of the beach on a warm weekend may have much wider relevance than it would appear at first. The saturation point is particularly low in wilderness or other areas we want to preserve in their natural state. Garrett Hardin gives an accurate and sensitive analysis of the dilemma:

> Wilderness cannot be multiplied; and it can be subdivided only a little. It is not increasing; we have to struggle to keep it from decreasing. But population increases steadily. The ratio of the wilderness available to each living person becomes steadily less —and bear in mind that this is only a statistical abstraction: were we to divide up the wilderness among even a small fraction of the total population there would be no wilderness available to any one. So what should we do? (7)

Rejecting price as a method of rationing, he suggests that access to wilderness areas be limited to those who are willing and able to go in on foot, carrying their provisions with them. (In special cases entry on horseback or by canoe might be permitted.) Some method of rationing is clearly essential to preserve the thing itself, the "wilderness experience" as Hardin calls it. Whether his method will be enough is perhaps open to question. Certainly the more population increases, the more difficult it will be to keep access within the necessary limits.

Redistribution of population is often proposed as a solution to the problem of population growth. I agree that, properly qualified, redistribution is a worthwhile objective—it is worthwhile even without population growth—and that we should be actively thinking about policies to bring it about. We should, however, recognize that it has serious limitations. It will not do much to protect wilderness areas. It must be assessed with regard to the welfare of people who already live in an area. We cannot simply found new cities wherever there is sparsely populated territory. In New England, for example, the Greater Boston area is not only becoming highly congested but is also spreading out in a way that makes it increasingly difficult for most of its inhabitants to reach open country. There is, however, still lots of thinly populated country in New Hampshire and Vermont. The advocates of redistribution suggest that, as population increases, we should stop growth of the Boston area and instead start a second Boston, or several Springfields and Hartfords, in New Hampshire or Vermont.

Would it solve the problem to allow New England to absorb more people without loss of welfare for the present inhabitants? The answer clearly is no. Many of the inhabitants of New Hampshire and Vermont are there because they do not want to live in or near a big city. And many of those who live in Greater Boston find it important to be able to get out into thinly populated country for weekends and vacations. Creating another Boston, or several Springfields, in New Hampshire and Vermont would impoverish life for both these groups of people.*

For the United States as a whole, the situation is different. Very few people go from New York or Los Angeles to Kansas or North Dakota for weekends or summer vacations. Large parts of these and other states could absorb more people without serious damage to recreational, aesthetic, or ecological values. Many areas have been losing population and would be glad to see a reversal of the trend. But here redistribution runs into a different sort of problem. People may not want to go where policy indicates they should. What many people want is to enjoy the advantages of living in the Washington–New York–Boston area or the San Diego–Los Angeles area and also to be able to get out of it with relative ease to beaches, mountains, lakes, and just plain countryside that are not so swarming with other escapees that they are not worth getting to. Perverse of them? They should be willing to live in North Dakota instead? Perhaps you will say they cannot eat their cake and have it, too. But the point is they can have their cake—or as much of it as is left—if population stops growing.

People could, of course, be told where they can and where they cannot live. Or financial and other incentives might be used to try to induce them to live where policy dictates. If

---

* If population continues to grow, redistribution may be a *pis aller*. That is different from saying that redistribution makes it possible to absorb more people without loss of welfare.

the incentives were large enough, they might be effective. But the loss of freedom involved in the use of compulsion and the cost of providing incentives should, at the very least, be compared with the loss of freedom and the cost of compelling or inducing people to have small families—which the advocates of redistribution rarely do. Moreover, although redistribution offers only a temporary and partial solution to the problems of population pressure, limiting family size offers a permanent and complete solution.

As a practical matter I think it would be a mistake to expect much relief from redistribution even in the short run, i.e., the next few decades.* After that, continued population growth will clearly swamp any benefits redistribution might bring.

Problems Created by Technology

Many people expect a technological *deus ex machina* to solve our environmental problems for us. They fail to explain, however, why technological development that in the past often had harmful effects on the environment will in the future follow only benign paths. Left to itself technological development will go in whatever directions seem most profitable—either in terms of return on investment or in terms of power and prestige for what Galbraith calls the technostructure (8).

In the past, consumers were free to buy any new gadgets the engineers came up with no matter how much damage they might do to the environment. Producers were free to adopt the cheapest methods without regard to the effect on the environment. The process still goes on. Only recently a new and serious environmental threat, the all-terrain vehicle, or ATV, has been launched on the market: "Through swamp, over ice, up mountains it rides—superblob, the latest in mechanized happiness. Light as a touch on its low pressure tires, the ATV jumps

---

* Even Eversley (6), in spite of his great enthusiasm for redistribution as a solution for Britain's population problem, admits that "despite everything successive governments have done to reverse the trend, the concentration into certain residentially attractive areas of the midlands and the southeast is becoming stronger."

through the air when the going gets rough. Soon, its makers hope, it will jump into backyards across America" (9). However, there are signs a change is in the making. We may be nearing the end of the era of blind, uncontrolled growth. Increasingly people, particularly younger people, are beginning to question the absolute goodness of growth itself.

Producers are the first to feel the pressure, though they will soon have to transmit it to consumers through higher prices or curtailed offerings.* The kind of thing that is beginning to happen is nicely illustrated by the following dispatch from Denver, Colorado, to the *New York Times,* December 9, 1969:

> It was once a fairly easy matter to bring a $65 million plant and 725 jobs into a small town. Townspeople celebrated their good luck, rolled out the red carpet and invited the Governor in to cut a ribbon. If the plant filled the air with smoke and the rivers with acrid wastes, few cared.
>
> But times have changed. Growing concern over the environment has taken precedence over economic development in just such a case in New Mexico and Colorado. . . .
>
> The issue is air and water pollution. The plant is a kraft paper mill proposed by the Parsons and Whittemore Corp. of New York. . . .
>
> Although officers of the company assured state officials that they would install the latest in pollution control equipment, their proposed plant was in effect expelled from New Mexico by public opinion and high anti-pollution standards. Even members of the Albuquerque Chamber of Commerce voted 2 to 1 against having the mill in their area. . . .

Many similar episodes have occurred. A group of students and faculty at the University of California in Santa Barbara have successfully protested the construction of a freeway across Goleta Slough on the ground that the Slough is "too valuable an ecological asset to be violated by a ribbon of concrete" (10).

* This point is worth stressing. People are too much inclined to the comfortable assumption that the costs of halting environmental degradation can be met out of the profits of industry. By and large this is an illusion. The costs will have to be met by all of us in our capacity as consumers and taxpayers, not just by those who own stock in particular industries.

The California Environmental Quality Study Council reported in February 1970 that its activities led to the reconsideration of two environmentally hazardous projects: the expansion of a fossil-fueled power plant in Huntington Beach and the construction of two oil refineries in the Coachella Valley (11). BASF, the German chemical producer, under pressure from a diverse group of environmentalists postponed building a new plant at Port Victoria in Beaufort County, South Carolina (12).

A larger-scale battle was fought in Congress in 1970 over a bill to allow increased timber cutting in the national forests. Supporters contended the bill was necessary "to meet the immediate lumber requirements of the nation's housing industry and to assure that future needs will be met through 'intensified forest management'." Opponents maintained that "the bill threatens America's national forests, scuttles historic multiple use practices and undermines prospective parks, wilderness, open space and recreation areas" (13).

The bill was defeated, partly because lumber prices had subsided from their peak the year before, but the industry has announced it is not giving up.

Direct interference with consumers' freedom of choice is not involved in any of these episodes, but hopefully it may soon follow. A vigorous effort was made to stop the supersonic transport, or SST. I hope a similar effort will be made to restrict severely—if not to ban—the less spectacular but perhaps even more obnoxious ATV.

How does population growth fit into this picture? The outcome of the struggle to protect the environment against the consequences of economic growth will depend in large measure on what kind of growth we have: rising per capita income with constant population or constant per capita income with increasing population. The larger the population component in growth is, the more the increased output will be for the necessities and long-established comforts of life. The more the increased output takes the form of necessities, the harder it will be to gain consideration for ecological, aesthetic, and recreational values if they stand in the way of expanding production.

For example, it has been relatively easy to ban DDT and related compounds in the developed countries. The standard of living leaves plenty of room to absorb the resulting increase in the cost of food. The less developed countries, on the other hand, protest that they cannot afford to give up DDT. They have at best only a slight margin over subsistence needs. With their rapidly growing populations they desperately need to expand food supplies. Any major obstacle, or any substantial increase in cost, could spell disaster. Confronted with a choice between the starvation of millions and serious damage to the environment, there is little doubt how most people and most governments would decide.

Or take the case of the demand for lumber. As the battle in Congress in 1970 showed, an increasing number of people are becoming concerned about the protection of our national forests. But if population continues to grow, it will be impossible to deny the urgency of the demand for more houses. Policies designed to protect the forests will run into heavy, and no doubt successful, opposition if they entail curtailing the supply of new housing for a growing number of families.

Shortly after the fight in Congress over the timber-cutting bill; the Boise Cascade Corporation ran a full-page advertisement that consisted of a picture of a baby carriage and the legend: "Challenge. Each new arrival dramatizes the urgency of an adequate supply of homes" (14). It is a reminder that if population keeps on growing, the shadow of the baby buggy will loom large over the environmental battles of the future.

To return to the debate between population and affluence, rising affluence is certainly a major source of environmental problems, but population growth is important too. Population growth through its effect on the labor force contributes to the increase in total output. If the increase in output is less than proportional to the increase in population, i.e., if per capita income is higher the smaller the increase in population, two further effects come into play: (a) the composition of demand is likely to be less harmful to the environment with fewer people but higher per capita income, even without conscious efforts at control; and (b) the growth of output will be easier to direct into environmentally harmless channels if it consists of the relative superfluities of a rising standard of living rather than the necessities of a growing population. This last consideration would become even more important if we should reach the point at which we decided that protection of the environment required curbing growth of total output itself.

Finally, population growth has a direct effect on the amount of space available to each person. As affluence increases, people spread out more, and their demand for space increases. But beyond a certain point—which has already been reached with respect to certain kinds of space, even in the United States—the consequences of a further rise in affluence are very different from that of a further increase in the number of people. In the case of rising affluence, what we might call the space standard of living remains constant whereas in the case of rising numbers it falls. The more population grows, the more drastic the fall becomes.

I conclude that we can stop arguing about whether affluence or population is the source of our environmental problems. Both are important. Moreover, there is going to be plenty to do on both fronts if future living conditions are to be tolerable.

References

1. Harvey Leibenstein. "The Impact of Population Growth on Economic Welfare—Non-Traditional Inputs, and Micro-Economic Elements," *Rapid Population Growth: Consequences and Public Policy Implications*. Baltimore: Johns Hopkins University Press, 1971.

2. Robert M. Solow. "Technical Change and the Aggregate Production Function," *The Review of Economics and Statistics*, Vol. 39 (August 1957), 312–20.

3. R. R. Nelson, "Aggregate Production Functions and Medium-Range Growth Projections," *American Economic Review*, Vol. LIV, No. 5 (September 1964), 575–606.

4. Clopper Almon, Jr. *The American Economy to 1975.* New York: Harper & Row, Publishers, 1966. Pp. 31–47.

5. Ansley Coale. "Should the United States Start a Campaign for Fewer Births?" Presidential address to the Population Association of America, April, 1968. *Population Index,* Vol. 34, No. 4 (October–December 1968), 467–74.

6. David Eversley. "Is Britain Being Threatened by Over-Population?" *The Listener,* Vol. LXVIII, Nos. 1999 and 2000 (July 20 and 27, 1967), 78–79, 110–11.

7. Garrett Hardin. "Effects of Population Growth on Natural Resources and the Environment," *Hearings before a Subcommittee of the Committee on Government Operations,* House of Representatives, Ninety-first Congress, First Session, September 15 and 16, 1969. Washington, D.C.: U.S. Government Printing Office, p. 94.

8. J. K. Galbraith. *The New Industrial State.* Boston: Houghton Mifflin Company, 1967.

9. *Business Week,* March 21, 1970, p. 27.

10. *Los Angeles Times,* December 14, 1969 and April 22, 1970.

11. Progress Report of the Environmental Quality Study Council, Sacramento, California, February 1970.

12. *Business Week,* April 11, 1970, p. 29.

13. *The New York Times,* February 5, 1970.

14. *Business Week,* April 4, 1970.

Discussion of Professor Sweezy's Paper

HANS H. LANDSBERG

Hans H. Landsberg is Director of the Resource Appraisal Program, Resources for the Future, Inc.

Professor Sweezy deserves praise for the courage with which he has opened up an area to investigation that has been conspicuous by neglect. As always happens in the absence of research, unsupported assumptions and what is sometimes referred to as "simple logic" take over. This paper is the first serious attempt I know of to advance a number of hypotheses. I shall agree with some and question others. In neither event shall I be able to furnish much in the way of support.

My major disagreement with the paper is in its failure to distinguish systematically between causes and effects in developed versus less developed countries. There are allusions, but no consistent dividing lines, because not only rates of population growth but income levels, historical context of development—and therefore demand structures—are so radically different in the two categories of countries that I find it unsatisfactory to discuss the subject under review in general terms.

Let me try to be more explicit. As I understand the principal thesis, it is that a rising economy combined with a slow rate of population growth tends to push disproportionately demands for luxuries (defined for simplicity's sake as goods or services that have an income elasticity of demand greater than one), and it is easier to keep these in check than a rise in demand for essentials that would be caused by faster population growth combined with lower per capita income.

I am not completely satisfied with the terminology and prefer to speak of discretionary and nondiscretionary expenditures; the latter embrace the kinds of demands that are "essential to living" in the context of the prevailing living standard at a specified time and place, although they might well be luxuries elsewhere.

Terminology apart, it seems to me that the initial income level from which advances are contemplated, as distinguished from rates of increase, is an extremely important independent variable. A southeast Asian or African country with an annual per capita income of $100 is in a totally different situation from that of the United States or a Western European country where per capita incomes are twenty to forty times higher. In low-income countries discretionary expenditures form an extremely small part of total expenditure. Food accounts for 60, 70, or perhaps 80 per cent of the family budget, and when clothing and shelter are added, little is left for other expenditures for most of the population. In those circumstances, population growth is bound to be by far the major variable in creating whatever environmental problems arise.

The situation is totally different in a country like the United States where on the average the food budget takes up about 18 per cent of family expenditure and the role of discretionary expenditure is much greater. In fact, it even invades segments of expenditures that would normally be considered in the non-discretionary category, such as food. The sharp rise in beef consumption this country has experienced in the last ten years is a good example. Had total beef consumption grown only in proportion to population growth, it would have grown by 35 per cent. Instead it grew by 120 per cent because per capita consumption rose by 75 per cent from 1960 to 1970. Thus, rising income produces a shift not only from nondiscretionary types of expenditure to discretionary types, but also from lower-priced to higher-priced items within expenditure categories.

Many examples of this kind can be given. They all demonstrate that in high-income countries the push for increased consumption and, concomitantly, increased generation of pollutants has been largely from the income growth and not from the population growth. This is not to say that slower population growth would not make it easier to manage the ensuing environmental problem, although even that is not necessarily so. Professor Sweezy and I agree that population growth is an important variable, but I think one has to go further than that and try to assess the relative roles more carefully. It is important for policy-making whether the income variable is twice as important or ten times as important. These distinctions become especially crucial when we deal with countries in different stages of development. To take proper account of them, income *levels* must be introduced as independent variables before one looks at the effect of income *changes*.

My second, though related, area of disagreement with the paper comes in the matter of dealing with the nature of the consequences of population and income growth—that is, what problem are we studying when we talk about the relative consequences of population growth and income growth in the less developed countries and in the developed ones? My main contention is that the problem in the less developed countries is largely not environmental in the sense that I feel the paper conceives it. In stressing the advantages that slower population growth holds out for less developed countries, one is not really as concerned over water, air, and landscape deterioration—in the way these concerns now prevail in this country—as over the low state of elementary living conditions, urban misery, rural misery, malnutrition, disease, filth, and a large variety of other ills that are of long standing but are, in most instances, greatly exacerbated by rapid population growth. One is faced not with adverse, unintended results of an advanced technology but rather with the persistent failure to apply or engineer appropriate and for the most part conventional technology.

In that context, rising per capita income is the *only* route that will lead to improvement in the human condition—so much so that it is hard to think of any way in which rising per capita income in the less developed countries would have an adverse effect until long into the future. To the extent that rapid rates of population growth make the attainment of rising per capita income more difficult, population growth is part of a vicious circle. It holds back a factor that is essential to the slowdown in population growth.

In the developed countries, on the other hand, because income growth in and of itself has created a new set of problems subsumed under the general heading of "pollution," the remedy surely lies not in increased growth of per capita income (though this does not spell "down with GNP!") and only to a limited extent in slower population growth. It lies predominantly in improving the way in which we introduce and manage technology and in building into the economy, which has hitherto been production and consumption oriented, incentives that will help direct demand into environmentally acceptable channels and will regulate access to a now-overloaded environment in accordance with standards that help to sustain it. This can be achieved with a wide variety of population-income mixes. Thus one can move toward such goals whether one does or does not have a basic conviction that population growth is "bad," that the place is too darned crowded, or that we produce the wrong kinds of things. For whether or not I agree with the author's preferences regarding the outcome of market decisions in these and other respects, I cannot see how they can in any event be fashioned into an analysis or policy prescription that is equally applicable to a society with a $100 per capita income and one with a $4000 per capita income.

This leads me to a third area of disagreement, which concerns the location of points of leverage for making improvements in environmental affairs. Limiting myself to developed countries, I find the detour via population control not only beset with difficulties of achievement for political, ethical, and other reasons but also highly inefficient. Obviously, we can deal with the undesirable side effects of the automobile, for example, more directly than through changing the rate of population growth, and I am not persuaded that the difficulties of modifying time-honored institutions and incentive systems—a development that will become necessary—will be any greater than those that would arise from population policies "beyond family planning."

This is not a plea for the "technological fix," the search for which I view with substantial misgivings, not only because it sometimes comes close to the search for escaping from the laws of thermodynamics but also because we have long learned that what looks innocent in the first instance may turn out to harbor some hidden threat. "R&D to the rescue!" often is a way of avoiding the obvious, such as devising efficient recapture of the used container or recycling the obsolete automobile or waste newspapers and magazines. I doubt that there is any disagreement between Professor Sweezy and myself regarding the uses or nonuses of technology, or its essential neutrality. Nor do I disagree that it is probably easier to regulate or lop off peaks of consumption caused by high per capita income when they are clearly responsible for clearly identified and controllable environmental damage.

The difficulty in appraising technology comes in—and here I differ from the paper's tenor—precisely the matter of identifying the adverse by-product. Often it is recognized only *after* it has shown up. Moreover, high incomes will seek outlets in one kind or other of what Professor Sweezy would call "superfluities." Must we then keep running forever, shouting "Halt the thief!"?

A separate problem associated with the high-income variant is that it sets up consumption patterns that lead to emulation by lower-income groups. The first two-car or three-car family on the block gives rise to more of them and changes the demand pattern way down the income line. When you have GNP growth by larger numbers with more slowly rising income, you are more likely to avoid this phenomenon. I do not know how large it looms, which suggests that I have not searched the literature or that here is a field of research that has not been explored.

I am also concerned with the implication throughout the paper that there are certain types of consumption that are socially sanctioned and others that are not. Use of the term "superfluities" presupposes a criterion that can be used to separate them from an opposite, perhaps "essentials." Obviously the market does not provide the distinction nor do we have any planning authority that does. Experience elsewhere with such authorities has not been happy. Yet few of us have not at one time or another elevated our own value systems to a general principle. This paper is no exception. Its author does not like the snowmobile or the all-terrain vehicle. In more general terms, he does not like what he calls "blind, uncontrolled growth." But he does not reveal his choice of controls, in character or in scope, and if he did, I might disagree with his choice of goods and services, and he with mine.

It is very fashionable to denounce the workings of the market system. Anyone defending it must be willing to be considered nourishing an ancient and discredited love of laissez-faire. Yet, to me, the arbitrariness implicit in terming certain consumption items "superfluities" represents a step backward, not forward. Let their price reflect their true social costs including environmental? Yes. Put constraints on their use to protect the rights of others or the quality of the environment? By all means. But if the market function is to be further *de*creased, obviously the scope of political decisions must be further *in*creased. My inclination would be to retard that process and instead build into market decisions the widest possible societal concerns, including those for a satisfactory environment.

There are limits to such endeavors. Economic incentives cannot produce miracles, if only because we have not found, and may never find, ways of translating all tastes and distastes, or benefits and dis-benefits, into dollar costs. Thus there is often no choice but to go the route of political decisions, but their results tend to be more rigid than outcomes in the market (1). Although we can always hope that education and full information will produce outcomes that are in our view salutary and have a chance of being sustained, that hope is not always borne out.

The difficulty of supporting the paper's general hypothesis regarding the respective roles of population growth and per capita income shows up clearly in the remarks on lumber demand. Contrary to the supposition made in the paper, in the current situation of the United States a specified future GNP resulting from high per capita income and low population growth could easily result in higher lumber demand for housing than a GNP that is derived from larger numbers and smaller income growth. In the latter event housing demand would tend to shift towards apartments, which use much less lumber than do single-unit dwellings. This example just goes to show how difficult it is to disentangle the effects of the two variables, not to speak of others, particularly technology.

Regarding technology, I find myself troubled by the paper's remarks on freedom of choice by consumers and producers—how they have prevailed traditionally and how their future curtailment is required in the interest of preserving the environment. There lurk somewhere in this view the presumptions that (a) if we only try hard enough we can perceive, prior to production and consumption, the dangers of a new technology; (b) chains of events are clearly understood; and (c) we can establish mechanisms that will tell us what to monitor. I am wholly in favor, and on record, as favoring the introduction of what is known as "technology assessment." But I am also aware of the immensity of the task and of a deceptive sense of prescience engendered by arguing from hindsight. Because society failed to perceive a danger before it arose is not to say that society was blind. In many instances there was no way of seeing, for a variety of reasons that it would take too long to recite and support. The fact that America's concern over the automobile focused for decades on safety rather than on its polluting characteristics is perhaps the best object lesson. In other instances the environment was simply not in need of protection—at a given level of loading. And in still others there were worthwhile trade-offs (as there are now in the less developed countries). It is prudent to consider technology as a gift horse to be well inspected, but it is one that often grows bad teeth long after it has been accepted into the stable.

My final point is directed to the paper's treatment of *congestion* as distinguished from *pollution*. I would go along with the proposition that congestion is primarily a consequence of population growth but would like to suggest that rising income makes congestion ubiquitous, or nearly so. The statistics on national park visits illustrate the point. Obviously, the steeply rising curve of visits owed something to rising population, but it was nothing compared with the effects of rising per capita income. Rising income allowed families to come from increasingly greater distances, bringing with them newly acquired or rented trailers and other equipment that enabled them to make the trip. Rising income allowed them to have enough paid leisure time—a concomitant of high income—to make the trip worthwhile, and it allowed them to find roads financed from high taxes. I do not doubt that growth composed of a larger but poorer population would have led to less crowding of national parks and other outdoor scenes than has actually been experienced. Thus, even in the matter of congestion, things are not clear-cut, although I also contend that where elbowroom pure and simple is concerned, population is of far greater importance than it is in other areas of environmental concern.

Let me close by re-emphasizing that this is a most valuable paper. It courageously plows ahead in ground that has been almost wholly uncultivated. I am certain that it will give rise to a good deal of badly needed research, so that the next time around we may be in a position to have tested some of the hypotheses that have been advanced. That my hunches are in different directions from those of the paper merely makes them worth stating, but no more. The important thing is to go from hunches to research.

Reference

1. J. W. Milliman. "Can People Be Trusted with National Resources?" *Land Economics,* Vol. 38, No. 3 (August 1962), 192–218.

5

Birth Control after 1984:
A Realistic Appraisal of Future
Contraceptive Developments

C A R L   D J E R A S S I

*Carl Djerassi is Professor of Chemistry at Stanford University
and President of Syntex Research Laboratories.*

> It is unmistakingly clear that unless something is done about
> the population explosion, we will be faced with an unprecedented
> catastrophe of overcrowding, famines, pestilence and war. . . .
> If we are to significantly help in the worldwide fight to curb the
> population explosion, there must be developed a simple and safe
> method that can be made available to populations on a massive
> scale.*

These are the words of the U.S. Senate's most vocal critic of
oral contraceptives, and it behooves us to consider what some
of the future contraceptive methods might be; especially what
it might take in terms of time and money to convert them into
reality. None of the many publications on this subject seems
to have concerned itself with such logistic problems. In that
connection it is instructive to note that in John R. Platt's list
(2) of world crisis problems only total nuclear or chemical-
biological warfare receives higher ratings than the problems
arising from the world's burgeoning population and that of the
four top priority problems only fertility control requires experimentation in humans for its ultimate solution.

* Statement by Senator Gaylord Nelson (1).

The surprisingly rapid acceptance during the last decade of intra-uterine devices (IUDs) and of steroid oral contraceptives in many developing and developed countries is principally due to the fact that their use separates, for the first time, contraception from copulation. It is clear that effective birth-control methods of the future must exhibit this same property. A long shopping list of new approaches to contraception could be developed from a recent report of a World Health Organization (WHO) scientific group (3), but for the present article, which will include an outline of logistic problems, determination of time and cost figures, and recommendations for implementation, I shall select only the following three topics:

(a) A new female contraceptive,* a "once-a-month" pill with abortifacient or luteolytic (menses-inducing) properties. I have selected such a method because it is scientifically feasible, it should lend itself to birth control in developed and developing countries, and it addresses itself also to the critically important subject of abortion. Some mention of prostaglandins will also be made in that connection.

(b) A male contraceptive pill.

(c) A draconian agent, such as an additive to drinking water. This was not selected to justify the Orwellian overtones of this article's title, but rather to place into realistic perspective the problems of developing such an agent, which is mentioned with increasing frequency as the final solution if voluntary methods should fail.

Specifically excluded from my list are sterilization and mechanical devices. I lack the technical familiarity to do justice to the former. Suffice it to say that if voluntary sterilization is to be used on a massive, nationwide scale, it must be reversible

* The FDA Advisory Committee on Obstetrics and Gynecology considers the long-term administration (up to three years) of synthetic progestational hormones through implants "one of the next developments in contraceptive methodology" (4). Without belittling its potential importance in birth control or the great deal of developmental work that needs to be done for years before such formulations can be used on a wide scale, such approaches do not fall within my definition of fundamentally new contraceptive agents. Rather, they represent new modes of administration of the usual steroid hormones and thus offer no basic advantages in further minimizing side effects.

and the operational procedure exceedingly simple. In the absence of complete assurance that vasectomies are reversible, backup methods would have to be provided such as the long-term (ten- to twenty-year) storage of viable sperm for possible insemination, coupled with foolproof methods (e.g., biochemical) for labeling such sperm samples.

I am also excluding devices such as IUDs even though, contrary to condoms or diaphragms, they also provide contraception divorced from coitus. Their rapid introduction into public use during the 1960s is due largely to the fact that, until now, clinical research with IUDs has fallen outside the scope of government regulatory agencies such as the Food and Drug Administration (FDA). It is highly likely that public* as well as scientific† pressure on government regulatory bodies will require that such devices also be included within their scope of control and that their clinical use be accompanied by the same cautions demanded for contraceptive drugs. I am emphasizing these arguments only to point out that the cost and time estimates I shall make of new chemical contraceptive agents most likely will also apply to new devices of the IUD type.

The Research Background for New Contraceptives

All the advances in fertility control considered by the WHO group (3) are based in one way or another on chemical approaches. As I pointed out earlier (10), this type of fertility-control research is exceedingly complicated, both in its preclinical and clinical phases; and the required manpower and financial resources are only available in the most technologically advanced countries. I emphasized that the new birth-control agents of the future, even though they may be used mainly in

* Note a long column by M. Mintz in the *Washington Post* (5).
† The mechanism of action of IUDs is incompletely understood and suggestions have already appeared in the literature (6) that their use may be associated with hyperestrogenism in women and with polycystic changes in their ovaries. Little is known about possible carcinogenic effects caused by the presence of foreign bodies in a woman's uterus for many years (7), although the relevance to humans of tumor induction by loops and spirals in rats has been questioned (8, 9).

the developing countries, will almost certainly be generated in North America or Europe. They will, therefore, be subject to the government regulatory bodies of those countries, and before constructing critical-path maps (CPM) for some new contraceptive agents, it is necessary to review briefly the conditions under which such new contraceptive agents would probably have to be developed. Since the FDA has such a crucial de facto power in many foreign countries, it is realistic to construct most CPM charts based on the American milieu, where most of the research on human fertility control is being conducted.

FDA Requirements and Animal Toxicity

Irrespective of the sponsor (industrial, governmental, or academic), no new drug can lawfully be administered to humans in the United States without an Investigative New Drug (IND) exemption issued by the FDA, although this requirement is at times overlooked by academic or individual clinicians. Such an IND application must outline the clinical protocols to be followed. For all practical purposes there exists no appeal from FDA decisions during this experimental phase, a state of affairs that is particularly restrictive for those investigators who abide strictly by IND requirements. Appropriately, animal toxicity data must first be presented, and the FDA's requirements (11) in this regard for drugs outside the contraceptive field are reasonable; in particular, the choice of the experimental animal is left to the discretion of the investigator.

Different FDA requirements (12) exist for contraceptives (whether steroids or nonsteroids), and they must be taken into consideration in any time-and-cost estimate for new fertility-control agents. These requirements are listed in Table 1. In contrast to conventional drugs, contraceptives must be tested in rats, dogs, and monkeys.

Nobody can argue with the requirement for animal toxicity data before administering a drug to humans, even in short-term clinical experiments dealing with only a few individuals. Nevertheless, specific definition of animal species is extremely unwise, for the sole reason for selecting any animal is to provide a model

Table 1. Animal toxicity studies for contraceptives:
estrogens and progestogens

Clinical study	*Animal toxicity study requirements*
IND[a] phase 1 (limited to a few subjects for up to 10 days administration)	90-day studies in rats, dogs, and monkeys
IND phase 2 (approximately 50 subjects for 3 menstrual cycles)	1-year studies in rats, dogs, and monkeys
IND phase 3 (clinical trial)	2-year studies in rats, dogs, and monkeys. Initiation of 7-year dog and 10-year monkey studies prior to start of phase 3. Reproduction and teratology studies in 2 species.
NDA (New Drug Application)	No further requirements, but must include up-to-date progress reports on long-term dog and monkey studies.

[a] Investigative New Drug.
Source: (12).

for extrapolation to the human. The unfortunate choice by the FDA of the dog as one of the required species for oral contraceptives has already been discussed (10) and has already resulted in the suspension of clinical experimentation with three different contraceptive agents, the most recent (January 1970) being the chlormadinone acetate "mini-pill." Even the simple requirement for "monkey" toxicity may be close to meaningless to reproductive physiology unless careful attention is given to the choice of the monkey species.

In order to gain as much knowledge as possible from animal studies, a species should be selected that most resembles man in its metabolic handling of that particular drug. For instance, Table 2 summarizes the excretion pattern and plasma half-life accumulated recently (13) in seven animal species for a new experimental (nonsteroid) drug. These studies with radioactive material (note this requirement in Figures 1 and 2 shown later)

Table 2. Excretion patterns and plasma half-life
of an experimental drug (13)

	Urine (*per cent*)	*Feces* (*per cent*)	*Plasma half-life* (*hours*)
Species		*Excretion*	
Man	94	1–2	14
Rat	90	2	4–6
Guinea pig	90	5	9
Dog	29	50	23–35
Rhesus monkey[a]	90	2	2–3
Capuchin monkey	45	54	20
Stump-tail monkey[a]	40	60	1
Mini-pig	86	1–2	4–7

[a] These two species belong to the same genus (*Macaca*).

were conducted in order to select the best animal model for
man, who excretes 94 per cent of the drug in the urine and dis-
plays a plasma half-life of fourteen hours. Table 2 demonstrates
that *for this particular drug* the mini-pig is at least as good an
animal model as the Rhesus monkey and, even more strikingly,
that the differences between the Rhesus and Capuchin monkeys
are almost greater than those of any other two animal species.

Another example can be cited from the extensive work of
Seal and Doe (14–16), which demonstrates the extreme species
variability of the corticosteroid-binding globulin (CBG) in
mammalian pregnancy. Table 3 contains only the data on man
and monkeys selected from the several dozen animal species that
have been studied. It is obvious from Tables 2 and 3 that if
Gertrude Stein had said "a monkey is a monkey is a monkey,"
she would have been dead wrong from a metabolic standpoint.

The reason that I have gone into such detail in toxicity requirements and metabolic differences in various animal species
is to illustrate a crucial point on which most future fertility-
control research rests. Unless all research is to be performed
directly on man—a suggestion that can hardly be entertained
with completely new agents—much more work needs to be
done in developing useful animal models that have some predic-

Table 3. Estrogen and pregnancy effects on
corticosteroid-binding globulin

Species	Control (ug per cent)	Post estrogen (ug per cent)	Pregnancy (ug per cent)
Man	22	70	55
Rhesus monkey	20	16	14
Green monkey	28	90	72
Squirrel monkey	5	80	80
Howler monkey	1.4		
Capuchin monkey	3.3		
Night monkey	5.8		
Spider monkey	3.5		

Source: (17).

tive bearing on man's biological response to a given agent. Such work will require major efforts on the part of investigators, major financial inputs (notably into primate facilities), and most importantly, some flexibility in the present FDA requirements (12) of rat, dog, and monkey tests. Although it is likely that the higher apes are probably the best models for human reproductive physiological behavior, insufficient biochemical work has been done to substantiate this claim. The funding for such work or for the requisite primate facilities is not included in Tables 5 and 6 (shown later). As pointed out already in Tables 2 and 3, the smaller monkeys frequently bear little resemblance to humans, but they are used almost exclusively because of ease of handling, availability, and cost. The latter is best illustrated in Table 4, which contains simply the approximate prices of monkeys and apes without taking into account the greatly increased handling and maintenance costs of the apes and their limited availability. Indeed, unless extensive breeding facilities are established, such exploitation of the higher apes may lead to their extinction (17).

It should be noted that all cost calculations for animal toxicity listed below (e.g., in Tables 5 and 6) are based on Rhesus monkeys and that appropriate corrections would have to be made if apes are to be employed. The current wide use of the

Table 4. Approximate price per animal

Animal	Price (dollars)
Monkeys (e.g., Rhesus)	75–100
Apes:	
Baboon	200
Chimpanzee	1000
Gorilla	2000–5000
Orangutan	2000–5000

Source: Private information from suppliers.

Rhesus monkey has also drawn the attention of a WHO scientific group, which commented that "although this monkey has considerable similarity to man, it shows differences in the timing and mode of implantation; in the placental production of chorionic gonadotrophin; and in the fetal, maternal, and placental production and metabolism of estrogen" (3). Under the circumstances one is almost tempted to ask what relevance to the human can be anticipated from studies with such experimental animals.

Role of Pharmaceutical Industry

Except for certain biologicals (i.e., special vaccines), essentially all modern medically prescribed drugs were developed by pharmaceutical companies. I know of no case in which all of the *work* (chemistry, biology, toxicology, formulation, analytical, and clinical studies through phase 3) leading to governmental approval of a drug (e.g., by the FDA in the United States) has been performed by a government laboratory, a medical school, or a nonprofit research institute. This does not mean that many of the basic discoveries leading ultimately to a publicly used drug are not discovered in nonindustrial laboratories or that certain important components (e.g., much of the clinical work) are not performed outside of industry. Nevertheless, it is a simple fact that in modern industrial nations pharmaceutical firms play an indispensable role in the development of any drug. Socialist countries have developed counterparts to the pharmaceutical industry, but so far they have had very little impact on drug innovation.

Both legislators and the public are frequently unaware of the creative elements of the pharmaceutical industry. This key function is not directly related to marketing. (Indeed, some pharmaceutical companies do no research but simply acquire their products from other companies.) The industry has the *unique ability* to organize, stimulate, and finance multidisciplinary research covering the entire gamut of scientific disciplines required in converting a laboratory discovery into a practical drug (e.g., as will be shown in Figure 1 and Table 5). The organizational efforts involved* in preparing a complete New Drug Application in the United States are completely outside the capabilities of nonprofit institutions and are not undertaken by government agencies, although the latter could presumably mobilize the requisite manpower and funds for such purposes.

At present all of the expenses associated with the development of a new prescription drug are borne by private industry and eventually recovered from sales. The ever increasing cost of drug development is certainly responsible in part for the progressively decreasing number of new drugs introduced in the United States. For the time being the present system still seems to work, even though major improvements will have to be instituted before long. All of the oral contraceptive agents em-

---

* In a symposium on "The Impact of Drug Legislation on the Drug Industry" held in August 1969, at the Gottlieb Duttweiler Institute for Economic and Social Studies (Zurich), Dr. Joseph F. Sadusk (of Parke, Davis & Co. and former medical director of the FDA) compared the 167 volumes (consisting of 72,200 pages) of a recent (1968) New Drug Application to the FDA on a new anesthetic agent with the much smaller applications (e. g., two volumes of 439 pages in 1959) of ten years ago. This illustration is not necessarily offered as a special variant of Parkinson's Law, but it points to the greater volume and complexity of supporting data required at the present time—much of it due to increased knowledge and availability of more sophisticated techniques. Of added interest is Sadusk's observation that the Canadian counterpart to the U.S. FDA application (72,200 pages) amounted to 67,128 pages, whereas the Japanese (2000 pages), British (857 pages) and Swiss (159 pages) were much shorter. Sadusk concluded with the question, "Is the public in those countries with greatly increased requirements better protected, and what is the proof if the answer is in the affirmative?"

ployed at present have been developed under such circumstances, but this circumstance is unlikely to hold for many of the future contraceptive agents.

Some of the special requirements that have been imposed on drugs used for fertility control are understandable and justified; similar requirements would undoubtedly be applied to any other drug (e.g., preventive medication in atherosclerosis) administered for long periods of time (usually years) to normal populations. These requirements are a response to our gradually increasing knowledge of human reproductive physiology in general, our accumulated experience with oral contraceptives in particular, and especially the surprisingly rapid acceptance by so many women of these new forms of birth control.

Unfortunately both the public and the government are not realistically facing the fact that development costs of such agents have escalated to such an extent that it is unlikely that the traditional course of drug creation will lead rapidly, or even eventually, to fundamentally new contraceptive agents. If the present climate and requirements had prevailed in 1955, oral contraceptive steroids would still be a laboratory curiosity in 1970. Yet it is obvious that toxicity and testing requirements will only become more stringent and time consuming rather than less so; additional criteria, such as checking for potential mutagenesis and making more sophisticated metabolic studies, will be added as logical consequences of accumulated new knowledge. Cost factors will escalate enormously. Therefore, as a foundation for future projections, we first need to review the origin and magnitude of present expenditures in contraceptive research and development.

Recent Research Expenditures for
Development of New Contraceptive Agents

From the late 1950s to the early 1960s the government spent very little on developing new birth-control agents. The overwhelming portion of the cost of developing oral contraceptives was met by three pharmaceutical companies. No published figures are available for these initial development costs, but retrospective calculations are useless in the light of today's requirements and knowledge.

A more realistic starting point is the second half of the 1960s which starts to approximate present-day circumstances. To my knowledge, research expenditures of the pharmaceutical industry in the area of reproductive physiology have never been collated. An incomplete personal survey among five pharmaceutical companies (Lilly, Ortho, Searle, Syntex, and Upjohn) has shown that their cumulative five-year expenditure (1965–69) in this field amounted to $68 million. Since my survey did not include all of the major American pharmaceutical companies active in this field nor any European firms, it is likely that the industry contribution during that period probably exceeded $100 million. This is an enormous figure by any standards. It is unrealistic to expect that larger sums or even the same sums will continue to be spent by this private sector when the eventual recovery of such expenditures becomes more and more distant and problematical (e.g., as shown later in Tables 5 and 6). Furthermore, this 1965–69 expenditure relates entirely to scientific work on birth control, whereas a substantial portion of government funds is devoted to ancillary activities (sociological and demographic studies).

The most encouraging recent initiative of the U.S. government has been the establishment of the Center for Population Research as part of the National Institute of Child Health and Human Development. However, its present quantitative limitation must be recognized immediately. According to Dr. P. A. Corfman, the director of the center, out of the total 1970 budget of $15.6 million, specific research projects account for $12.9 million, with $9 million of this going for contraceptive development (18, p. 6414). The only other significant government source is the Agency for International Development, whose budget for developing new methods for fertility regulation was negligible (about $100,000 in 1968) until 1969 when approximately $5.9 million was obligated for such purposes; the estimated figure for fiscal 1970 is $6.5 million (19).

Two of the most important private groups working in fertility research are the Population Council, with an annual research budget of about $2 million, and the Ford Foundation, which has been expending $4.5–7 million annually since 1966 in support of research and training in reproductive biology (20). An unstated proportion is allocatable to research directed specifically towards developing new contraceptive agents.

These cumulative expenditures are a reference point in evaluating the estimated research costs given below and the likelihood that the required funds will, in fact, become available.

Future Birth-Control Developments for the Female

All of the new contraceptive methods introduced during the past twenty years have been designed for the female. The reason is not just that she is more receptive to new approaches (presumably since unwanted pregnancies affect her much more directly than the male) but rather that there exist more hints to rational contraception from our knowledge of the female reproductive cycle than from the male process. Furthermore, it is possible to interfere with the female cycle at numerous stages, starting with ovulation and ending with embryogenesis. One survey of potentially useful approaches to fertility control in the female lists chemical agents interfering with ovulation, pituitary gonadotrophin secretion, fertilization, implantation, and finally embryonic development (3). Rather than scan our over-all knowledge of such approaches—which can be found throughout the scientific literature*—I have selected one such method in order to subject it to a type of critical systems analysis. Such a detailed presentation for one agent, which so far has not appeared anywhere in the literature, should be very useful in research and budget planning for other contraceptive methods as well. Most importantly, such an analysis will draw attention to the weak points in our present system of contraceptive drug development and other drugs as well. The set of recommendations listed at the end of this paper is largely an outcome of the present analysis. As an important example of

* An extensive bibliography will be found in (3).

future contraceptive methodology in the female, I have chosen a "once-a-month" pill with luteolytic and/or abortifacient properties since there are at least four advantages of such an agent over presently used ones:

(a) Administration of one pill a month is clearly more convenient than daily administration. This applies to major fertility-control programs in developing countries as well as to highly motivated individuals in advanced countries.

(b) Periodic short-term administration of a drug may be expected to give rise to fewer long-term side effects primarily because the agent is intended to act more specifically on a well-defined biological process.

(c) Since the agent will be effective in incapacitating the corpus luteum, irrespective of whether fertilization has occurred, it does not matter whether the woman is pregnant or not.

(d) Hopefully the agent may be active anytime during the first eight weeks after fertilization so that it can also act as an abortifacient. It could then be taken bimonthly. In case of drug failure another agent (possibly prostaglandins) should be available for subsequent chemical abortion or else surgical termination of the pregnancy should be available as a backup measure.

A CPM map for the development of such an agent is reproduced in Figure 1, and a more detailed description of the individual steps combined with estimated costs is given in Table 5. Three major additional comments are required for a full evaluation of this chart. The first concerns the teratology (malformations) studies, which are extremely important in any agent affecting embryonic development. The unsupported assumption is made that the FDA would permit phase 1 clinical studies without animal teratology. Irrespective of the correctness of such an assumption, such studies and the subsequent phase 2 and phase 3 clinical research can be performed only in a location where, in case of method failure, surgical abortion can be employed. The work leading to the determination of the eventual clinically effective dose will require progressive lowering of the dose until a level is reached in which failure is observed. From an investigative standpoint, it would be desirable

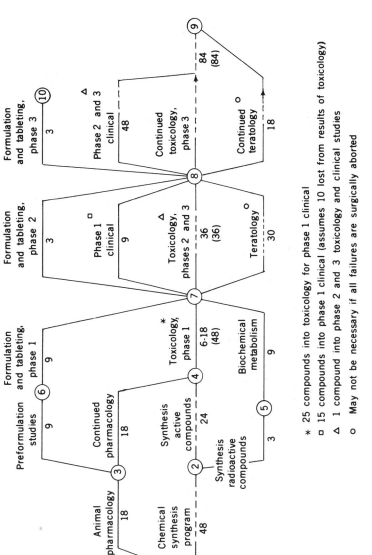

* 25 compounds into toxicology for phase 1 clinical
□ 15 compounds into phase 1 clinical (assumes 10 lost from results of toxicology)
△ 1 compound into phase 2 and 3 toxicology and clinical studies
o May not be necessary if all failures are surgically aborted

Figure I. Critical-path map for development of a luteolytic or abortifacient agent.

Table 5. Cost-and-time analysis of
luteolytic or abortifacient agent

Job identity	Function	Duration of function (*months*)	Cost including overhead (*thousands of dollars*)
1	Start of project		
1 to 2	Chemical synthesis of compounds in 0.5 to lg. amounts for biological screening program (4 chemists at $45,000/chemist/year).	48	720
1 to 3	Development of biological models to test luteolytic or abortifacient compounds. Use of synthesized compounds in test systems in rodents and monkeys to determine mechanism of action.	18	200
2 to 4	Synthesis of larger amounts of active compounds selected in biological test systems to be used in preformulation, formulation, phase 1 toxicology, and clinical studies.	24	200
2 to 5	Synthesis of radioactive material of the most active compound in biological tests for use in biochemical metabolism.	3	10
3 to 4	Continued biological studies on mechanism of action of active compounds.	18	150
3 to 6	In vitro and in vivo studies of stability, solubility, and absorption of active compounds to assist formulation and tableting.	9	100[a]

Table 5. (*cont.*)

Job identity	Function	Duration of function (*months*)	Cost including overhead (*thousands of dollars*)
4 to 7	Toxicology for phase 1 clinical—assumes that since only acute therapy is envisaged, FDA will not require toxicology as for current oral contraceptives. It will be sufficient to study LD 50 in 60 rats and 16 dogs per compound, using 25 compounds; 15 compounds are expected to be satisfactory for phase 1 clinical.	6–18	125
	If usual phase 1 contraceptive toxicology is required (Table 1), the following numbers of animals are needed for 25 compounds: 12,000 rats, 2400 rabbits, 800 dogs, 5400 primates for LD 50, 90-day toxicology, teratology, and abortifacient (repeat abortion through F_1, F_2, and F_3 generations) studies.	[48]	[14,000]
6 to 7	Formulation and tableting for phase 1 clinical studies.	9	100[a]
5 to 7	Metabolic studies in rodent or primate and human with synthetic radioactive material already prepared. Both oral and intravenous administration may be studied.	9	25
7 to 8	Formulation and tableting for phase 2 clinical studies.	3	50[a]
7 to 8 to 9	Toxicology and teratology for phase 2 and 3. Although	36	2,700

Table 5. (*cont.*)

Job identity	Function	Duration of function (months)	Cost including overhead (thousands of dollars)
	FDA may require very limited studies for clinical phase 1 because of acute dosing, it has been assumed that toxicology required for later clinical work will be as severe as current oral-contraceptive development, involving long-term teratology and repetitive abortion studies of 5 compounds for 1 year: 160 rats, 32 dogs, and 32 primates (phase 2); the best of these 5 compounds 2 years in 240 rats, 7 years in 64 dogs, and 10 years in 80 primates (phase 3).	84 to completion of all toxicology[b]	400
	If usual phase 2 contraceptive toxicology is required, the following numbers of animals are required for study of 1 compound: 800 rats, 160 dogs, and 160 primates for 1 year.	[36]	[315]
	If usual phase 3 contraceptive toxicology is required, the following numbers of animals are required for study of 1 compound: 240 rats for 2 years, 64 dogs for 7 years, and 80 primates for 10 years.	[84][b]	[400]
7 to 8	Phase 1 clinical studies. Assumes 15 compounds satisfactory in toxicology. Administer single dose to a	9	600

Table 5. (*cont.*)

Job identity	Function	Duration of function (*months*)	Cost including overhead (*thousands of dollars*)
	small number of women to create abortion first or second month of pregnancy. Select best compound for phase 2 and 3 clinical studies. With 1-dose level and costs of $660 per woman per cycle, with 3 cycle studies, total for 15 compounds equals $300,000. Therefore for 2-dose levels costs are:		600
8 to 10	Formulation, tableting, and cost of material for phase 3 clinical studies, including cost of material for long term toxicity.	3	300[a]
8 to 9	Phase 2 and 3 clinical studies of best compound will be combined. Assume requirement of 1000 women studied for 10,000 cycles.	48	500
Total time and cost to NDA filing:		120–204[b]	6,780[b]
Preparation of NDA and master file:		6	60
Grand total (without toxicology of Table 1):		126–210[c]	6,840
Grand total (with toxicity of Table 1):		210	18,330

[a] Costs for formulation, stability, and analytical work (including usual overhead) can be calculated in general on the basis of $150,000 for any new drug in a conventional dosage form or $270,000 for a new drug in a novel dosage form (e.g., silastic implant). The present costs were calculated on this basis. Allow for some work on rejected compounds as per cost of drug.

[b] Two-year rat, dog, and primate studies necessary for NDA, but must have ongoing 7-year dog and 10-year monkey studies (see Table 1).

[c] The development time is calculated, not by summation of all times in the time breakdown, but rather from the CPM chart, following the longest course of development. When the usual FDA contraceptive toxicology (see Table 1) requirements are given as a possible alternative, the duration of study and associated extra cost are given in brackets.

if such drug failures were permitted to proceed beyond the fourteenth week of pregnancy before undertaking surgical abortion so as to examine the human fetus for teratology. This is a difficult requirement with respect to availability and co-operation of patients. Otherwise, one would have to depend on monkey data, which are obviously not as informative.

The second comment on Figure 1 and Table 5 pertains to the time estimates. These are ideal figures, and the aggregate of about 126 to 210 months (bottom of Table 5) may not be realizable because it involves almost perfect coordination and even telescoping of various steps in the CPM scheme. For instance, the preliminary toxicology (steps 4 to 7) on twenty-five compounds will involve rejection of several compounds because of serious toxicity, as well as rejection based on phase 1 clinical data (steps 7 to 8). The six to eighteen months estimate for the initial toxicology leading to the selection of the final compound is, therefore, very optimistic. But this time analysis offers the first justification for the title of my paper since the middle of the 1980s is already an optimistic target date when such an agent could receive the final stamp of government approval (under current regulations) and be disseminated to the public.

The third comment refers to the cost estimate. For reasons given in Table 5 there are major uncertainties with respect to the ultimate cost of toxicology since this depends on factors such as the choice and cost of the animals (see Table 4), as well as on the frequently changing government regulations. A further and greater uncertainty is the estimate for phase 3 clinical studies (steps 8 to 9). Much larger numbers of cycles may be required in response to demands* that virtually all actual and potential side effects of such drugs should be known prior to government approval for marketing.

This may be the single greatest hurdle and uncertainty in any

---

* As an illustration of the magnitude of such costs, a current study of ten thousand women on various medical effects associated with oral contraceptives sponsored by the National Institutes of Health Center for Population Research involves an annual cost of $1 million (18, p. 6397).

planning of new contraceptive developments; for this reason I make a very special recommendation at the end of this article. Irrespective of the final cost figure ($7 to 18 million in Table 5), it must be emphasized that allocating such a sum of money by a government or private agency in the form of grants to various nonindustrial laboratories cannot possibly accomplish the desired goal of producing an agent ready for wide public use. This is because the cost and time estimates in Figure 1 and Table 5 are based on the availability in one organization (i.e., research divisions of large pharmaceutical companies) of all the manpower, facilities, and logistic support required for the type of activity and schedule outlined in the CPM chart. If these facilities had to be created *de novo* and the required infrastructure had to be supported exclusively from funds allocated to such a project, the final cost would have to be multiplied several times. Finally, whatever the over-all cost figure, it should probably be at least doubled because, as has already happened with the currently used types of oral contraceptives, an agent may be rejected at a late stage of phase 3 clinical trial.

Prostaglandins

The importance of abortion as a method of fertility control has been emphasized numerous times (21).* In areas of the world where population growth was reduced dramatically within a short period of time (such as Japan and eastern Europe), it was done principally through access to surgical abortions. Clearly the availability of a chemical (i.e., nonsurgical) abortifacient

* The lay press (22) as well as the Senate hearings (18) contain the unsupported statement that if abortion were available as a backup procedure in case of contraceptive failure, then less dangerous oral contraceptives could be used. As yet we have no evidence that it is easier to develop a "safe pill" that needs to be only 90 per cent effective rather than 99.9 per cent. The history of the present oral contraceptive suggests that this is not the case because lowering of the recommended dose (i.e., presumed lesser danger) may still give full protection and yet be unacceptable as a result of other side effects such as uncontrolled breakthrough bleeding. Similarly, clinical testing of an estrogen-free "mini-pill" with a slightly greater pregnancy rate than the usual oral contraceptive was recently suspended by the FDA because of factors that had nothing to do with efficacy.

would be highly desirable. Therefore (aside from the hypothetical agent described in Figure 1 and Table 5, which on the basis of present leads may well turn out to be a steroid), some mention of the prostaglandins (frequently abbreviated as PG) is warranted, especially since they are chemically distinct from the steroids and offer another illustration of the long time sequences inherent in birth-control research.

The isolation and chemical structure elucidation of the prostaglandins was effected by Bergstrom and collaborators (23) in Sweden in the 1950s. By 1957 one pharmaceutical firm, the Upjohn Company, had already started a program in this field, which has reached multimillion-dollar proportions after thirteen years. Numerous other firms in the United States and in Europe have since become active in this field. However, no drug containing any of the prostaglandins has yet been introduced into medical practice. Quite recently an Upjohn group demonstrated a luteolytic effect of PGF_{2a} in the Rhesus monkey, especially the pregnant one, with termination of pregnancy occurring in the majority of animals treated eleven to fifteen days after ovulation (24). At about the same time two European clinical reports (25, 26) appeared on the use of PGF_{2a} and PGE_2 as abortifacients after intravenous infusions in women at various stages of pregnancy. The success ranged from fourteen out of fifteen to three out of eleven patients, but the differences were probably associated with different infusion rates and concentrations. The side effects were generally diarrhea and vomiting, and there is reason to believe that the abortifacient action of the prostaglandins in humans is not related to the luteolytic action observed in monkeys (24).

In spite of extensive press coverage and optimistic headlines (27–29) accompanying these initial clinical trials, it must be recognized that these are only preliminary leads and that many problems of a time-consuming nature must be overcome before the prostaglandins can be considered practical candidates as abortifacients. A few of the more obvious ones are:

1. The prostaglandins have actions on almost all body systems (23) and although their use as abortifacients will involve

only short-term administration, extensive clinical work will be required to determine possible side effects in a representative group of women.

2. A great deal of research has been performed in the past few years in academic and industrial laboratories on the synthesis of the various prostaglandins. Whereas various successful approaches have been reported, none has as yet lent itself to large-scale synthesis, and the availability of adequate amounts of various prostaglandins is still a bottleneck that will take time to resolve.

3. The requirement for intravenous infusion limits their use to hospitalized patients. Such a drug would still represent an important advance in developed countries where surgical abortions are carried out in hospitals, but alternative means of administration must be developed if one of the prostaglandins is to be used in the manner and on the scale envisaged for the type of agent described in Figure 1. Intramuscular administration (26) is a possibility, but major emphasis in future research must be placed on formulations active by the oral or intravaginal routes. Until now there has been no success in achieving oral forms with any of the naturally occurring prostaglandins, and work with synthetic congeners or special formulations would be required. This would put such compounds only at the beginning of the CPM chart in Figure 1, with most of the time-and-cost estimates outlined in Table 5.

4. If intramuscular, and especially oral, administration of prostaglandins become realities, then out-patient use will presumably be their widest application. This implies the definite possibility of incomplete follow-up and raises the specter of potential teratogenesis if abortion should be unsuccessful. Irrespective of possible FDA requirements, teratology studies in primates must be performed at some stage.

Male Contraceptive Agent

The condom or withdrawal prior to ejaculation are the only practical contraceptive measures currently available to the male.

As pointed out by the WHO scientific group (3), "an agent that could safely and effectively inhibit fertility in the male, without risk of interfering with spermatogenesis and libido, would find practical application in fertility regulation." The report then proceeds with a lengthy list and an associated bibliography of chemical agents that have been shown to have some effect on the fertility of male animals (notably rats) and concludes that "none of the chemical agents is suitable for use in man, owing to known or potential toxicity. Similarly, immunological processes present hazards when used in man, and they suffer from a lack of specificity. *Consequently, no systematic method of fertility control in man is available at present.*" (Italics mine.)

The CPM chart (Figure 2) and accompanying Table 6 contain a longer time estimate for the discovery of suitable leads that may give rise to compounds warranting clinical investigation. It would be highly desirable if several programs (each of them costing about $3 million) of the type outlined in Figure 2 under steps 1 to 2 to 4 to 8 and 1 to 3 to 7 were instituted in several laboratories at the same time in order to increase the chances that a useful agent might emanate from such research. Nothing will stimulate future research on a practical male contraceptive agent more than the discovery of viable and significant chemical leads, but even then 1984 appears to be an exceedingly optimistic target date for a male contraceptive pill ready for public use.

Three other difficulties associated with the development of a chemical contraceptive drug in the male must be recognized. The first is that our basic knowledge of the reproductive biology of the male is even less advanced than that of the female and that a great deal of fundamental work needs to be done, much of it probably in subhuman primates. This is also the reason why a substantial number of the first series of grants by the National Institutes of Health (NIH) Center for Population Research were issued in support of research dealing with maturation and fertilizing capacity of spermatozoa.

The second difficulty is with the actual clinical work and has so far not drawn the attention of planners in the birth-con-

Table 6. Cost-and-time analysis of critical path map for
male antifertility agent[a]

Job identity	Function	Duration of function (*months*)	Cost including overhead (*thousands of dollars*)
1	Start of project		
1 to 2	Chemical synthesis of compounds for biological screening (4 chemists at \$45,000/chemist/year).	60	900
1 to 3	Use of compounds synthesized, in modified Jackson bioassay to discover compounds affecting fertilizing capacity of sperm stored in epididymis, followed by studies in primates.	18	150
2 to 4	Synthesis of compounds found active (assume 25) in bioassay screen.	24	225
2 to 5	Radioactive labeling of best compound from 1 to 3.	3	10
3 to 6 to 8	Preformulation, formulation, and tableting for phase 1.	12	200
3 to 7	Continued animal pharmacology.	24	200
5 to 8	Studies of biochemical metabolism of the labeled compound prepared (2 to 5).	9	25
4 to 8	Toxicology for phase 1 clinical studies (assumes 25 compounds studied) including LD 50, 90-day toxicity, and teratology in 4000 rats, 1500 rabbits, 800 dogs, and 500 primates.	24–36	1700
8 to 9	Formulation and tableting for phase 2 clinical.	3	50

Table 6. (*cont.*)

Job identity	Function	Duration of function (*months*)	Cost including overhead (*thousands of dollars*)
8 to 9	Phase 1 clinical studies with 15 compounds. For each compound use groups of 5 males at 3 widely spaced dose intervals for 6 months. Studies of sperm mobility and fertilizing capacity will require evaluation together with effects on spermatogenesis.	9/compound (max. 48)	450
8 to 9	Toxicology and teratology for phase 2 (assumes 5 compounds studied) 1-year toxicity in 800 rats, 160 dogs, and 160 primates, and continued teratology.	24	315
9 to 10	Formulation and tableting for phase 1 studies, including cost of material for jobs 9 to 12.	3	300
9 to 11	Phase 2 clinical studies. Expansion of phase 3 studies to 50–100 men to quantitate dose requirement for 5 compounds.	24	500
9 to 11 to 12	Continued toxicology for phase 3 clinical studies with 1 compound includes 2 years in 240 rats, 7 years in 64 dogs, 10 years in 80 primates, and continued teratology with 1 compound.	96	400
11 to 12	Phase 3 clinical studies. Increased numbers of men in trial (possibly 1000) with studies of mechanism of ac-	48	800

Table 6. (*cont.*)

tion, of fertility return upon cessation of dosing, and of any fathered offspring from escape pregnancies.		
Total time and cost to NDA filing:	144–240	6,225
Preparation of NDA and FDA master file:	6	60
Grand total:	150–246	6,285

ᵃ See footnotes to Table 5.

trol field. The human spermatogenic cycle, from spermatogonium to ejaculate, lasts approximately twelve weeks. It is likely that testing, including pretreatment-control and posttreatment-recovery observations, may last up to six months depending on the point at which the particular drug attacks this sequence. Pilot testing could presumably be carried out in groups of five males at each of three widely spaced dose levels for each agent (see step 8 to 9 in Figure 2). Observations should combine evaluation of effect on spermatogenesis and/or sperm motility together with observations of organ toxicity and other side effects. *At the present time, there appear to be available in the entire country facilities for evaluating only two drugs at a time.* The complications would be even greater in phase 2 and phase 2 clinical studies. Women can easily be collected for clinical studies through their association with Planned Parenthood clinics and individual obstetricians or gynecologists; there exists no simple mechanism to collect similar groups of males for clinical experimentation. The prisons and armed forces are the only convenient sources and results would have to be based largely on examination of masturbation sperm samples rather than on an evaluation of fertility control in an average population.

This leads to the third difficulty, the male's generally lesser interest in, and greater reservations about, procedures aimed at decreasing his fertility. Tablet taking, if the agent is to be administered orally, would be even less reliable than it has

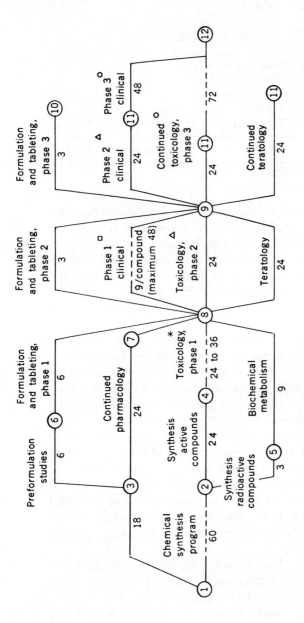

Figure 2. Critical-path map for development of a male anti-fertility agent.

* 25 compounds into toxicology for phase 1 clinical
□ 15 compounds into phase 1 clinical (assumes 10 lost from results of toxicology)
△ 5 compounds into phase 2 toxicology and clinical studies
○ 1 compound into phase 3 toxicology and clinical

proved to be in women, and efficacy can probably only be determined on a large scale by following marital couples. However, if a male contraceptive pill were developed, it might be possible to introduce the motivating factor through the female, at least in stable, monogamous relationships.

The single greatest objection to the present oral contraceptives is the essentially continuous administration of a potent agent to fertile women for many years. Clearly the same objection will be raised with a male contraceptive pill if it has to be consumed continuously by fertile males for many years. However, if both a female and a male contraceptive were available the two partners could alternate (e.g., every three to six months) in their use of a contraceptive pill and thus avoid continued exposure to one agent for prolonged periods of time. Such a regimen is likely to work only in educationally advanced, motivated groups, and it is probable that the female partner would bear the principal burden of enforcing it.

"Orwellian" Contraceptive Approaches

Some laymen, legislators, and scientists concerned with the economic and environmental effects of rapid population increase have started to imply that drastic government-imposed birth-control procedures may have to be introduced during the next decade if voluntary use of conventional methods fails to stem the human tide. I would like to use the adjective "Orwellian" for such externally imposed extensions of voluntary fertility control—which have been reviewed extensively by Berelson,* together with incentive programs, tax benefits, and many other features. Clearly the most all-encompassing and frightening is the first entry in Berelson's list of involuntary fertility-control methods—a temporary sterilant added to water or staple foods. I would like to consider briefly some of the practical problems associated with the development of such an agent that reduce the concept to an absurdity.

* See (30) and extensive bibliography cited therein.

1. The substance should be active either in the male or the female, but only in their reproductive years. It must be active over an enormous dose range, since food or water intake can vary greatly in twenty-pound children as compared to two-hundred-pound adults, and must be tasteless. It must be specific for the human.

2. If added to food, it would have to be incorporated by the supplier rather than consumer in order to insure universal administration. Even then, a dissenter could simply eliminate a given food from his diet and thus escape the contraceptive effects unless it were universally required (e.g., salt). In any event the contraceptive additive would have to be stable to processing (baking, heating, sterilization), packaging, and shipping (oxidation, light).

3. In view of the universal ingestion of water, it would seem to be the better vehicle, although even here it would be feasible only in central water-supply systems and not in wells. This requirement alone probably eliminates at least half of the world's population. However, regardless of the method of incorporation into the water, the contraceptive agent would have to display chemical stability in contact with pipes and other metals; light and oxidative stability in holding tank or reservoir; temperature stability during cooking or refrigeration (e.g., possible precipitation from solution); lack of chemical interaction with minerals (e.g., hard, soft, and softened water) and with commonly consumed foodstuffs during cooking; and absence of concentration problems arising from food processing, as in the preparation of frozen juice or soup concentrates. Even if these virtually insuperable obstacles could be overcome, let us not forget the tremendous difficulty encountered in adding even as simple an agent as fluoride to municipal water supplies.

4. The question of "side effects," which has gained so much notoriety—as in the recent "Nelson hearings" on oral contraceptives in the U.S. Senate (18)—is insoluble. No drug is devoid of side effects and, in this particular instance, the agent should have minimal side effects not only in the sex and age group in

which it is supposed to be active, but also in all other age groups and in the opposite sex. In contrast to any human drug, which generally is simply a contaminant of the person's microecology, the "Orwellian" contraceptive added to food or water would be a general environmental pollutant. It would have to be considered a pesticide, albeit one that is directed primarily at humans. It is exceedingly unlikely that such a compound active in man would be ineffective in at least some other animal species. In fact, since initial biological screening for such an agent would not be carried out in man but first in animals, *an agent truly specific for the human would completely escape detection.*

5. If such an "Orwellian" contraceptive were completely effective, then its effects would have to be reversible through the administration, presumably by license, of a second agent. The likelihood of discovering such an agent is slight, yet its availability is an absolute prerequisite before the sterility agent can be employed. The other alternative would be to develop a contraceptive that significantly reduced but did not abolish fertility, with the level of escape then setting the birth rate. Such a property might make an agent acceptable from a demographic, but hardly a personal, standpoint.

In the light of these special problems, which would have to be superimposed on the already formidable difficulties (see Figures 1 and 2) associated with the development of any systemic chemical fertility-control agent, it is perfectly clear that the creation of such a universal birth-control agent is outside the realm of possibility in this century. My conclusion should be contrasted with that of Ketchel (31, 32), who makes the optimistic but completely unsupported prediction that within five to fifteen years methods will be developed for controlling the fertility of an entire population.

Immunological approaches, though probably slightly easier to implement in an Orwellian society than an additive to food and water, are still so far away (3) that they do not merit serious consideration within the context of this paper. We are thus brought back to reality with only two reversible methods that have any possibility of being introduced on a massive scale by government edict during the next twenty years, provided the political realities enumerated by Berelson (30) and also Ketchel (31, 32) are faced. In the male this would be vasectomy and in the female, administration of a sustained-action contraceptive of the estrogen-progestin type (4). Reference to vasectomy has already been made in the introductory section of this article.

General Recommendations

The inevitable conclusion reached from the data in Figures 1 and 2 and Tables 5 and 6 is that the pharmaceutical industry must remain involved in the massive effort required to bring a fundamentally new female or male contraceptive agent to fruition in the 1980s. Furthermore, for reasons outlined in detail in an earlier article (10), most of this work has to, and will, be done under rules and regulations established by the FDA and similar government regulatory agencies of the most technologically advanced countries. If this premise is granted, then the following recommendations should be taken into consideration.

The first three recommendations would encourage research irrespective of the sponsor (industrial, governmental, or academic) of such drug trials. The last two would provide specific incentives for continued investment by the pharmaceutical industry in contraceptive research. This needs to be done for three reasons: First, the organizational abilities of the pharmaceutical industry are a *sine qua non* for the development of a practical birth-control agent. Second, given that major advances in birth control will be based on chemical methods, then access to the large and highly productive organic chemical research groups in the pharmaceutical industry are indispensable prerequisites (see steps 1 to 2 in Figures 1 and 2). This has already been recognized by nonindustrial groups like the ·Population Council and the NIH Center for Population Research. Third, unless some incentives in the contraceptive research area are introduced soon, it is unlikely that the present rate of industry expenditure for research in this field (probably $15–20 million per annum) will be maintained; indeed it is likely to decline, and it may reach a noncritical level in a short period of time. This would be a tragedy, except in the eyes of those who dismiss or ignore the population problem. Therefore, the fourth and fifth proposals are made with the purpose of insuring industrial laboratories some likelihood of a profitable recovery of their research investment and of reducing the risk inherent in ten- to fifteen-year research projects.

If the problems that prompted the following five recommendations are not taken into serious consideration, birth control in the middle 1980s will not be very different from that of 1970.

1. *Conflicting dual role of FDA*. The U.S. Food and Drug Administration, as well as government regulatory agencies in other countries (e.g., the Food and Drug Directorate in Canada), have two principal functions, which are potentially conflicting.* This conflict has particularly serious consequences for future research in contraceptive technology, whether such research is performed by industry or by some other sector. A definition of this conflict and a possible resolution should, therefore, receive the highest priority.

The first function, which clearly should not be abolished, is that of protector of the consuming public regarding drugs on the open market. The FDA must protect the consumer from harm and fraud, it must maintain and enforce appropriate analytical standards, and it must assume the function of policeman or watchdog. This historical function of the FDA is at least partly incompatible with a more recent one—namely, its role in passing on all clinical protocols by having a de facto veto on all clinical work with experimental drugs. It is at this premarketing stage of a drug's development that the maximum flexibility commensurate with scientific caution and medical responsibility must be maintained. The agency responsible for such protocols

* Some brief comments are made on this point in a National Academy of Sciences report (33).

must consider its main function to be the stimulation of research and drug development rather than just policing it.

Thus, the role of the FDA seems to have moved from that of protector to that of guarantor; Congress, the press, and consumer-protection groups are responsible. Yet it must be recognized that this role of guarantor is an impossible one. No drug can be *totally* effective and *completely* safe, and no agency of government can guarantee that it will be. It is illuminating to examine the roles of other regulatory agencies. The Securities and Exchange Commission requires that a company coming under its jurisdiction make certain disclosures about its financial operations, but it does not guarantee the investor that a company will prosper. Similarly, the Federal Aviation Administration (FAA) certifies that aircraft meet certain safety requirements, but it does not guarantee the traveler that it will not crash.

Every contraceptive drug will have side effects, as does any drug. The FDA must recognize the benefit of a drug as well as the risk. The FDA reviewer's incentive to weigh the benefits of approving a drug is nowhere near his risk in approving it and later having to defend his position to his superiors under pressures from the press or Congress. Consequently, the understandable emphasis has been on hypercaution, bureaucratic delays, and enormously escalating requirements. For every example in which such hypercaution proved ultimately justified, there are probably dozens of examples in which it led to long delays or total abandonment of potentially important drugs.

The consumer also suffers from the delusion that drug safety and drug efficacy are all-or-nothing propositions. The fact that people experience side effects from "safe" drugs should be no more surprising than the fact that occasionally some people die when "safe" airplanes crash. This evaluation leads to the following recommendation, which may not only be beneficial in facilitating and stimulating research on contraceptive drugs but also on other drugs in preventive medicine that involve long-term administration to a "normal" population.

The FDA (as well as similar regulatory agencies in other

countries) must announce a realistic role and declare that their approval is not a guarantee, that drug side effects are always possible, and that the final decision as to whether the benefit of a drug in a particular patient outweighs the risk is that of the prescribing physician. If the physician cannot be trusted, emphasis should be placed on improving and sustaining medical education in the country because in the end the physician must carry the main burden of responsibility. (It would take too long to go into the issues concerning the sources of drug information now used by physicians and the constructive measures that might be introduced to improve them.)

For drugs of the contraceptive type, the IND-NDA process as it exists is totally inadequate and should be modified. The existing phase 3 clinical program should be reduced to meticulously planned, moderate-sized clinical studies for a limited time (two years would be adequate in most instances) that would disclose whether a new agent has any conspicuous toxicity. Efficacy could clearly be established under such conditions. The question then arises whether the drug has any low-incidence toxicity. The oral contraceptives have taught an important lesson, well known to statisticians, that large samples are needed to demonstrate small effects reliably* and that it is extremely difficult and costly to accumulate such samples in a premarketing phase.

It is at this stage that the FDA could introduce the concept of *conditional approval,*† somewhat analogous to the FAA's Certificate of Provisional Airworthiness. During this time of use-testing the agent could be marketed, and some of the profits from the sales could be used for structured prospective studies of large numbers of the patients on the medication. The FDA could assign a permanent monitor to co-administer such pro-

* At the January 23, 1970, hearings of the Senate Subcommittee on Monopoly, Dr. D. Seigel of NIH, in response to a question about the number of subjects required to determine the doubling of the risk of breast cancer, indicated that 85,000 person-years would be needed for a statistical evaluation (18, pp. 6403 and 6420).
† Such a proposal has been advocated by, among others, my colleague Professor J. Lederberg (Department of Genetics, Stanford Medical School). For some relevant comments, see his article in (34).

grams. This would be far superior to the collection of anecdotal reports of side effects because it is very difficult to judge whether they are drug-related. Under such a new scheme one avoids the need to collect tremendous quantities of information on people who are well and reacting favorably to the drug during the phase 3 clinical trials. Instead, attention is focused during the "provisional-approval-for-marketing" phase on the few individuals who do poorly, and it is possible to determine more quickly whether their reactions are drug-related. If the drug survives a well-designed prospective follow-up study, it could be given full approval by the FDA and accordingly released from continuing large studies financed by the sponsor. As can be seen from Figures 1 and 2, implementation of such a recommendation could markedly speed up the time required to develop a practical contraceptive agent.

2. *Legal liability.* This problem is particularly serious in the United States, but it is also becoming noticeable in Europe. Attention should be paid to the liability question since it is extremely likely that contraceptive drugs of the type outlined in Figures 1 and 2—if they are developed at all—will be introduced first in North America and Europe (10). The problem is particularly acute in the birth-control field because of the wide population spectrum that is exposed to such drugs and because the "1984" birth-control agents are particularly susceptible to this hazard. These facts merit two comments.

The first refers to the peculiar American phenomenon of enormous liability suits—which are certainly not limited to the drug field. Liability insurance costs for the physician and for drug firms have risen to such an extent that their impact on the cost of drugs and of medical care must be taken into consideration. Such liability suits are particularly difficult to try in the birth-control field. In contrast to a car accident or a clearly incompetent surgical operation, cause-and-effect relationships are frequently difficult to establish when an agent (such as a male contraceptive pill) is administered for many years while the person is exposed to many other drugs and environmental hazards. Even though a case might be made that government approval of a drug ought to carry with it some assumption of co-responsibility for liability or that the consumer should take out special-risk insurance as does the air traveler, this area is outside the present jurisdiction of the FDA.

However, the second comment is clearly related to the FDA. The FDA requires on occasion that all patients on an experimental drug that has been discontinued during the premarketing phase must be followed up for extensive periods of time. The impeccable logic of such a position in many cases—especially when the drug treatment, the disease, and the follow-up time are clearly defined—need not be argued. However, this same position has now been taken several times by the FDA with certain oral contraceptives. Since the follow-up time after discontinuance of the drug may well extend to twenty or more years, during which the person will take many other drugs and may be exposed to a variety of other conditions, any information from such a required study is virtually meaningless. Even if it were useful, the logistic and financial burden for what amounts to de facto lifetime free medical care should not necessarily have to be borne by the developer of the drug. He has probably already spent millions of dollars on nonrecoverable research costs (since the experimental drug was never marketed), and because of his research activities in a field such as reproductive physiology, he may have to deal with much larger patient populations during the clinical experimental phase than in any other area of drug research. The same problem will clearly arise in other areas of birth control (e.g., male contraceptive pill); serious thought should be given to the possibility that a government agency assume the responsibility for follow-up procedures on discontinued drugs (in contrast to a similar situation in which a marketed drug is discontinued).

3. *Appeal procedure.* As pointed out in this and an earlier article (10), all clinical research performed in this country is subject to disapproval by FDA personnel. Disapproval of the initiation or continuation of clinical trials essentially cannot be appealed, yet disapproval is frequently a result of hypercaution rather than exceptional scientific insight. An appeal procedure

of the type outlined earlier (10) is urgently required in the birth-control field; the absence of such appeals is already having serious repercussions, and major research projects are often discontinued.

4. *Patent protection.* Consideration should be given to a possible revision of the patent lifetime of drugs in the birth-control area and other fields that require very long-term, premarketing investigation. At present, the life span of a patent in the United States is seventeen years. If a pharmaceutical firm invests millions of dollars in research over a period that consumes most of the lifetime of the patent (a circumstance that may easily happen when ten to fifteen years of premarketing research and development is required), then a crucial incentive element is removed. One possibility is to offer use-patent protection for such products for perhaps 10 years, starting with the date of NDA *approval.*

5. *Government-industry interaction.* As pointed out earlier, the costs of developing a new contraceptive agent have risen so dramatically that they are not only beginning to outstrip the financial capabilities of an individual pharmaceutical company, but they greatly reduce the chance to recover such expenditure after approval for public sale. For instance, if ten to fifteen years of research by one company costs $10 to 30 million and results in a "once-a-month" pill, is it likely that the public, the press, or possibly even the legislatures will tolerate a price of several dollars for a single pill when the final manufacturing cost of the chemical ingredient may only amount to 5 or 10 per cent of the price? Yet unless such prices for single pills were charged, the prospects for recovery of the research expenditure—let alone a profit on the investment—would be negligible.

The understandable reason for these tremendous costs and lengthy experimental time periods is that a drug administered to large portions of the normal population must have a minimum of risks. The chances of developing such drugs are correspondingly smaller, and it is only reasonable that the public (i.e., the taxpayer via the government) should bear part of this development cost for what could really be equated to an insurance policy. The special features responsible for the extraordinary costs of birth-control drugs are the lengthy toxicity requirements (completely unlike those of other drugs and concentrating largely on subhuman primates) and the large and lengthy phase 2 and phase 3 clinical trials that are accompanied by an ever-increasing number of clinical laboratory examinations. It is this aspect of the research, and not the chemical, biological, short-term toxicological, or even phase 1 clinical studies, that should be funded by the public. One way of partially funding such research is inherent in my first recommendation.

Another possibility is that a pharmaceutical company have the option of applying to a government agency for full financial support of long-term toxicity studies (which could actually be performed elsewhere under contract) and all phase 2 and phase 3 clinical work. If the research should lead to a commercial product, the company would be obligated to repay the accumulated financial support on an annual royalty basis of not more than 5 per cent in order not to affect the price of the drug too drastically. If all of the money is repaid and the drug is still being sold commercially, it might be reasonable to expect a continued royalty payment on a reduced basis (e.g., 2 to 3 per cent) for the life of the commercial product. During the first years of such a system funds would only be outflowing from the government agency, but after a certain period an equilibrium would be reached. Under extremely favorable circumstances this might even turn in favor of the government agency.

Such a proposal may appear unprecedented in the drug field, in spite of the fact that this industry spends a higher proportion of its gross income on research than any other, but it actually has a striking precedent in the U.S. government's original decision (prior to Congressional veto) to underwrite the development of a supersonic transport (SST) in this country. The socially redeeming features of the SST and its effect on the environment can hardly compare with a drug in the birth-control field. The monetary equivalent of a few SSTs per annum could have a remarkable effect in the birth-control field and at the same time serve as an indication of what the national priorities really should be.

My fundamental purpose in making this proposal is not to argue the advantages of the free-enterprise drug industry or to protect its profits; it is to assure the continued development of drugs that are vital to human well-being. For this to be possible, we must decide either to create an effective partnership between government and industry based on the model of other major technological efforts—such as the space program—or undertake the difficult and even more costly steps that would be involved in a socialization of that part of the drug industry that requires long development cycles.

Conclusions

1. Eric Blair* can rest easily in his grave because birth control by governmentally imposed methods—such as incorporation into drinking water—is totally unfeasible by 1984.

2. Fundamentally new birth-control procedures in the female (e.g., once-a-month luteolytic or abortifacient) and a male contraceptive pill probably will not be developed until the 1980s at the earliest, and then only if major steps of the type outlined in the present paper are instituted in the early 1970s. During the next decade development of practical methods of birth control without important incentives for continued active participation by the pharmaceutical industry is highly unlikely, and without them birth control in 1984 will not differ significantly from that of today.†

* Alias George Orwell.
† I am grateful to many persons in academic, industrial, and government circles for comments, but I am particularly indebted to Drs. J. Bennett, S. A. Bessler, K. Dumas, R. Havemeyer, R. Hill, and E. Segre for their valuable contributions.

References

1. "Environmental Quality: Family Planning. Part 2, Adequate Funding Levels for Research." *Congressional Record,* 116 (28) Washington, D.C.: U.S. Government Printing Office, February 27, 1970. Pp. S2611–S2612.
2. John R. Platt. "What we must do," *Science,* Vol. 166 (1969), 1115.
3. "Developments in Fertility Control." *World Health Organization Technical Report Series,* No. 424. Geneva, 1969.
4. U.S. Food and Drug Administration Advisory Committee on Obstetrics and Gynecology. *Second Report on Oral Contraceptives.* Washington, D.C.: U.S. Government Printing Office, August 1, 1969.
5. M. Mintz. "IUD Hazards," *Washington Post.* March 5, 1970.
6. A. Pakrashi and G. Ghosh Ray. "Contraceptive Mechanism of IUD's," *Journal of Reproduction and Fertility,* Vol. 19 (1969), 357.
7. W. B. Ober, et al.. "Endometrial Morphology and Polyethylene Intrauterine Devices," *Obstetrics and Gynecology,* Vol. 32 (1968), 782.
8. C. M. Southam and V. I. Babcock. "Induction of Subcutaneous Tumors in Rats by Plastic Loops and Spirals," *American Journal of Obstetrics and Gynecology,* Vol. 96 (1966), 134.
9. P. A. Corfman and R. M. Richart. "Induction in Rats of Uterine Epidermoid Carcinomas by Plastic and Stainless Steel Intrauterine Devices," *American Journal of Obstetrics and Gynecology,* Vol. 98 (1967), 987.
10. Carl Djerassi. "Prognosis for the Development of New Chemical Birth Control Agents," *Science,* Vol. 166 (1969), 468.
11. E. I. Goldenthal. "Current View on Safety Evaluation of Drugs," *FDA Papers* (May 1968), 13.
12. E. I. Goldenthal. "Contraceptives, Estrogens and Progestogens: A New FDA Policy on Animal Studies," *FDA Papers* (November 1969), 15.
13. Private communication from Drs. E. Forchielli, R. A. Runkel, and M. D. Chaplin, Syntex Research, Palo Alto, Calif.
14. U. S. Seal and R. P. Doe. "Vertebrate Distribution of Corticoste-

roid-Binding Globulin and Some Endocrine Effects on Concentration," *Steroids,* Vol. 5 (1965) 827.

15. U. S. Seal and R. P. Doe. "The Role of Corticosteroid-Binding Globulin in Mammalian Pregnancy," *Proceedings of the Second International Congress on Hormonal Steroids,* Milan, May 23–28, 1966. Amsterdam: Excerpta Medica Foundation, 1967. P. 697.

16. U. S. Seal and R. P. Doe. "Metabolic Effects of Gonadal Hormones and Contraceptive Steroids," *Effects of Gonadal and Contraceptive Hormones on Protein and Amino Acid Metabolism,* H. A. Salhanic, D. M. Kipnis, and R. L. Van de Wiele, eds. New York: Plenum Press, 1969. P. 277.

17. J. Hallaby. "Primate Overkill," *New Scientist* (October 19, 1968. P. 93.

18. *Hearings before the Subcommittee on Monopoly of the Select Committee on Small Business,* United States Senate, Part 15, "Oral Contraceptives" (Volume 1). Washington, D.C.: U.S. Government Printing Office, 1970.

19. Private communication from Dr. J. J. Speidel, Office of Population, Agency for International Development Bureau for Technical Assistance.

20. O. Harkevy and J. Maier, *Family Planning Perspect,* Vol. 2 (1970).

21. G. Hardin. "The History and Future of Birth Control," *Perspectives in Biology and Medicine,* Vol. 10 (1966), 1.

22. *U.S. News and World Report.* March 2, 1970, p. 37.

23. S. Bergström, L. A. Carlson, and J. R. Weeks. "The Prostaglandins: A Family of Biological Active Lipids," *Pharmacological Reviews,* Vol. 20 (1968), 1.

24. K. T. Kirton, B. B. Pharriss, and A. D. Forbes. "Luteolytic Effects of Prostaglandin F_{2a} in Primates," *Proceedings of the Society for Experimental Biology and Medicine,* Vol. 133 (1970), 314.

25. S. M. M. Karim and G. M. Tilshie. "Therapeutic Abortion Using Prostaglandin F_{2a}," *Lancet,* Vol. 1 (1970), 157.

26. U. Roth-Brandel, et al. "Prostaglandins for Induction of Therapeutic Abortion," *Lancet,* Vol. 1 (1970), 190.

27. *The New York Times,* January 28, 1970.

28. *Time,* February 9, 1970.

29. *Washington Post,* March 14, 1970.

30. B. Berelson. "Beyond Family Planning," *Science,* Vol. 163, 533.
31. M. M. Ketchel. "Fertility Control Agents as a Possible Solution to the World Problem," *Perspectives in Biology and Medicine,* Vol. 11 (1968), 687.
32. M. M. Ketchel. "Should Birth Control Be Mandatory?" *Medical World News* (October 18, 1968), 66.
33. National Academy of Sciences, *Technology: Processes of Assessment and Choice.* Washington, D.C.: U.S. Government Printing Office, July 1969. P. 169.
34. J. Lederberg. "Biomedical Research: Its Side Effects and Challenges," *Stanford M. D.,* Ser. 6, No. 3 (1967), 13.

Discussion of Professor Djerassi's Paper

J O H N R. P L A T T

John R. Platt is Professor of Biophysics, Mental Health Research Institute, University of Michigan.

I am fascinated by Carl Djerassi's suggestion at this conference that we need work on an aphrodisiac pill to increase the libido in men. I am sure that all of you have heard the definition of the perfect contraceptive. It would be a pill that would be effective; it would taste like Scotch; it would be an aphrodisiac, and it would turn the eyeballs blue. Now, somebody is supposed to ask me, "Why should it turn the eyeballs blue?" The answer is, "So you'll know that the girl took it." I can imagine an extensive trade in blue contact lenses if this ever comes to pass.

I am struck by Professor Djerassi's remark about the cost of monkeys, chimpanzees, and gorillas that are needed as experimental animals. Modern biology really has a potential method for dealing with this problem if only someone will take the initiative to do the research. The device is "genetic copying." I have already been urging some of the groups at the National Institutes of Health to mount a major research and development project on this to provide us with more uniform experimental rats and mice, but the application to primates might be even more valuable. Something like $40 million a year is spent on laboratory mice and rats in this country, and if one could use the same techniques for copying mice by nuclear transplantation that are now used for copying frogs, for example, one might have genetically identical mice for many of these studies. Of course, one does not want or need genetically identical animals in every study. But there are some studies in which a group of identical animals would be of great advantage in cutting down the statistical variations in results, and thus would cut down the number of animals needed (for instance, to test a chemical compound or to compare two compounds). I think that research and development on genetic copying would pay for itself in laboratory mice alone.

It is also clear that the advantage of new methods of getting just twenty or thirty of those $2000 gorillas would support a couple of years of a professor's salary to develop a genetic copying method that could be extended to the higher apes. This could solve the problem of breeding, as well as the problem of depopulating East Africa of its gorillas. I am quite serious about this. I think that massive studies in genetic copying of higher animals, both for increasing the protein supply in the world and for making available identical laboratory animals for improved studies, would have enormous payoffs—at the multimillion-dollar level. If there were an opportunity like this in the oil industry, there would be six companies in the field drilling by tomorrow morning. But not biologists! They do not seem to see the biotechnology that is far more important to the world—and even to the laboratory—than the next thousand studies on DNA or some other kind of "pure research."

The second thing that I think is worth commenting on is the complexity of the solutions that Dr. Djerassi suggests.* Have we really explored the *simple* possibilities as carefully as we should? Both research men and doctors know so much and are so committed to large, careful studies that they may dismiss simple methods or folk remedies or new ways of using older drugs that have already been tested. It took a long time to realize that the best treatment for burns seems to be an ice cube, that one of the simplest low-cost contraceptives appears to be a loop of plastic, and that one of the best abortifacients is a warm, concentrated salt solution injected in the uterus, at least for hospital use. I certainly would like to see careful research on whether the salt-solution method could be adapted for home use. Who knows? Perhaps old herb women have been doing it for a thousand years. I do not know whether the salt should be sodium chloride, magnesium sulfate, or some other salt, or what the teratogenic effects might be in case of failure. I don't know whether the

* See also (1).

effects would be any more serious physiologically than an enema or an emetic, but I can imagine that there are simple techniques that we have not looked into sufficiently.

There are also rumors about the effects of single high doses of well-known drugs, such as dicoumarol and atabrine, as abortifacients that deserve to be looked into. But these are drugs that have been extensively tested already and are in large-scale daily use by millions of people, so that a statistical analysis of conceptions among patients on high doses of these drugs might quickly show up any appreciable contraceptive or abortifacient effect. If they worked, the side effects from an occasional high dose following a missed period might be much less serious than the side effects from daily application of our present hormone contraceptives.

Rumors still continue about simple plant products (such as the barbascos and *Dioscoreae* of Mexico) that were used by primitive tribes either as contraceptives or abortifacients and that were a natural part of food supplies in certain parts of the world. I have never seen these rumors seriously and statistically either confirmed or denied. There are many valuable plant products whose medical effectiveness was once regarded as old wives' tales; digitalis and quinine are but two examples. It would seem that one or two million dollars spent to track down these rumors and to try to identify any such plant products—and their effects— could be more valuable than the same money spent on new, synthetic drugs. Such an approach might even bypass the Food and Drug Administration's rules that cause the difficulties Djerassi has listed! If there *is* some tribe in Mexico or India or Africa that already knows about such products and has had them in its "family-planning armamentarium" for some time, they are automatically among the "generally-recognized-as-safe" drugs —at least for that part of the world—and they could go on the "safe" list!

Let me suggest a third direction, which is also tangential to Djerassi's suggestions. In his research on nonsteroid compounds, Dr. Roger Guillemin is studying the chemical messengers that go from the hypothalamus to the pituitary. Some of these are believed to be small compounds such as tripeptides, which appear to control natural hormonal products in the body, yet they probably have less physiological side effects than the direct application of the hormones themselves. A careful study of these other sites of action is definitely needed. Someone once counted seventeen different places in the conception sequence of males and females at which intervention could take place. I am not sure that more than a few of these have been carefully examined.

One specific point in the conception sequence that seems to be particularly important for research is the egg cortex. When the first spermatozoan enters the egg, the egg cortex hardens almost instantaneously, blocking out all the other sperm and thereby limiting the offspring to only one complete set of chromosomes. One wonders if the egg cortex could be hardened in advance so that even the first sperm could not get in. It is almost certain that the trigger compound that hardens it is some component in the outer membrane of the sperm, possibly a polysaccharide, a small protein, or some other small trigger molecule that is released on contact with the egg. The isolation and identification of this trigger compound should not be a difficult problem because essentially all the experiments can be done in a laboratory dish. The outer coatings of the sperm would be stripped off to find out which of perhaps a dozen or a hundred products is the one that causes the egg to harden. As far as I know, these compounds have not been identified, and there seem to be only three laboratories working on this cortex-hardening problem. Again, one or two million dollars might significantly increase the chances of finding new solutions. We ought to have as many laboratories working on contraception at this basic research level as we have working on new carburetors or on reducing pollution in automobiles: It is a more important problem for the nation and the world.

But the most important method is the contraceptive method that has been dismissed by many as "Orwellian" or "Draconian" (1, 2): the adoption of contraceptives in foods. This has been seriously misrepresented in most conferences and most writings on the subject because of the failure to recognize that this can also be a *voluntarily* chosen method just like all of our present contraceptives. I am not interested in imposing a dictatorial method on the world; I am very concerned about side effects and the long-range effects of the large-scale application of compounds to populations. But I am also concerned about our inability to do very much about the population explosion by using our present methods. We have blinded ourselves to the possible degree of public acceptance and to the enormous increase in effectiveness that would result if we could find oral contraceptives that could be put in salt or other foodstuffs and that could be used voluntarily.

Let me therefore say some favorable things about putting contraceptives in salt. I suggest that Djerassi might not have been so negative had he applied the same analytical reasoning to the good things that could be said about this method as he applied to his critical-path sequence. I agree that this method might not work because of lack of effectiveness or uncontrollable side effects, or because the public or their representatives would not accept contraceptives in food—even on a voluntary basis. But since more methods are needed for population control, important additional possibilities should at least be explored in the laboratory.

I agree with Djerassi and others that no contraceptives for large populations should be put into water. It would be both a waste and a danger because water goes to industries and is drunk by animals. The foods that contraceptives could be put into should be so delicious or so expensive that they are not normally thrown out to the chickens or the barnyard animals. They should be factory produced or commercially marketed, even in primitive societies, which limits them to foods such as salt, sugar, beer, special breads, polished rice, betel nuts, and perhaps a few others.

Among these, salt is a necessity in every population and, in general, is not manufactured in the home or on the farm but in factories serving large areas. We know how dependent on it populations are—Gandhi's famous march to the sea to break the British salt monopoly and get free of the British factories that were manufacturing it is a good illustration. If there were an effective and safe contraceptive that could be put into salt, it could be put in at a small number of factories, possibly one or two hundred, all over India, for example. It could be monitored by a small number of biochemical technicians, perhaps with master's degrees, just as chlorine and fluoride in our water, Vitamin D in our milk, iodine in our salt, or other "public-health" compounds are monitored in the United States.

This means that such a method would be exceedingly cheap compared with any of our present contraceptive methods, which involve individual application, prescription, or medical examination. If individual examinations or medical applications were needed for birth control in a country the size of India, with over 100 million women of child-bearing age, about 100,000 paramedical personnel would have to be trained and kept in the field. To do that, several hundred training centers would have to be set up, staffed by hundreds or thousands of doctors —who must themselves be trained in advance.

Each step in this process—training the doctors, preparing the centers, training the paramedical personnel, and so on— could take five, seven, or even ten years in order to get the present type of contraceptives out into all the villages. The result is that to the ten or fifteen years needed, as in Djerassi's research and testing program (1), there must be added twenty or thirty years to organize sufficiently to reach the population, which is increasing all that time. But a method such as an additive to salt, which would require only factory application and about one hundred biochemists, could be a thousand times cheaper and in use ten to twenty years earlier—hundreds of millions of babies earlier.

But the most difficult thing in considering this food-additive method is the "Draconian" aspect that Djerassi and others have emphasized—yet this is the aspect that is also the most unnecessary. What we should be talking about is a *voluntarily* chosen contraceptive that can be put into salt, so that people who *want* to have babies can simply go down the street to the "other store" and buy the other salt or the antidote. This is what we have already with our present methods—a voluntary choice to use them or not to use them. To require *more* from a new method just for the sake of claiming that it is "Draconian" is excessive and unfair to these other, neglected possibilities.

Thus, in Berelson's recent article comparing different contraceptive possibilities (2), he recognized that the use of contraceptives in food is likely to be both the cheapest and the most efficacious method, but he indicated it is the one least possible to adopt politically or to apply administratively, and the one most morally and ethically offensive. Why is it the least possible method to apply administratively? Why is it the most "Draconian" or unethical? It is because we have talked about it as though it *had* to be compulsory. We do not insist on calling our other contraceptives, or iodine in salt or vitamins in bread, compulsory.

Attacks on this method are therefore a serious and even dangerous mislabeling of a potentially useful method. Suppose an effective contraceptive could be offered that could be taken by everyone as an additive in normal salt, but that couples who wanted children could get an antidote or untreated salt. I think many American suburbs would vote to adopt such a method in preference to their present clumsy and unpleasant methods of contraception.

In fact, when it comes to aesthetics and morals, our *present* methods of birth control are not all that good. Condoms have to be applied and interrupt a moment when you would like a certain love interest in the partner. Diaphragms require either precalculation or interruption. IUDs have a high percentage of rejection. Jellies and foams have chemical smells and odd lubrications. Pills require you to be able to count the days. There may be millions of young women in America who have signs on their pillows, the bathroom mirror, or the door of their rooms that say—"Don't forget it," or "Start again Wednesday!" And when these methods fail, abortion is the next step for millions of married and unmarried women.

Is this what is to be held up as an aesthetic and ethical ideal, compared to taking contraceptives in food? Our present methods are so antipsychological, so hostile to all the charm, affection, spontaneity, and intimacy of the love relation that it is surprising we have adopted them as widely as we have. It shows how widely and rapidly contraception might spread if we invented some really easy, inoffensive, or pleasant ways to do it. So, I think something that could be put into salt and chosen voluntarily would be less offensive than many of the things we do and advocate today.

In addition, I believe voluntarily chosen contraceptives in food would not be as politically impossible as Berelson seems to think (2). This method was first suggested publicly by Dr. Homi J. Bhabha, of the Indian Atomic Energy Commission, at the 1962 Pugwash Conference, and not by an American with aims of "genocide." Bhabha is said to have discussed this with Nehru, who said that if there were a safe and effective chemical of this kind, he could get the Indian parliament to adopt it. The Indian parliament might not agree to this now, but there is a new atmosphere in many legislatures in the last eight years, so that adoption is not as far-fetched a notion as we supposed when we insisted on making the method compulsory.

I agree with Djerassi's emphasis that we need a compound that does not have harmful side effects on small children and old people and that does not put hair on girls' chests or cause trouble with men's hormones. But is this absolutely impossible? Let me suggest that if we could find the compound that serves as the "trigger function" in hardening the egg cortex, for example, it would only work on an egg cortex. There are no egg cortexes in small children, men, or women after menopause. I think that the side-effect problem is very important, but it is a problem to be approached by a scientific analysis of what the possibilities are, rather than ruling them all out in advance.

It is worth emphasizing that the dosages of contraceptives for a general population might be much less than the dosages required to give 99 per cent reliability in each individual case. It is possible that the effects are nonlinear and that our present hormone dosage might be cut by a factor of 10 to 30 and still give a significant *average* decrease in birth rate. Couples that wanted to be *sure* not to have children would then add their own individual contraception, and the side effects of larger doses to the general population would be greatly reduced. This is also the answer to the problem of individuals whose need for salt (or any other carrier food) is much greater or less than the average. They could be warned or prescribed for on an individual basis, as we prescribe for diabetics today, without affecting the average improvement in birth control.

In conclusion, let me emphasize what seems to be the most important aspect of this method. If a couple had to go down the street voluntarily to get the "other salt," this would mean *every child would be a wanted child.* It would mean that the decision to have children would be a *positive* decision, preferably by both the mother and the father, instead of a negative decision because someone is too lazy to get up, or because the store ran out of pills, or because you forgot to count the days.

"Every child a wanted child" is surely a most moral slogan for us to adopt. It has been adopted already in some population-planning programs. I would like to suggest that we all adopt it and try to get our research *aimed* at adopting it; that is, aimed at automatic contraception. Then *conception* would require the singular choice. It is not clear how much this would cut the birth rate, but I have seen estimates that as many as two-thirds or three-quarters of the babies born in the world are not wanted *consciously in the daytime* by both partners at the time of conception. The rate of abortion in countries that have made abortion easy has increased from 40 to 100 per cent of the live births, suggesting the enormous fraction of children who were not wanted, at least by the next morning. My feeling is that if we made the rule "every child a wanted child," the birth rate might drop almost immediately by about a factor of 2.

Is it not worth rethinking our conventional prejudices and researching these neglected possibilities—these cheap, simple, *moral* possibilities?

References

1. Carl Djerassi. "Prognosis for the Development of New Chemical Birth-Control Agents," *Science,* Vol. 166 (October 24, 1969), 468–73.
2. Bernard Berelson. "Beyond Family Planning," *Science,* Vol. 163 (February 7, 1969), 533–43.

Discussion of Professor Djerassi's Paper

PHILIP A. CORFMAN

Dr. Philip A. Corfman is Director of the Center for Population Research of the National Institute of Child Health and Human Development, National Institutes of Health.

In discussing Professor Djerassi's paper I take the following points as given: (a) The world needs new contraceptive methods of all kinds as rapidly as possible; (b) Governments, international agencies, and industry must work together in the development of such new methods; and (c) We must make accommodations between governments and industry that are compatible with the goals of each.

Djerassi's principal argument is that present circumstances are so difficult for industry that no progress in contraceptive development is possible without major accommodations. It should be noted, however, that Djerassi limits his field of discussion to chemical contraceptives entirely dissimilar to any now in use and thereby excludes variations of steroid contraceptives and IUDs, both of which hold promise for significant innovation. Readers may fail to recognize these limits and may extend the argument to fields in which significant advances are likely to take place before 1984.

I agree with several of Djerassi's points:

1. We need better animal models for contraceptive development. This is an issue of immediate importance, particularly since important decisions have been made based on the observations that some progestogens seem to cause breast tumors in beagle dogs. Industry can make a significant contribution to this problem.

2. Djerassi's rationalization of the contraceptive development process is an important contribution. The critical-path charts seem a bit pessimistic, and they do fault fundamental re-

search; but the charts are useful. I hope that Djerassi expands on this work.

3. I agree with his analysis of the difficulties in developing male contraceptives, particularly in relation to the lack of adequate testing facilities.

4. The analysis of the difficulties in developing a universal sterilizant is a *tour de force*. I agree that such a goal is both scientifically and operationally ridiculous.

There are several points of disagreement:

1. I believe that Djerassi faults the significant contribution of nonprofit agencies to contraceptive development, and for this reason, I do not agree with his implication that all the expenses of drug development are borne by industry.

2. I do not agree with his denial of the importance of the contribution by non-Western countries to contraceptive development. Significant work has been done in South America, Japan, and other parts of Asia, for example. This point applies particularly to IUDs and other nonchemical methods (which are outside of the scope of the argument), but such countries are developing an increasing competence and willingness to work in the chemical field as well. Note, for instance, the recent work on prostaglandins done in Uganda.

3. I believe it is mistaken to say that the rapid introduction of IUDs is due solely to the lack of FDA authority. This may have facilitated such development; but the time was ripe for the development of new contraceptives, and new agencies had become heavily engaged in this field.

4. I do not agree that all new methods must be independent of coitus or that sterilization must be reversible. I believe our goal should be to develop a variety of methods that will be acceptable to different population groups.

5. I do not believe it is correct to say that the FDA has become an international agency or that other countries are totally dependent on FDA decisions. Several countries delayed approval of oral contraceptives for some time after the FDA approval, and Japan and the Soviet Union still do not permit the general use of these agents. But even if the FDA were an "international

agency" in Djerassi's sense, I do not believe one should fault the agency because its legislative responsibility is to the American people.

Let me close with an observation or two. The first concerns the dilemma that has arisen concerning progestogens and breast tumors in beagles. The most expeditious way to resolve this problem is for scientists from industry and elsewhere to demonstrate, if they can, that the beagle is a poor model for the study of these agents. Some recent unpublished work indicates that this may be true. What concerns me is that this work was not done several years ago when the issue first became apparent.

There is no doubt we need new contraceptives and that industry, the FDA, the National Institutes of Health, and private agencies all must participate. Our goal is the development of a variety of effective and safe methods that are acceptable to different populations. This goal will be achieved most rapidly if we work together as scientific colleagues and partners.

6

Rapid Population Growth and the Social Structure

D O N A L D   F.   H E I S E L

Donald F. Heisel is Staff Associate, the Population Council.

This paper will concentrate on an issue that is a little less broad than the title would indicate; it is the relationship between emerging patterns of differential fertility and broad status or class differences within a society that is experiencing rapid population increase. Many important aspects of the relationship between population change and social organization are not included; for example, no reference will be made here to the relationship between status differences and mortality or migration nor to the demographic aspects of the family, marriage, or sex roles in general. These omissions are made not on the grounds that they have less priority but simply because a catalogue of issues, each only briefly touched on, will be less useful than a more thorough discussion of a single matter. Moreover, it will become quite clear that even with a narrower focus a sharp and clear picture is difficult enough to come by.

Differential Fertility and Social Class

The issue of the relationship between fertility and social class is by no means a new one. Since the early statements of Malthus and Marx it has been raised often. Most recently, it has come up in a variety of modified forms as one part of a debate about the general international activity in the family-planning movement. The broader debate, which challenges the place of family planning as an appropriate element of the whole pattern of relationships between the developed and developing nations, seems to be growing in intensity. As a component of this sometimes rather sharp and polemical dialogue, the issue deserves attention.

Ideally, the discussion should encompass the whole of the less developed world. I shall restrict it mainly to sub-Saharan Africa, however, because that is the region I know best. Moreover, Africa may well be of special interest in regard to this question. A good case can be made that much of sub-Saharan Africa emerged from the colonial experience with a less rigid class structure than much of the rest of the developing world. Social mobility may be somewhat more possible in the region at this time. This is not to say that the social distance from a peasant village to the elite urban centers is not one of awesome magnitude; however, it is a gulf that can be crossed, given the appropriate circumstances.

Another point of particular interest is that sub-Saharan Africa has the highest aggregate fertility of the major regions in the world.

No single description of the social structure will apply equally well throughout all of the region. In particular, this discussion does not refer at all to South Africa, Rhodesia, or the areas of Portuguese domination. On the other hand, some of these comments may have relevance for societies outside sub-Saharan Africa, especially where far-reaching social change has led to a large-scale shift in the class system.

The Lack of Data

The subject of differential fertility has received relatively little serious attention in the less developed world—and almost none in sub-Saharan Africa. One of the most important reasons is that we lack the data needed to illuminate the subject. Throughout sub-Saharan Africa the task of estimating with reasonable accuracy the crude birth rate for a nation as a whole is one that challenges the best demographic techniques. There are substantial regions where a full-scale census has never been carried out and where sample surveys of demographic data are incomplete and by now considerably out of date, and there is nowhere in the region a functioning system of vital registration for a whole country or for any representative areas of a country. All demographic data—total size of population, infant mortality, age-specific fertility, or any other piece of information—must be examined first in terms of reliability and only second in terms of substantive significance.

Obviously, if it is a major task fraught with difficulties and pit-falls to know the crude birth rate or the rate of natural increase, then it is far more difficult to know the specific rates for any given subgroups. However, this is precisely what we must try to do in order to study differential fertility.

In addition to problems with demographic data, it is worth noting that meaningfully conceptualizing class or status differences in a modern African society is by no means obvious or simple. References to an "urban elite" or to the "traditional peasantry" provide crude but useful approximations. Yet there is much that needs to be explored to obtain a clear understanding of how the class system works in the various countries of sub-Saharan Africa. The system has elements of flexibility in the face of very rapid social change and is of course uniquely African. Linkages in any given country between patterns of stratification and other major groupings, such as the extended family, linguistic and ethnic communities, and religious groups, need very careful consideration to be useful and not misleading. We should not fail to recognize, though, that in this discussion the terms used for the patterns of stratification are no more than rough approximations.

There is another range of factors that I believe has discouraged the study of differential fertility in the less developed countries. The theoretical framework of most discussions of the consequences of rapid population growth has tended to be, for generally good reasons, an aggregate approach. Thus, discussions of the economic consequences of rapid population growth have usually referred to the most natural unit of economic planning: the national aggregate. The familiar discussions of the effects of rapid population growth on per capita income, welfare expenditures, the dependency ratio, and so forth refer mostly to the population as a whole. Similarly, research on attitudes concerning family size—the surveys of knowledge, attitude, and practice of contraception—often places emphasis on obtaining an estimate of the national-average ideal number of children. A maternal- and child-health approach also usually stresses aggregate considerations.

It may be very much to the good that attention has largely been focused on aggregates in the study of economic consequences. In general, such consequences can be stated with some reasonable degree of clarity. But when we turn to implications for the social structure, things typically start getting a bit woolly, and it becomes necessary to engage in a discouraging amount of speculation. Nevertheless, in my judgment it is essential that we look at the social-structural consequences and do the best we can to understand them.

This matter is important because, as said earlier, it is an issue in the growing debate over the relationship between the less developed areas and the urban industrial nations, especially the West. In Africa, Asia, and Latin America one cannot go very far without encountering serious questions about the motives, methods, and consequences of the urgency with which the need for family planning is being stressed by outsiders. One might almost argue that it is precisely the recent successes in getting a few national family-planning programs launched in the region that has led to the emergence of a new opposition. The United Nations and its agencies, including the World Bank; a substantial number of northern European countries; a number of extremely important voluntary agencies; and the U.S. Agency for International Development—all stress the need for population control or family planning, and that makes the idea suspect in some important circles. My impression is, for example, that in Africa an increasing number of people are beginning to ask why it is that so many outsiders seem to be so very interested in getting Africans to have fewer children. Associated with this suspicion are very real concerns about what the implications of fertility reduction might be for their social system apart from the desired economic or medical effects. Serious people are worried about what the availability of contraception will mean for traditional sex roles, sexual mores, and the respective positions of the various classes and subgroups. Such fears may not always strike an outsider as serious; but they must not be taken lightly, for it is not easy to prove that they are groundless in every case. The issues of fertility control, social organization, and differential fertility in sub-Saharan Africa must be carefully examined precisely because people there are concerned about them.

The importance of differential fertility can also be approached in another way. In this view, there are two main considerations justifying careful attention to differential fertility: the evidence of differential fertility and policy implications.

The Evidence of Differential Fertility

First, I believe it is clear that a pattern of substantial differences in fertility associated with social class has already appeared throughout much of sub-Saharan Africa, although the evidence is not always hard. Fragmentary data from some censuses and demographic surveys indicate that women with a relatively higher level of formal education have substantially lower fertility in a given age group. In the Kenya census of 1962, for example, the difference in reported average number of children born to women by age 35 to 39 was almost 1.5 children. Women with nine or more years of education had about 4.5 children whereas women with one to four years of schooling had about 5.9.

To the extent that there are errors of reporting in such data, they probably understate the difference. The more highly educated women are more likely to report births with greater accuracy. With the less educated the average tendency would almost certainly be to omit some of their children, possibly those children who died soon after birth or those who have grown up and moved away. In general, data like these indicate an inverse relationship between fertility and social class, which comes through clearly despite errors and misreporting.

The pattern of differential fertility is also revealed in data from KAP * surveys comparing responses of elites with those of rural agriculturalists. Surveys in Ghana have shown that respondents who are members of an urban elite are much more likely to have had experience in the use of contraceptives than are other members of the society. Another study in Nigeria showed that the practice of contraception rose steeply with the education of wives—from 5 per cent among the uneducated to 71 per cent among those with university and other post-secondary-school training (1).

It is obvious that such a pattern of differential fertility can have almost no impact on the aggregate vital rates. The number of women enjoying the levels of education and status that are associated with significantly lower fertility is so small that their demographic effect on the aggregate is almost nil. However, the social and economic implications of such differences are of considerable importance and deserve careful attention.

This pattern of differential fertility is probably a relatively recent development in sub-Saharan Africa. If the data—and this is a very big "if," for the demographic history of Africa is far less known than its present—point in any direction, it is toward relatively small differences in fertility associated with social status in precolonial and colonial times. Some fertility differences were almost certainly present, but they seem to have been chiefly associated with variations in health conditions between regions and with differing cultural patterns (such as average age at first pregnancy or the extent to which a postpartum taboo was maintained). Variations in fertility were neither generally nor notably linked to class differences so far as one can detect on the basis of the available data. (Evidence for this is largely indirect; references to family patterns and fertility in the large body of anthropological literature dealing with earlier periods make virtually no reference to differential fertility associated with any sort of social classes.)

Before the period of rapid demographic growth began, fertility

* The abbreviation KAP refers to *k*nowledge of contraceptive technology, *a*ttitudes toward its use, including ideal family size and desire for additional children, and *p*ractice of contraception.

tended to be high and relatively homogeneous within a given group. The high levels of fertility were matched by high levels of mortality, in the classical model of a pretransitional population. Then, sometime following the end of World War II, sub-Saharan Africa embarked on the path of rapid demographic change that characterizes much of the developing world today. Mortality began a sustained decline in most, but not all, areas of the region, and it continues to the present day. Aggregate fertility has remained high, and populations are now growing typically at the rate of over 2 per cent and in some cases over 3 per cent per year.

However, among some groups fertility as well as mortality has begun to decline relatively sharply. Not surprisingly, this seems to have taken place primarily among the upper-status, better educated members of society. One must suppose that formal education is a major factor because it suggests both new values in place of traditional ones and, perhaps even more important, provides the literacy, which gives one access to modern medical technology. The educated person who can read a magazine in French or English has a much greater chance of learning that fertility can be planned with relative ease by people all over the world.

The essential point is that in sub-Saharan Africa, despite what are probably the highest levels of aggregate fertility in the world, differential fertility inversely related to social class has unmistakably begun to appear. The very fact that the pattern of differential fertility exists, quite apart from its impact on aggregate fertility, leads to the second main reason justifying careful concern.

Policy Implications

Analysis of the patterns of differential fertility can reveal some of the most important linkages between the demographic characteristics of a population and the organization of the society. In the long run, we are concerned with the broad issues involved in the organization of society. For example, interest in population and the policies aimed at influencing population trends— migration and mortality controls, as well as family-planning or pronatalist policies—are justified by their implications for the whole social structure. This is most obvious in the cases of fertility and migration policies; it is difficult to imagine anyone advocating family planning or alien exclusion laws for some presumed intrinsic merit. Even control of mortality—despite the universal desire of human beings to enjoy as long and healthy a life as possible—is hardly considered an unqualified end in itself. If it were, ministries of health would not be as weak and underfinanced as they usually are.

The goals that population policies most often refer to are those involved in the process of development. But development itself is not a process that can be defined in simple one-dimensional terms. It is a characteristic of the whole social and economic structure.

Furthermore, although using the per capita gross national product as a crude index of development sometimes makes it sound as if mere aggregate national economic power is the sole concern, this clearly cannot be the case. Development is a meaningful concept only if it refers to a situation in which the positive benefits are available in some significant measure to all members of the society. If there are gross inequalities and no real opportunities for social mobility, no matter what the per capita gross national product or its rate of increase, the situation is better described as exploitation than development.

The importance of internal differentiation of status in society carries over to fertility as well. Fertility cannot be viewed merely as one of the variables determining the rate of natural increase or the age distribution of a population. These are extremely important, but they are not the whole story. Fertility is also a characteristic that varies in a systematic way with other important characteristics.

Policies directed toward influencing the level of fertility in a society, whether antinatalist or pronatalist, must take into account more than the effect of the rate of population increase on aggregate economic behavior, the total number of workers, or the percentage of people 65 years of age or older. It is essential to consider the direct implications of any fertility-oriented policy for the social organization, including the status system. The decision of whether to have a family-planning program and what kind to have should be related to more than the desired gross national product or any other aggregate index.

In some of the discussions of population problems and programs in developing countries, reference has been made to the relationship of selected aspects of fertility patterns to status inequality within a developing society. Interestingly enough, the arguments do not at all arrive at the same conclusions about the advisability of fertility-control programs.

For example, in the report of the Pearson Commission, one of the six particular difficulties cited as being created by very rapid population growth refers directly to economic inequality. The report argues that in the developing countries:

> The distribution of income is unequal, and population growth tends to make it more so by raising land values and rents while depressing wages. As ownership, too, is usually very unequally distributed, the bulk of the population may fail to participate in whatever improvement occurs.

The conclusion drawn by the commission is that:

> . . . it is clear that there can be no serious social and economic planning unless the ominous implications of uncontrolled population growth are understood and acted upon. (2)

Another example with a more direct reference to differential fertility and social class is the argument that high fertility among the poor leads to a cycle of poverty. It is asserted that mortality declines as a result of public-health measures and general improvements in hygienic conditions, and that all members of the society benefit to at least some measurable degree. Declines in fertility, however, are reasonably accessible only to the better educated and more affluent in the early stages of a demographic transition. Therefore, it is the poor who carry the burden of rapid population growth; their children have fewer advantages and are in turn more likely to remain poor themselves. Thus opportunities for social mobility are restricted and differential fertility acts to reinforce a class system and possibly also to slow down the process of development.

Stated in its most extreme form, this argument has at times been pushed to the point of asserting that the lack of family planning is a major cause of poverty or, conversely, that poverty can be cured by family planning.

Both of these arguments support the position that it is the poor who stand to benefit most through family planning. Thus, it is in the interest of social equality that contraceptives be made available to the less educated, the peasants, and the poor.

Other arguments have led to quite different policy conclusions. One position is that it is in the best interest of development not to engage in special efforts to make the means for fertility control available to the peasant majority in the society. It is usually put forth verbally as an extrapolation from the ideas developed by Boserup (3). It is argued that the economic pressure caused by increased density of population will eventually stimulate innovative behavior on the part of the peasants. One important kind of innovation would be migration from economically depressed rural areas and thus the creation of a more stable and highly motivated urban or plantation agricultural labor force. Other innovations would include the adoption of improved agricultural technology on small farms. Such innovations are argued to be an unavoidable prerequisite to development. Eventually, after development has gotten underway—a process prompted in part by demographic pressure—a decline in fertility will spread from the elite to the peasantry and the pressure will be eased.

There is another quite different argument that tends toward a similar policy position. In this case, the recommendation of family planning for the poor in a country is seen as, at best, a somewhat irrelevant gesture and, at worst, as a malicious and reactionary attempt to distract the peasants from recognition of the essential task of revolution. In effect, this argument holds that a concern for fertility control is really a matter of offering sex in place of social justice. Once the needed changes have taken place and

> . . . there is greater economic security, political participation, elimination of gross class division, liberation of women, and respected leadership, humane and successful population programs are at least possible. Without these conditions, genocide is nicely masked by the welfare imperialism of the West. (4)

Pushed to a more extreme position, this kind of argument would presumably hold that family planning should be withheld from the poor in order to foster other social changes.

These then are four arguments that base themselves on the issue of the relationship between fertility and social inequality in a situation of rapid population increase. Two arrive at a position that encourages a family-planning program and two do not. However, all four are somewhat indebted to speculation, and not one of them stands as a convincing guide to policy.

The Need for Research

In order to make the necessary policy decisions in a more informed and rational manner for sub-Saharan Africa, it is essential to have the results of further research. The rest of this discussion will outline the data and analysis needed to clarify the issues further. The needed research falls into two categories: improvement of the basic sorts of demographic and sociological data required in order to establish major parameters, and specific research projects that could help clarify important aspects of the relationship between differential fertility or family size and systems of social stratification.

Referring to the need for more and better census data in Africa may appear to be such an obvious point that it does not justify the time spent on it. The conclusion that more and better data are needed is hardly a unique or challenging one for a scholar to arrive at. However, in the present case it is more than just a pious nod in the right direction. The need is truly acute, and there are substantive issues that can have ramifications for basic policy. Underenumeration and underestimation of the rate of population increase can produce a very unreal evaluation of the effectiveness of economic policies.

Throughout a considerable portion of sub-Saharan Africa, no true census of population has ever been taken. In some of the unenumerated countries there have been demographic sample surveys; but like most of the censuses, most of these surveys were taken a long time ago, and the age of the data alone makes them of dubious value. For example, in much of West Africa smallpox has been nearly eradicated during recent years, and great progress has been made in the control of measles. However, estimates of the death rate and of the rate of population increase are still based almost entirely on data collected ten or more years ago. It is apparent that planning for development with reference to demographic conditions becomes nearly impossible. Moreover, it must be remembered that sub-Saharan Africa is undergoing a demographic revolution; in effect, the data become old before their time. The absence of reasonably sound data is a great stimulus to uninformed debate over erroneous data. This is a simple point requiring no deep insight— but it is of overwhelming importance.

Of equal importance is the question of reliability of demographic data once they have been collected; no reports in sub-Saharan Africa can be taken at face value as accurate. Levels of error are among the highest in the world for standard demographic items such as age and number of children ever born. For social and economic characteristics such as marital status, religion, or occupation, conceptual problems and errors of reporting are such that the value of the data is doubtful. In recognition of such difficulties, attempts have been made to simplify enumeration forms. In this way a few items of the greatest value can be more reliably measured than could poor data covering a broad range of variables.

For example, in the 1969 censuses of Kenya and Uganda, detailed information was reduced to a bare minimum. Apart from the basic demographic items for all individuals—age, sex, relationship to head of household—only race, nationality, birthplace, educational attainment, marital status, and a battery of questions designed to establish estimates of vital rates were asked. There were no questions concerning economic activity, and the number of social characteristics was sharply curtailed. Such a schedule has been recommended for use in some West African countries as well.

An even more extreme example can be found in the case of the Democratic Republic of the Congo (Kinshasa). Here, for a variety of reasons including mistrust of sample estimates, a registration listing of all persons that is maintained by the civil administration will be employed in place of an enumeration of individuals. The procedures are designed so that only summary tabulations will be produced.

Such expedients may be unavoidable. Clearly, if some items have to be sacrificed, they should be nondemographic. One effect of dropping social or economic items is that analysis of the demographic behavior of subgroups such as social classes will have to be severely curtailed. Much information that would illuminate important patterns of differences will be lacking. In assessing the trade-off between quality of information and quantity of variables considered for any individual, it is important not to unduly narrow the scheme to purely demographic variables. What is needed at this stage is not only more censuses or demographic surveys in more countries but also a good deal of careful experimentation and thought about what questions to ask and how best to ask them. In so doing, the importance of being able to detect the significance of classes or strata in society ought not be neglected. Moreover, the variables referring to such strata will have to be developed so as to be the most meaningful ones for the various societies of sub-Saharan Africa.

The process of determining which questions to ask can be considerably assisted by the continuing development of sociological and anthropological research into the structure of contemporary African societies. What is especially needed to clarify the issues is a thorough examination of just which concepts are most useful in dealing with the patterns of social differentiation in a given society. This will require an analysis of the differences within and between the various social groups and strata as well as an understanding of how they reinforce or conflict with each other. For example, the significance of tribe or ethnic group, the extended family structures, religion, formal education, and occupation need to be sorted out much better so that it will be possible to make more meaningful use of the demographic data. The conclusion that more data are needed is hardly an intellectual breakthrough. However, it is one of the blunt truths in sub-Saharan Africa, and it bears repeating.

Continuing development of such basic demographic and sociological data is necessary for the determination of the most effective and appropriate population policies. However, they will not be sufficient by themselves.

The most important single additional piece of information needed is an answer to the question "So what?" That is, we need a measure of the relative importance of differential fertility to the stratification system, all other things being equal. An evaluation of such relative importance is necessary to keep us from claiming either too much or too little for the variable in which we are interested. In other words, it can help to keep us reasonable.

Limited Special Studies

It is intriguing to think about building some great vast theoretical model that would produce all such desired results. By linking up all the relevant variables in our model we could, in theory, routinely produce estimates of how much stratification is generated by a given amount of differential fertility, how much poverty is produced in the class system by a given rise in the rate of natural increase, or how much free primary education would have to be provided to offset a given amount of differential fertility. It would be a very useful model indeed.

However, the prospects are scant for such a device at this time. Its development requires knowledge of very many complicated feedbacks and interactions, so it is hard to see it having useful results for a long time to come. Before we can get to such a grand, unified control of our subject, it is necessary to explore a number of specific issues through a series of more limited special studies. I should like to describe several that I believe are very important for sub-Saharan Africa.

For example, two adaptations of the widely used KAP-type survey have proven to be of considerable use in providing information needed in the early stages of an action program. Such studies have often shown that even within what superficially appears to be an unpromising population, there is a substantial unmet desire for family planning. Typically, they report findings such as "*x* per cent of women in their childbearing years do not want more children." This finding has frequently served to inspire the confidence of decision-makers that not all peasants have many children just because they want them and that if contraceptive services are offered, they will be used. Studies can help to reduce uninformed opposition and may hasten the development of action programs. In addition, KAP surveys carried out early in a program have proved useful as a benchmarker against which comparisons can subsequently be made. This can provide a measure of some aspects of the program's impact.

In such operational uses of these data, emphasis is appropriately given to estimating averages for the total population. However, existing KAP data can almost certainly be used to produce still more information about the relationship between fertility and social status than has been drawn out up to now.

It might be rewarding to carry out a systematic examination of KAP data with emphasis shifted to social-status variables as related to attitudes and behavior concerning fertility.* It might be possible to learn a good deal about the critical points at which attitudes and behavior are significantly altered. The determination of such critical points for single status variables or for variables in combination would appear to be very useful as a guide to policy. This shift in emphasis is a relatively modest one, but it might help to extract additional useful information from the body of KAP data.

A second further use of KAP surveys is to give particular at-

* Caldwell opened this line of inquiry in early surveys carried out in Ghana. See (5).

tention to folk contraceptives and induced abortion. These issues have been raised in some of the surveys already done but have not been explored very thoroughly. The ethnographic and anthropological literature is far less helpful on the subject than one might expect. Nevertheless, I believe there is a growing feeling that there are phenomena of some considerable importance in sub-Saharan African. In particular, induced abortion is probably much more important than previously realized.

My experience, which corresponds with that of others, is that knowledge of methods said to induce abortion is very widespread in Africa. Most frequently the methods involve the use of an herb or a chemical substance that will induce abortion when eaten or drunk. Materials from the traditional pharmacopoeia, as well as modern drugs, are referred to. Mechanical methods are mentioned far less frequently and seem to occur mainly in urban areas.

Traditional methods of contraception appear to be of somewhat less and declining importance. Often the methods described are defined as useful only before an individual is completely married. Other methods are associated with practices of witchcraft.

In both induced abortion and some of the methods of traditional contraception, an element of personal danger and antisocial behavior is clearly perceived.

Further research needs to be done on the use or even just the awareness of such methods, its association with status, and its implications. A specific KAP survey of folk contraception and induced abortion is needed. This is an important issue because, if these methods are viewed as dangerous or immoral but no alternatives are readily available, the whole idea of fertility control may become negative. Furthermore, I suspect that such perceptions are very much associated with the social status of the individual. For example, the educated elite should be relatively free of such perceptions because they have access to knowledge of alternative methods.

A quite separate area that would surely repay the research attention it receives is the cluster of issues involved in the pattern of relationships between parents and children, inheritance, land tenure, and fertility within and outside the traditional family system. William Goode, in his world survey of family patterns, suggests that the family in sub-Saharan Africa is undergoing quite acute strain (6). Comparisons sometimes made with the Caribbean and Latin American marriage patterns appear to be apt. The questions are, broadly, why should this come about in sub-Saharan Africa, and what are the likely consequences?

Very little is known about the economy of the family at different levels of society. It would be extremely useful to know the effects of increased land pressure on African peasant society when it leads to an inability of the parents to assure a meaningful inheritance—for instance, how it affects the age at marriage and the marital stability of the children. This is a complex matter depending in part on the number of children in the family, the system of land tenure, the rules of inheritance, the availability of other possible occupations, and the concepts of illegitimacy. However, there is strong circumstantial evidence that the problem is associated with family breakdown in sub-Saharan Africa. Similar questions arise with the problem of low-income parents trying to cope with an inflation in the price of brides. If such economic pressures within the peasant family do lead to a rise in the proportion of births outside the system of traditional marriage, the effects this would have on over-all fertility are still not known. It is possible to develop speculations that would imply a rise in fertility, a decline, or no effect at all. Conversely, the effect that the introduction of a family-planning program would have is also not known.

There is also evidence of a trend of a rather different nature but also of great importance. In the Sudan, Henin has convincingly demonstrated that the transition from nomadism to settled agriculture, especially in an irrigated area such as the Gezira, is associated with a marked increase in fertility (7). There are a large number of resettlement and irrigation schemes being considered or actually developed in sub-Saharan Africa, and many hopes are contingent upon their success. If the improved conditions of life for peasants participating in such schemes generally leads to higher rates of population increase and to higher fertility, then the relationship between family structure, land tenure, and population growth may be even more complex and more important than appeared at the outset.

It is in the context of just such agricultural and family systems in transition that current demographic pressures have arisen. Although attempts to deal with the rapidly rising population certainly cannot wait for research to clarify all of the various issues involved, it is also risky to proceed as if such issues did not exist. They are a matter of grave concern to people in the societies of sub-Saharan Africa and deserve careful attention.

A final area to which I would like to refer is that of the relationship between the number of children in a family and the formal educational system. This is a matter of great significance in sub-Saharan Africa precisely because formal educational qualifications are so closely tied to social status and the possibility of social mobility. The great need for formal education is manifested by the fact that almost all higher level economic and political activities are transacted in a foreign language—English or French—that most often must be learned in school.

In virtually all of sub-Saharan Africa, formal education requires payment of tuition directly by those responsible for the child for all years, from the beginning of primary through the end of secondary school. Thus the link of formal education to the economic status of the family is quite direct. A question of major importance is how the lower-status family that aspires to mobility for its children responds to the system. It will make a considerable difference, for example, if a family with limited resources provides a small amount of education to all of the children or a good deal of education to only one or two. The solution adopted should have implications both for patterns of social mobility and for the readiness with which limitation of births is viewed as having relevance for achieving greater mobility.

A closely related issue is the degree to which responsibility is felt, beyond the nuclear family itself, to assist children financially in obtaining an education. The number of children one has some responsibility for in addition to one's own biological children has important implications for the relevance of fertility limitation by a couple. It is also one of the very important ties between the survival of the extended family system, social class, and social mobility.

It is widely believed in Africa that the cost of education is one of the major considerations leading to the adoption of family planning by peasant couples. (This seems generally to be supported by evidence from KAP surveys.) It seems clear, though, that the relationship is not entirely simple. In my judgment, the issue has complications and ramifications that call for serious further attention.

Conclusions

The conclusions drawn from this discussion are essentially simple. Fertility control is already available to and used by the elites in almost all societies; this fact is of considerable importance to the whole question of whether family planning should be withheld from, offered to, or urged upon peasants at any given point of time. More broadly, in regard to any proposed population policy, the implications for social mobility and the patterns of social inequality must be considered. Actions taken or not taken in response to the demographic revolution in an area such as sub-Saharan Africa can have profound consequences for the basic structure of the society. It is essential that we concern ourselves with those consequences if our actions are to be meaningful, effective, and humanly responsible.

References

1. John C. Caldwell. "The Control of Family Size in Tropical Africa," *Demography,* Vol. 5, No. 2 (1968), 615.

2. Commission on International Development, Lester B. Pearson, Chairman. *Partners in Development.* New York: Frederick A. Praeger, Inc., 1969, p. 58.
3. Ester Boserup. *The Conditions of Agricultural Growth.* London: George Allen & Unwin, 1965.
4. Steve Weisman. "Why the Population Bomb Is a Rockefeller Baby," *Ramparts,* Vol. 8, No. 11 (May 1970), 47 ff.
5. John C. Caldwell. *Population Growth and Family Change in Africa.* Canberra: Australian National University Press, 1968.
6. William Goode. *World Revolution and Family Patterns.* Glencoe, Ill.: The Free Press, 1963.
7. R. A. Henin. "The Patterns and Causes of Fertility Differentials in the Sudan," *Population Studies,* Vol. XXIII, No. 2 (July 1969), 171–98.

Discussion of Dr. Heisel's Paper

E D W I N   S.   M U N G E R

Edwin S. Munger is Professor of Geography at the California Institute of Technology.

Dr. Heisel's paper follows one tendency that occurs in this and other discussions: When talking about specifics, one usually starts talking about specific areas. However, many of Dr. Heisel's remarks on Africa are germane to many less developed countries. I am not qualified to comment about differential fertility; my own concern is political geography in sub-Saharan Africa, and I would like to apply some of his ideas to the future political and economic pattern in Africa.

Dr. Heisel has wisely repeated an old saw that I shall re-emphasize, and that is: We need more information on Africa. In a sense, the civil war in Nigeria took place because no one knew how many people there were and no one could trust anybody to find out. Nearly everyone cheated on the census, and finally a war developed with the result that possibly a million people are dead or malnourished. A similar situation could arise in other parts of Africa. Having information can be a life-and-death matter.

There is less stratification in Africa than in most of the developing world, as Dr. Heisel brought out. One aspect of this is the extended-family system. Many observers believe that Africans want to have large families so that they can be guaranteed care in their old age. It is my observation that many people in black Africa have not worried much about this. However, as Africans move from being a largely rural people with an extended-family system to urban people with a nuclear family—a more Western-type family, without the advantage of the extended-family system—they are going to start to worry, and more people may want to have larger families simply to give them protection in their old age. But experience is showing that with modernization women really want to limit family size more than men, whose pride is often involved.

Dr. Heisel stresses, and I think the point important, that many in black Africa and other parts of the developing world seriously question the motives of white nations that promote population limitation. I had a long interview in August 1970 with President H. Kamuzu Banda of Malawi, who told me with great pride and to my shock:

> Well, there were some people from the United Nations came here and they wanted to talk about population planning. I threw them the hell out of the country in forty-eight hours. . . . I'm not going to have any of that nonsense around here. . . . We've got 4 million people in Malawi. We could have 20 million people. We have the land. . . .

His reasons were primarily political because he envisions Malawi including a good deal of Mozambique territory. The fact that Malawi has one of the lowest per capita incomes in Africa, about $40, made no impact.

The suspicion is very strong that the affluent nations are interested in population control in Africa so they will be less hindered in their exploitation of Africa's still untapped mineral resources. Dr. Heisel stresses the relative insignificance of class differences in Africa, but I would put more stress on the ethnic differences, for these are terribly important. It would be difficult to be a Yoruba going to eastern Nigeria to advise the Ibos that they should have fewer children. One can argue that one of the causes of the tragic war in Nigeria was the tremendous growth of population in eastern Nigeria, coupled with superior education, that led to an outflow of 40,000 or 50,000 Ibos to northern Nigeria. One may argue that the lack of population control led to this Ibo emigration and that Ibos should now control their population so they will not have to move out for employment. But I would not want to be the federal official in charge of giving out that information. This will be a very touchy issue for the federal government in Nigeria. The Ibos will believe it is a policy for their elimination. The same holds for other ethnic groups in Africa.

For some years most African countries will probably try to solve problems of population not by population-control programs but by removing aliens. I was in the Ivory Coast in 1953 at a period when there was severe pressure on employment. All of a sudden there was an uprising and 12,000 Africans who were aliens fled the country. Many had lived there a long time. Those who were not killed went back to countries such as Dahomey, Guinea, Ghana, and Togo. Ghana, burdened with large unemployment, has sought to curb population by deporting, in some cases under rather cruel circumstances, thousands of people who have lived and worked in Ghana, spent their whole lives there, and consider themselves Ghanaians.

In East Africa, with its excellent common market, Kenyans are losing jobs in Uganda to citizens. Rhodesia, which has had a problem of unemployment because of the sanctions, has required workers from Mozambique to return to Mozambique, a country which has suffered from demographic anemia for a long time, with a steady loss of people to South Africa and Rhodesia. In Zambia the problem occurs in reverse; President Kenneth Kaunda, on grounds of principle, does not want people from the Barotse province in the far south (where South African employment has been a principal source of income) to go to South Africa to work under oppressive political and social conditions for higher wages, so he has prohibited the export of labor from Zambia. The result has been separatist stirrings in Barotseland and the loss of seats by the ruling party.

I am sure Dr. Heisel would accept this one correction: He talked quite often of sub-Saharan Africa when I really think he was speaking of black Africa or Africa between the Sahara and the Zambezi. He is quite right in excluding the areas of white domination from his considerations. However, I do think there is quite a bit that can be learned about the 15 million black people in South Africa for whom better figures are available than for most of sub-Saharan Africa, where politics have interfered. Much can be obtained regarding the differential growth rates of the black, Coloured, and the Asian populations of South Africa that may have application further north. In South Africa, of course, great suspicion of population control is held by the educated Africans. Comments from prominent members of the National Party recommending bonuses for larger white families and larger budgets for birth control for the black population, the Coloured population, and the Asian population can be blatantly racist.

Some interesting work that is going forward deserves mention. Simon Ominde, chairman of the Geography Department at the University of Kenya in Nairobi, has done an outstanding study on the migratory movements in Kenya, particularly in rural areas. Professor Norman Miller of the American Universities Field Staff edits the *Journal on Rural Africa,* valuable for its concentration on rural Africa.

In conclusion, Dr. Heisel's excellent paper raises questions that have few answers given the state of knowledge of sub-Saharan Africa. Demographic trends do now and will continue to affect the political stability and economic growth of Africa, and knowledge of them can have immediate application to the field.

7

The Present State of
Family-Planning Programs

BERNARD BERELSON

Bernard Berelson is President of the Population Council.

In this appraisal of the present state of family-planning programs, I will try to answer the questions: Where do we stand? Where do we go from here? In my view, the present state is simultaneously impressive, frustrating, uneven, inadequate, and doubtful or unknown. The prospects are promising and dubious. In this paper I shall seek to justify these adjectival conclusions.*

First a few words about the nature of the task and its difficulty. By "family-planning programs" we mean those deliberate efforts, usually governmental in funding and administration, to provide birth-control information and services to the target population on a voluntary basis. The end objective is to lower fertility (among other objectives, e.g., maternal health, child health, reduced resort to nonmedical induced abortion). Given that task, the inherent difficulties are so numerous and so great that it seems virtually insoluble (which indeed it may be, by some definitions of "solution").

There are *political* difficulties: lack of convinced and in-

---

* I am indebted, as always, to Dorothy Nortman of the Council staff for her good help in the preparation of this paper. I asked her for many hard-to-get data and she was able to provide most of them, for which thanks are due and hereby given.

A small portion of this material was used in a presentation I made at an Organization for Economic Co-operation and Development meeting of donor and recipient organizations in the population field in November 1969.

formed will within the government, fear of political liabilities in promoting the program, governmental instability, ethnic competitions, resistance to perceived neocolonialism, and concern with military power.

There are *bureaucratic* difficulties: "standard operating procedures," jealousy of any new and popular program, a widespread bureaucracy to be activated, and the press of other business upon already overburdened staffs.

There are *organizational* difficulties: lack of trained personnel to run the program, thin channels of communication to the people, lack of a medical infrastructure to attach the program to, occasional opposition or indifference of the professional medical community, dispersal of the population into many small villages, and the heavily rural complexion of the society.

There are *economic* difficulties: costs of the program, the competition for funds with the going establishment, and the requirements of finance ministries.

There are *cultural* difficulties: the weight of tradition, the inertia of high fertility built into the family system over centuries, the lack of popular education, the subordination of women, early marriage, and high marriage rates.

There are *religious* difficulties: active in some places, passive in others, and meant to influence both the people and, perhaps even more, the government.

There are *personal* difficulties: illiteracy and ignorance, the ancestral need for sons, the social-security need for sons, social pressures toward parenthood, the superstitions and customs attached to menstruation, the sensitivity of sex-related behavior, peasant resistance to change, the invisibility of social support on so private a matter, and remoteness of rewards.

There are, finally, the difficulties of *sheer size:* tens of countries and each a new venture, hundreds of staff directors to be recruited and trained and located effectively, thousands of clinical facilities to be established and operated, a few hundred thousands of staff workers to be recruited and trained and located effectively, a few hundred millions of individual couples to be informed and served, many hundred millions of births to be averted,* and billions of dollars.

When the matter is put that way, one would only stand in awe of the problem were it not for the heavy consequences—for the individual child, for the family, for the community, for the developing nations, and for humankind. We are undertaking a virtually unprecedented effort at deliberate social change of a very great magnitude. Where do we stand? Where do we go from here?

Where Do We Stand?

Let us begin our appraisal by evaluating the record against seven criteria: needs, magnitudes, comparative programs, costs, targets, trends, and birth rates.

By Needs

There are four necessary ingredients (aside from money): the political will at the top to support the effort, the interest and motivation among the people to accept the practice, the technology for application in the individual case, and the organization to implement the policy by bringing the technology to the service of the motivation. Where do we stand on them, compared with, say, 1960?

With regard to *political will,* there are two basic points. The first is that in the past decade policy-makers have shown a great upsurge in awareness, interest, and policy determination on "the population problem." In 1960 only three developing countries had antinatalist population policies (all on paper), only one government was offering assistance, and no international assist-

* By a rough calculation and simply to indicate the order of magnitude: 1.125 billion births must be averted between 1970 and 2000 in the entire developing world (including mainland China) in order to get from a birth rate of 40 to 20 per thousand per year or, with anticipated declines in mortality, to get from a growth rate of 2 per cent to 1 per cent. If the developed world reached a net reproduction rate of 1 by the year 2000 and the developing world got there by 2050, the world's population would be stable in 2100 at about 15 billion.

ance organization was working on family planning. In 1970 nearly twenty-five countries on all three developing continents, with 67 per cent of the total population of the developing world, had policies and programs; and another fifteen or so, with 12 per cent of the population, provided support in the absence of an explicitly formulated policy (Table 1). Five to ten governments

Table 1. Governmental policy on family planning in developing countries

Population size (*millions*)	Policy and/or program and date started	Support but no policy	No support, no policy
400 and more	China (mainland), 1962 India, 1952, 1965 [a]		
100–400	Pakistan, 1960, 1965 [a] Indonesia, 1968		
25–100	Philippines, 1969 Thailand, 1970 Turkey, 1965 United Arab Republic, 1965 South Korea, 1961 Iran, 1967	Nigeria, 1969	Brazil Mexico Burma
15–25	Morocco, 1965	Colombia, 1967	Ethiopia North Vietnam South Vietnam Congo (Kinshasa) Afghanistan Sudan
10–15	Taiwan, 1964 Ceylon, 1965 Nepal, 1966 Kenya, 1966 Malaysia, 1966	Venezuela, 1965	Algeria Peru North Korea Tanzania
Less than 10	Ghana, 1969 Tunisia, 1964 Puerto Rico, 1969	Chile, 1965 Cuba, (?) Ecuador, 1968	Africa: 26 countries

Table 1. (*cont.*)

Population size (millions)	Policy and/or program and date started	Support but no policy	No support, no policy
Less than 10	Singapore, 1965 Jamaica, 1966 Trinidad and Tobago, 1967 Mauritius, 1965	Dominican Republic, 1967 Hong Kong, 1956 El Salvador, 1967 Dahomey, 1969 Honduras, 1965 Nicaragua, (?) Costa Rica, 1968 Panama, 1969 The Gambia, 1969 Barbados, 1967	Asia: 19 countries Latin America: 7 countries

ᵃ Program reorganized in 1965.

now offer external support (though only two in any magnitude). And the international assistance system is formally operational in the United Nations Population Division; the United Nations Development Program (UNDP); the World Health Organization (WHO); the United Nations Educational, Scientific, and Cultural Organization (UNESCO); the United Nations Children's Fund (UNICEF); the Food and Agriculture Organization (FAO); the International Labor Organization (ILO); the Organization for Economic Co-operation and Development (OECD); and the World Bank, plus regional offices.* Even if some of this development is merely international fashion or response to funding opportunities, it is still a truly historic development—a large one and, as Table I shows, a very recent one.

The second point is that in many cases this achievement is still more apparent than real, more word than deed. A policy is not a program, and a lightly held policy can hardly even be called a policy. So in several of the countries favoring family

* Also worth noting on the international front is the lessened impact of the two major ideological disputes over population and family planning, centered on Marxism and Roman Catholicism.

planning, and indeed in a few of the international organizations favoring it, a question arises about the strength of the will to effect fertility decline: Do they really mean it?

With regard to *interest and motivation,* we have assembled a great deal of evidence from surveys in the past decade, contravening earlier belief, to the effect that there is some degree of interest among the people, even among illiterate and uninformed villagers. Knowledge about the matter is low, but attitudes are generally favorable; the interest is in stopping births rather than in spacing them (the latter is a more sophisticated form of family planning that came later in the West as well); the wanted number of children is larger than in the modernized developed world but smaller than couples now have; the better-educated and the better-off, typically in the cities, are farther along in this aspect of modernization, as they are in all others; and the proportion who want no more children now rises sharply with the number already had (Figure 1). Thus, at least by verbal profession, there does seem to be a market for family planning in the developing world—not overwhelming, but not trivial either.

With regard to the *contraceptive technology,* we are much better off than in 1960 but still not really well off. We have the contraceptive pill, which has worked well in the developed countries but not well in the developing (and which is presently suffering from medical doubts). We have the intra-uterine device (IUD), which has in a relatively few years become the single best (reversible) contraceptive method for the developing world; it illustrates how technology matters in this field, not only in itself but indirectly, by stimulating development of the organization to deliver services. We have better methods of sterilization and abortion. We have much more research aimed at discovering and testing better methods—better forms of IUDs, a "once-a-month" pill, a chemical abortifacient, a "morning-after" pill, an injection or an implant.

With regard to *organization and administration,* we have made at least a start wherever there are favoring policies, and we have made impressive progress in a relatively short time

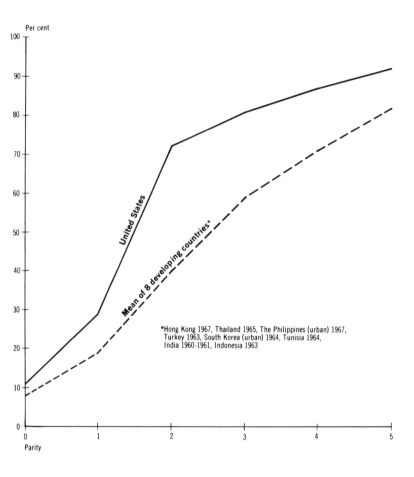

Per cent

United States

Mean of 8 developing countries*

*Hong Kong 1967, Thailand 1965, The Philippines (urban) 1967,
Turkey 1963, South Korea (urban) 1964, Tunisia 1964,
India 1960-1961, Indonesia 1963

Parity

Figure 1. Percentage of respondents not wanting more children,
by parity.

where the will has been strong. But over-all, organization and administration have been and remain a problem. The programs are usually located in health ministries, which typically are not strong ones in developing countries. There are administrative weaknesses, not least the burden of frequent administrative changes, and bureaucratic obstacles. The record by country shows a wide range of performance, simply in getting in position to carry on a program. How ready are the countries to deliver information and services, as indicated by their capability to reach the target population? This is not an easy question to answer reliably and systematically, but a rough estimate can be made based on the distribution of personnel and facilities (Table 2). The range is about as great as it can be, even within the category of official policy, and the median is only about 50 per cent. There is a slight correlation between capacity and duration—the programs in the higher countries are two or three years older than in the lower ones—and in several of these countries, urban areas are much better served than rural areas. Over-all, the distribution does show that many countries with favorable policies on paper in fact lack programs. Thus, even the mandated effort has actually been carried out in only a limited number of cases, usually the more advantaged ones—which has led a highly knowledgeable observer to say that the family-planning effort, like Christianity, has not failed, it has just never been tried. In several settings, it is more correct to say that family planning has not really been implemented than to say that, once implemented, it cannot be effective.

The consequence in program effectiveness is reasonably clear (Figure 2): There is a good correlation between capacity and actual achievement, as measured by the proportion of married women of reproductive age (MWRA) who used contraceptives received from program sources in January 1969. And there are ready explanations for individual countries off the trend: Kenya, Ceylon, and the United Arab Republic (U.A.R.) have incorporated family planning into their general medical services, but more by fiat than by fact. But on the whole—and this is an im-

Table 2. Estimated organizational capacity of programs
to reach target population
with family-planning information and services [a]

From 85 to 100 per cent:

Ceylon	95
Singapore	95
Taiwan	95
South Korea	90

From 55 to 85 per cent:

Pakistan	75
United Arab Republic	75
Kenya	70
India	65

From 25 to 55 per cent:

Malaysia	50
Thailand	40
Tunisia	40
Iran	40
Colombia	35
Dominican Republic	30

25 per cent and below:

Chile	25
Salvador	25
Venezuela	25
Turkey	15
Indonesia	10
Morocco	5

[a] What the tabulation says, for example, is that approximately 95 per cent of the target population in Ceylon is in principle reachable by the organized program. The estimate of organizational capacity to reach the target population is based on the proportion of facilities and personnel currently in place. Two factors have an important influence on this capacity: the target ratio of population to facility-personnel and the extent to which facilities and personnel capable of providing services already exist in the country when the program is adopted. These estimates do not evaluate the quality of the target itself nor the extent to which existing facilities and personnel are actually in use. They are only estimates of organizational capacity based on the targets set by the program administrators.

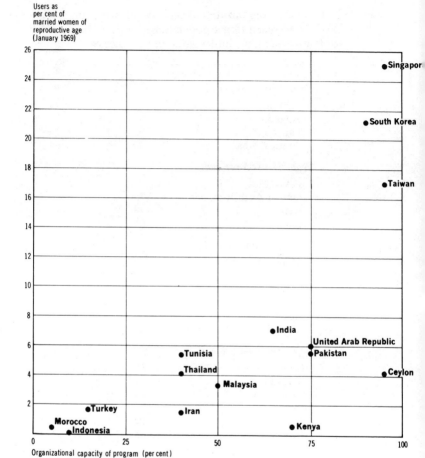

Figure 2. Relation of organizational capacity or program and achievement in use of program contraceptive.

Table 3. Percentage of family-planning services and supplies
provided to current users by the program (January 1969)

	(*per cent*)
India	87
South Korea	84
Ceylon	76
Tunisia	66
U.A.R.	60
Malaysia	57
Turkey	57
Thailand	56
Taiwan	53
Iran	50
Kenya	50
Morocco	40
Singapore	24

Source: (1).

portant and encouraging point that speaks to the "reality" of
existing motivation—effort does pay off.*

By Magnitudes

In the developed world, almost all contraceptive practice
(that is, contraception involving supplies or services) derives
from the private sector. In the developing world more contraception depends on government programs, thus attesting to the importance of the efforts under consideration. Even here, however,
the private sector is by no means insubstantial. By the best
available estimate, something over half the current users of
family-planning services in a number of developing countries
are provided contraception through the public programs, but
with a wide range (Table 3). The median in these countries is
nearly a 60 : 40 public-to-private ratio, so both are clearly important.

* My colleagues William Seltzer and Dorothy Nortman properly point
out that Figure 2 does not take account of the time-and-effort factor in
programs. A revised and complementary attempt along these lines is
presented as an appendix to this paper.

Table 4. Estimated users of supplied contraception[a] in the world, excluding mainland China, Soviet Union, and eastern Europe

	Users supplied by private sector	Users supplied by public sector	Total users	Rough estimate of proportion of eligible MWRA (per cent)
	(millions)			
Developed countries	30–35	2–2.5	32–40	30
Developing countries	4–5	6–6.5	10–12	5
All countries	35–40	8–10	42–52	12

[a] In the developed world, the major methods are the pill and the condom; in the developing world, the major methods are the IUD and the condom.

As a rough estimate of the magnitudes involved, note the proportion of all MWRA covered by supplied contraception (Table 4). That of course does not include rhythm or *coitus interruptus,* or abortion or sterilization, in which case the proportions rise to approximately 75 per cent in the developed world and perhaps 25 per cent in the entire world. In the absolute, it is almost certainly true that abortion and sterilization together account for far more averted births in the developing world than all the methods of supplied contraception combined. As someone has observed, we should never forget the psychological attractiveness of a single-act certainty over a multiple-act probability.

As to magnitude of supplied contraception, the national programs in eighteen developing countries have actually provided family planning to about 15.3 million acceptors, or about 10 per cent the total MWRA, with a range of 0.3 to 45 per cent. This has been done over an effective program life for these eighteen countries of four years, on the average. Is that achievement to be considered "only" or "fully"?

By Comparable Programs

How have family-planning programs done as compared to public-health programs at a similar age of development—appreciating that all the public-health programs have been aimed at the universally accepted goal of death and illness control, whereas in the case of family planning both ends and means are often in question. A colleague who has had considerable experience in such matters concludes:

> I know of few, if any, newly started public health programs which have been so widely accepted and implemented, in so many developing countries within a period of so few years, or have in general progressed as well as has family planning since about 1963–64, indicating the time when large-scale reasonably effective control programs became possible both technologically and financially. (2)

And he compares public-health programs in environmental sanitation and thereby control of some of the infectious and parasitic diseases, smallpox, venereal disease, tuberculosis, and leprosy. He goes on:

> There is no doubt that malaria control programs have achieved a great deal of success in recent years, but we have to bear in mind the many steps and the length of time which were required to achieve this success and even today the problem is far from solved. . . . Given a similar stage in the development of national programs, those for population control suffer little, if any, by comparison.

In both public health and family planning, a good proportion of the ultimate effect has come and will come from nonprogrammatic factors, such as improvement in nutrition or shift toward modernization. In any case, this seems an instructive comparison with what would seem to be the easier job of improving the health of a community.

By Costs

Are such programs economic? Are the returns worth the costs? There is a rough consensus among economists that an averted birth, viewed strictly from the economic standpoint, is worth at least one to two times the annual per capita income, or $100–200 in a typical developing country. How much have these programs actually cost? Not very much. National efforts cost only a matter of cents per capita (Table 5)—a median around

Table 5. Governmental allocations for family-planning programs (latest available year, usually 1969)

Per capita (U.S. cents)	*Countries*
Less than 2	Indonesia, Kenya, Morocco, Nepal
2–4	Iran, Turkey
5–8	Malaysia, South Korea, Taiwan, U.A.R.
9 or more	India, Pakistan

5 cents which translates into about 30–35 cents per MWRA. Internal program costs in the established programs in Korea and Taiwan range around $3.00 per acceptor and $5.50 per current user. The most comprehensive and sophisticated analysis of costs in this field, recently completed,* finds that a "couple-year-of-protection" (CYP) costs roughly the same amount in most countries (especially when differences in per capita income are taken into account):

Chile, 1968	$6.95
South Korea, 1968	4.36
India, 1968	3.10
Pakistan, 1967	2.79
Taiwan, 1968	2.21

As a rough order of magnitude, assume three to four CYPs for

* See (3). Another recent study on India (4) found a much higher ratio of return (present value of monetary saving) accruing from averted births to the cost of averting them, in the order of 60 : 1 for recent years.

one averted birth—in which case the cost-to-benefit ratio for family planning ranges from 1 : 10 to over 1 : 30.

By Targets

How have the programs done when measured against their own targets? This straightforward question is not easy to answer because of absence of data, lack of continuity between the targeted category and the data, unspecificity of the target, and imprecisions of temporal interpolation. But we do have (or can derive) the needed information on ten particular programs, and again the range is extremely wide, from above target to far from it (Table 6). Moreover, the proximity to target is closely related to the degree of effort expended on the program (as indicated in Table 2). Naturally, any interpretation must be weighed against the requirement of the target itself, which in the case of Singapore, for example, is particularly severe.

By Trend

Here again the picture is mixed (Figure 3). A few countries still appear to be building the program (Chile, Thailand, Turkey), but more seem to have hit a plateau of acceptance (Ceylon, Hong Kong, South Korea, Taiwan, Tunisia, and Singapore). The data are not fully available from India and Pakistan but at best a plateau is probably indicated there as well. The interpretation partly depends upon absolute levels of performance—increases cannot be sustained indefinitely—but the situation does require attention, especially since the demands of the next years will not decrease in most countries. And not one program started since 1965 has really been "successful."

By Fertility Effect

The effect on the birth rate itself is the ultimate test, and at the same time a very difficult one to appraise because of technical problems—lack of decent data on the birth rate; inability to isolate the program's impact from a whole welter of other factors; inability to evaluate the program's indirect effects (what happens outside the program but as a result of program

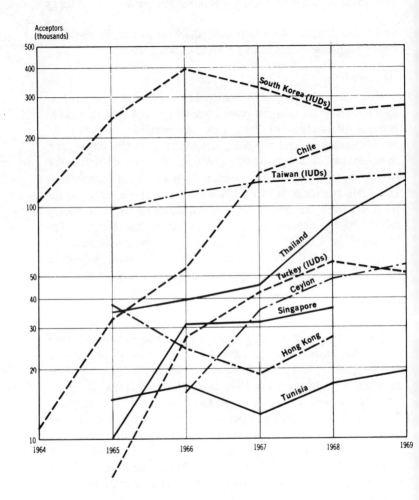

Figure 3. Trend in annual acceptors, by country (all program methods, unless method specified).

activity); inability to handle the so-called substitution effect (what would have happened in the absence of a program); and inability to separate credit for accelerating declines from "causing" them. But there are some pieces of evidence:

1. An analysis conducted for OECD on "the demographic impact of family planning in developing countries" concluded that the programs accounted for 2.3 million averted births in 1968, or a decrease of "1.3 points, or approximately 3 per cent, off the birth rate" of 43.8 per thousand (excluding mainland China). The analysis rests on several assumptions, naturally, and yields what the author calls a "very limited success"—though that impact could also be reasonably interpreted as a substantial one indeed (5).

2. In Hong Kong the crude birth rate has been falling for a decade, from about 35 to about 20. According to a sophisticated analysis:

> . . . the 1961–1965 period contrasts with 1965–1967. . . . Most of the earlier decline probably can be attributed to changes in age and marital status distributions (particularly the former); but almost none of the recent birth rate decline is due to these factors. Almost all of the 15 per cent decline in the birth rate in 1966 and 1967 can be attributed to a genuine decline in the fertility of married women. . . . The 1965–67 declines occurred at a time and in age patterns which make it plausible to interpret the change as due to a significant degree (but certainly not entirely) to the activity of the Hong Kong Family Planning Association. . . . (6)

3. In South Korea the crude birth rate fell about ten points during the 1960s, by best estimate, due partly to increasing age of marriage, partly to increased use of induced abortion (at least an estimated 20 per cent of 1968 pregnancies), partly to a contraceptive program that has reached nearly 50 per cent of the MWRA, and partly to increased urbanization and industrialization (women in the labor force) (7). On the effect of the large IUD program alone, one analysis credits it with a decline in the crude birth rate of about 10 per cent (8).

Table 6. Achievement of family-planning programs compared to targets through end of 1968 [a]

Country	Program target	Target prorated to users/acceptors	Percentage of target actually achieved
South Korea	1,800,000 IUDs (1962–71)	1,080,000 IUDs	113
	150,000 sterilizations (1962–71)	90,000 sterilizations	
	171,000 orals (in 1968)	171,000 orals	
Taiwan	600,000 IUDs (1964–69)	600,000 IUDs (June 1969)	92
Pakistan [b]	5,000,000 users (by 1970)	4,000,000 users	83
Malaysia	Natural growth from 3% (1966) to 2% (1985)	90,500 users	60
Ceylon	750,000 acceptors (1966–75)	225,000 acceptors	44
Singapore	CBR [c] from 32 (1964) to 20 (1970)	82,000 users	37
India [d]	CBR from 41 (1965) to 25 (1976)	10,000,000 users	30–40
Turkey	2,000,000 acceptors (1965–72)	800,000 acceptors	17
Morocco	CBR from 50 (1965) to 45 (1972)	114,500 users	10
Dominican Republic	CBR from 48 (1967) to 28 (1977)	54,000 acceptors	10

[a] To convert birth or growth rate targets into family-planning acceptors or users by the end of 1968, total population was projected from the initial target year to 1968, and the number of women of reproductive age was projected at the initial growth rate. The crude birth rate targeted for 1968, as applied to the projected 1968 population, yielded the target births for 1968, and total births divided by the number of MWRA projected for 1968 yielded the 1968 general fertility rate (GFR) to meet the target. By assuming this GFR to be a weighted average of no fertility for users and the base-line fertility for nonusers, MWRA were dichotomized into users and nonusers. The procedure is considered to yield findings of a reasonable order of magnitude.

[b] The figure for Pakistan is probably on the high side because of overreporting, perhaps by as much as a fourth to a third.

[c] Crude birth rate.

[d] The figure for India is particularly problematical because of unavailability of firm data; at the same time, the achievement is compared to the newly designated target (in 1969) of reaching a birth rate of 32 by 1974—in which case our procedure

4. In Taiwan, according to one study, the birth rates in local areas are significantly related to program acceptances, even beyond the influence of nonprogram factors (9); and in another careful study, the decline in fertility among IUD acceptors was over 30 per cent greater than among their counterparts (10).

5. In Tunisia, a detailed analysis concluded that contraceptive usage (about two-thirds from the program) accounted for about a third of the decline of the birth rate during the period 1963–68, or for about 1.5 points or 3 per cent (with later marriage and change in age structure accounting for the remainder of the estimated 5-point decline) (11).

The evidence is not full or finally convincing, but it is beginning to come in and to show a moderate but still heartening result in the desired direction. With less stringent data on the impact of the program on information, attitude, and acceptance, it does carry a certain plausibility.

Finally, by way of summarizing the past record and the prospect, what is to be defined as "success" or "failure" in this field? What is the required goal and when is it to be reached? Let me mention four reasonable goals in order of decreasing demand and measure our chances against each of them.

First, if the goal is zero growth by the year 2000, then I am confident the goal will not be reached in the developing world, and probably not in the developed world either.* We have noted the tremendous task of bringing the growth rate in the developing world down to 1 per cent, let alone zero—averting over a billion births in thirty years. In any case, we are just beginning to see a fascinating historical phenomenon in the countries now closest to zero growth that has the characteristics of what psychologists call an approach-avoidance conflict in individual behavior: The farther one is from a goal the better it looks, but the closer one gets to it the less attractive it becomes. Psychologists know that an approach-avoidance conflict is a stable one; that is, it is very hard to resolve. So if zero growth within the next few decades is "absolutely neces-

* Even a net reproduction rate of 1 in the United States now would not bring zero growth to this country by the end of the century (12).

sary," whatever that means, then we may be in for a dark future.

Second, if the goal is to take 1 to 1.5 points off the growth rate in the developing world in the next twenty years, or roughly 15 to 18 points off the birth rate, then it seems to me we have a differential chance at that. My own view is that in the favored countries—those with higher literacy and popular education, with good communication channels, and with a decent medical network—this goal can be reached. In the middle countries, my answer would be "perhaps," depending upon (a) how fast general development moves ahead and (b) how markedly the contraceptive technology improves in the intervening period. In the unfavored countries, the answer may be no, or close to it.

Third, if the goal is to bring about the ultimate fertility decline faster than it would otherwise occur, by a nontrivial number of years, then on the evidence of South Korea, Taiwan, Singapore, Japan, and selected places in India and Pakistan, we probably have a decent chance to gain a few decades on what would occur to fertility in the absence of such programs, particularly if the subject countries have the will to do so.

And finally, fourth, if the goal is to get organizationally ready to do the job more effectively whenever circumstances truly permit, then the prospects seem good indeed, since we have already moved some distance toward that goal.

Where Do We Go from Here?

If that is where we are, what is ahead? Here it is convenient to distinguish between *within* family planning and *beyond* family planning. *Within* refers to efforts to lower birth rates directly by seeking to extend effective family planning on a voluntary basis by provision of services and information (including persuasion to the small-family norm). *Beyond* refers to efforts to lower birth rates indirectly by instituting social or economic measures that would themselves influence people toward diminished fertility.

Within Family Planning

There are several things that can be done that should make a difference.

1. *Full, continuous, and informed implementation of mandated programs.* As suggested above, we need to do what we know needs to be done. There is not a going program that cannot be significantly improved in management, most by a good deal. We know what the common improvements are—better training, better supervision, better informational programs including population study in the schools, better fiscal arrangements, fewer bureaucratic controls, more experimentation for feedback into program, far better evaluation, and so on. Indeed, perhaps the first need is for the field to get its own house really in order; that in itself could make a substantial difference. This is not the place to go into the specifics, but the fact is that the present policies are not being pursued energetically, systematically, or fully, and doing so would seem to be one of the best places to go from here.

2. *Improvements in contraceptive technology.* Contraceptive technology is better today but by no means good enough. A logistically easy, effective, simple, one-time, reversible, trouble-free, culture-free, doctor-free, coitus-free, inexpensive technique would make an important difference. This would be especially true now that the means of delivering the technique are available or in the process of being built up, thanks partly to the most recent technological development, the IUD.

3. *Extension of the means for fertility limitation.* Beyond contraception, but within family planning, is legalized, medically supervised induced abortion. This is a sensitive subject but an important one. Legalized abortion now exists in several countries in varying degrees of liberality and appears to be increasingly acceptable (namely, India and the United States). Illegal, nonsupervised abortions are common throughout the world—literally millions a year by best estimates—and indeed represent the stimulating factor for contraceptive programs in

Latin America. Probably nowhere has abortion been legalized for demographic reasons, but it has always had a demographic effect.* Indeed, someone has said that although some contraceptive programs have failed, all abortion programs have succeeded, in the double sense that they have had large numbers of acceptors, wherever suitably available, and have made a demographic difference. Here again, if countries find this an acceptable means of population limitation by their own standards, the technique becomes critical since medical doctors are already insufficiently available where they are most needed and hence a nonsurgical means of terminating pregnancy is needed.†

4. *Extension of the urban postpartum concept.* Whether it is the highest point of motivation for family planning or not (and it may well be), certainly a very good time for family-planning advice and services is the immediate postpartum period. A demonstration program including over 125 hospitals in the developing world has had good results, including reaching

---

* As in the well-known case of Japan, for example, and the lesser-known case of Rumania, where stringent restrictions on abortion suddenly introduced in November 1966 (along with some pronatalist social measures) resulted in a birth rate a year later over 2.5 times greater (34.2 as against 13.4, now down to the mid-to-low 20s).

† Christopher Tietze has shown, with regard to medical safety, that "in terms of the risk to life, the most rational procedure for regulating fertility is the use of a perfectly safe, although not 100 per cent effective, method of contraception and the termination of pregnancies resulting from contraceptive failure under the best possible circumstances, i.e., in the operating room of a hospital" (13). Here are the data on "illustrative annual rates of pregnancies and of deaths associated with contraception, pregnancy, and induced abortion per 100,000 women of reproductive age in fertile unions."

	Pregnancies	Deaths
No contraception, no induced abortion	40,000–60,000	8–12
No contraception, all pregnancies aborted out of hospital	100,000	100
No contraception, all pregnancies aborted in hospital	100,000	3
Highly effective contraception	100	3
Moderately effective contraception, no induced abortion	11,800–13,000	2.5
Moderately effective contraception, all pregnancies aborted out of hospital	14,300	14.3
Moderately effective contraception, all pregnancies aborted in hospital	14,300	0.4

younger women, but there are another 350–400 hospitals of some size potentially available. The extension is desirable on all grounds, including the involvement of medical schools and the medical community. A current estimate is that the maximum cost of institutionalizing family planning in all such hospitals would be about $40 million over a ten-year period.

5. *Extension of the postpartum concept to the rural areas.* The postpartum program is now essentially limited to the cities of the developing world since that is where the delivery institutions are. But the large proportion of the population is rural. The idea is to provide some degree of maternal and child health care (MCH) plus family planning to every pregnant woman in the society, out of humanitarian and medical, not just demographic, concern. A feasibility study was recently completed in eight to ten countries to see what such an effort would require in people, training facilities, physical facilities, transport, and all the rest, including money. Preliminary data suggest costs in the range of about 60 cents per capita per year (14).

6. *Incentive programs.* Several countries have used payments to program workers, from the field to the doctor's office, to promote and/or effect family planning on a piecework or bonus basis. But here, "incentive" is used to mean payments directly to the target population for initiating or practicing contraception or for periods of nonbirth. To a large extent, especially for those with deferred payments, such plans are put forward as surrogate for the social-security value of children or sons. A number of such schemes have been proposed,* but for various practical reasons none has yet been tried in the field. To my mind, their potential value is limited, but some experience should be gathered wherever feasible and acceptable.

7. *The private sector.* Here there are two possibilities. First, we have seen (Tables 3 and 4) that the private sector is an important part of the distribution of contraception to people in the developing world. There is a great reservoir of talent and energy in that sector that could in principle contribute to the legitimate extension of the practice. It would be good to

* For a general review, see (15). As later examples, see (16–18).

find ways to encourage private industry along this line.* Second, there are industrial pathways that could be utilized (as they have been in Japan)—the tea estates on the Indian subcontinent, the agro-industrial estates in the Philippines, and similar enterprises with credibility and a service network among large numbers of people.

Beyond Family Planning

There are numerous ways to attack "the population problem" other than by direct promotion of family planning, ways in which the primary motive power comes from social factors that in turn promote fertility limitation. Where do we go on them?

1. *Development—social, economic, educational, informational, and health.* There is no doubt that general development would have an effect on birth rates—through industrialization and a rising standard of living, for people always seem to choose affluence over fertility, within the family and within the nation; through popular education, by making the future real, and hence making any kind of planning sensible; through nutrition and health, by lowering infant and child mortality, in the absence of which lowered fertility is unlikely; through mass communications, by making it possible to reach the masses with a message; and through a general modernization in attitudes, by breaking up the traditional cake of custom in which high fertility is embedded. There is no real question about all that, but the related questions are two-fold: Can development come fast enough, given the population burden? Is investment in that route better in cost-to-benefit terms than investment in family planning itself? The first question is at best problematic. As for the second, the budget for population and family planning in most countries is less than 1 per cent of the national development budget and would appear to be better invested, from the standpoint of development, where it is; that 1 : 99 mix is preferable to 0 : 100. With regard to popular education, for ex-

* For some suggestions to this effect, see (19).

ample, the family-planning budget would buy one more day of school in Taiwan and Singapore, two and a half days in Ceylon, and seven to nine days in South Korea, Pakistan, and India (20). Presumably, the family-planning program is doing more for fertility decline than those extra hours in school would do.

2. *Tax and welfare benefits and penalties.* Here again, a number of proposals have been made on paper but few effected in practice—withdrawal of maternity benefits, withdrawal of family allowances, withdrawal of large-family requirements for public housing, tax on births after a given number, tax benefits for the smaller family, withholding of educational benefits, and pensions for parents of small families as a social-security measure. Most social-welfare systems now in effect have a certain pronatalist cast, but at best it is doubtful that they have had a pronatalist effect. The current proposals vary in detail but all seek to turn the system in an antinatalist direction. Here are a few examples: the opening of public housing to couples with few or no children in Singapore; the imposing of a much larger fee for delivery of the fourth and subsequent child in Singapore's major government maternity hospital; the removal of maternity and tax benefits in Pakistan; the consideration in the U.A.R. of restricting educational and subsidy benefits to the first two children; the consideration in Iran of a revision of the child-benefit plan to decrease the amounts for later children; a proposal in Malaysia to limit maternity benefits to the first three children; a proposal in Colombia (defeated twice) to obligate girls for social service after their schooling; and the incorporation of population or family-life materials into the school curriculum in several countries. It is too early to say whether such measures are, or since most are still proposals, would be, demographically effective. In any case, as population pressures grow, countries may move further in this direction when they can. But not only are there ethical issues (e.g., protecting the child from the penalty) and political problems, but the practical problems are enormous. As has been said, if a country could administer such complex systems for demo-

graphic ends, it probably would not need to do so in the first place.

3. *Shifts in social institutions.* Such basic changes can be seen as part of general development and hence desirable as basically supporting fertility decline. At bottom, they involve the emancipation of women, one way or another. The first mode usually advanced is to delay the age of marriage from around the current 16 to, perhaps, 20 (as currently being considered in the U.A.R. and some other African countries). This would have a worthwhile effect on the birth rate at least in the short run, but the problem is how to bring it about, since passing a law, although good, is not sufficient where the problem is greatest. Another mode is the promotion of female participation in the nonagricultural labor force; again worthwhile, and possible in limited situations (currently in the urban areas of Korea), but difficult to implement in the typical rural areas of the developing world.

4. *Coercion.* Proposals are being seriously made by responsible men that "the population problem" is too great to be left to the inevitable failure of voluntary contraception, that the right to free individual choice of numbers of children does not exist because of what the economists would call the "neighborhood effects," and that the "privilege" to reproduce can be, and at present must be, limited by the state to a level acceptable for the society as a whole. Again, plans have been put forward, but apart from other obstacles—ethical, administrative, and technological—there is no political climate for such an enterprise.

People in this field have been diligently looking for something to do "beyond family planning"—something practicable and ethical, economic, and with some chance of effectiveness, even on an experimental or demonstration basis. On the whole, we have not found it, and we continue our search.

At the same time, it is worth noting that whatever else one does in order to effect the necessary fertility decline, either in general development or in measures other than family plan-

ning, some means of contraception is required as instrument.*
If age of marriage is raised or popular education extended or
employment of women promoted, contraceptive practice is still
required to make those favorable conditions fully responsive in
fertility behavior. So if this movement, in the long view of
history, turns out to have provided only the instrument, with
all the engine power coming from the developmental or social-
structural changes, that still will have been a major contribution and will bring about the decline faster than otherwise.
And if family planning is not "enough," what is that can be
done? The empirical question remains as to how the same
amount of money and effort could have a greater demographic
impact, given the realities, and most of us in the field are looking for an answer.

Conclusion

In summary, where we stand is indicated by my initial ad-
jectives. The present state of family-planning programs is:

Impressive. A great deal of program development has occurred in a very few years and with relatively small resources
in both personnel and funding. Indeed, a great social movement has been instituted against formidable obstacles and without any major political disruptions in an historical eyeblink.

Frustrating. Many things that we know need to be done and
in principle can be done are simply not being done because of
lack of will or bureaucratic limitations or personality conflicts
or lack of funding or some other unworthy reason.

Uneven. A few countries have been able to achieve important targets and sustain the forward movement, even to the
point of suggesting that they may reach a take-off point in the
foreseeable future, whereas others have been unable to do so
or have not really tried (and the same can sometimes be seen

---

* As Spengler says, "the arrangements cannot succeed unless the means
to control family size are widely available and very cheap in relation
to the incomes of the masses." (18, p. 1238)

within a country, as in India, where the performance by states varies by a factor of at least three (21), and varies in different areas of program operation).

Inadequate. Not only has "the population problem" not been "solved" by family-planning programs in most of the countries at issue, but also, and more realistically, the efforts in several key countries are not adequate to the requirements of the task.

Doubtful or unknown. We simply do not know how well or badly things are going in several places for lack of a proper system of evaluation with feedback to guide the administration of the program (let alone the lacunae deriving from the difficult and still-unsolved technical problems of measurement).

And the prospects are at the same time:

Promising. Awareness of consequences is still growing; the technology is likely to improve and/or expand, the programs are gaining both acceptance and experience, effort has been shown to matter, and the momentum is still running in this direction though not so strongly as in the mid- and late-1960s. Anything done now makes the task easier later on, other things equal, because of the group support engendered and the subsequently averted births of currently averted births. And, as Kirk says, "the speed of (the demographic) transition, once firmly begun, has accelerated over time" (22).*

* In Kirk and Sanderson (23) there is the following remarkable tabulation, showing the number of years historically and currently required for countries to reduce their annual crude birth rates from 35 to 20, 1875 to present. It shows that the later the reduction of crude birth rates began, the less time it took.

Period in which birth rate reached 35 or below	Number of countries	Years required to reach birth rate of 20		
		Mean	Median	Range
1875–99	9	48	50	40–55
1900–24	7	39	32	24–64
1925–49	5	31	28	25–37
1950–present	6	23	23	11–32

Countries included are 1875–99—Austria, Australia, England and Wales, Finland, Italy, Netherlands, New Zealand, Scotland, United States; 1900–24—Argentina, Czechoslovakia, Germany, Hungary, Japan, Portugal, Spain; 1925–49—Bulgaria, Poland, Rumania, U.S.S.R., Yu-

Dubious. The problem itself is terribly resistant, the positive results tend to be concentrated in the more favorably situated countries where traditional fertility patterns are beginning to break up under social pressures; we may be hitting a plateau of effort and results at the same time that we encounter more women in the reproductive ages as an echo effect of the post-war baby boom, and the measures beyond family planning are unlikely to be helpful in the short run.

We are thus in a mixed position that is difficult to appraise with confidence. With so much having gone on in so many places in so few years, we do not altogether know where we now are. We are trying to digest our experience to date, to assimilate it, to balance the achievements and the shortfalls, and to appraise alternatives even as we seek to advance beyond what we now do. Nor do we lack for critics on all sides —politicians who suspect the whole enterprise of impure motives, international civil servants who think the whole "population problem" has been oversold, financial supporters who want more results, program administrators who want more freedom, self-interested operators who seek to turn the family-planning movement to their own ends, demographers who feel the effort has become captured by the medical men, medical men who feel the effort has been captured by the demographers, social scientists who say that family planning will never work in the absence of deep structural changes, and doctors who say it will never work in the absence of a complete medical infrastructure. If one does not close his eyes and ears, as of course he should not, then he is beset with conflicting and usually un-

---

goslavia; 1950–present—Ceylon, Chile, Hong Kong, Puerto Rico, Singapore, Taiwan. "The initial and terminal dates were determined by three-year averages rounded to 35 and 20 respectively. . . . [In] some countries, including all of those entering the transition since 1950, the reduction of the birth rate has not yet reached 20. In these cases, the decline in the birth rate after reaching the 35 level, or data for at least seven years, was projected by linear extrapolation of the average annual rates of decline" (22, p. 95).

The authors also "suggest that the threshold for fertility reduction is itself changing over time, i.e., a lower level of socio-economic development than was historically necessary in Western Europe is now required to 'trip off' the same fertility reduction" (23, p. 8).

realizable advice and derives only a little comfort by rationalizing that he seems to have a position somewhere near the "norm of the middle."

All of this leaves us in the "Yes, but . . ." stage. Since this great effort is a continuum of challenges, there is always a convenient position for critics: Whatever we have been able to do, there is always something that we have not yet done. Do we measure initial acceptors reasonably well? Yes, but we cannot get good continuation rates. Did we demonstrate something in Taichung? Yes, but that's only one city. Do we have an impressive program in the rest of Taiwan? Yes, but Taiwan isn't India. Is the IUD an improvement over earlier contraceptives? Yes, but the removal rate is high. Is there now a much larger investment of personnel and funding in this field? Yes, but it is not enough. Is family planning itself worthwhile? (a) Yes, but it ought to go on within the health context; or (b) Yes, but it really needs stronger social measures to succeed. Did a program have a fertility effect? Yes, but it would have happened anyway. Given the nature of the effort and the many specialized interests with an investment therein, there need be no cause for surprise in such responses—and, as I have tried to suggest, the reality includes sufficient material to justify both the "Yes" and the "but."

What do we now need? As starters, we need three things— and there is not much room for substitution; all three are needed.

We need the will, expressed in governmental action, to do the job with appropriate means. At present, if I am not badly mistaken, there is a discontinuity of will between the donor and the recipient agencies: they do not fully share the common objective of population control. The irony is that, with a few exceptions on each side, the donors are more committed than the recipients, yet it is the latter who must do the job. One cannot substitute its will for the other's. Presumably, enough is shared so that together they can, if they will, usefully get on with the task.

We need funding. For family planning alone, a good deal can be done for 5–10 cents per capita per year, properly applied. But greater funding is needed for going the medical route via extension of the MCH infrastructure throughout the society and perhaps for some of the social measures beyond family planning. Large sums could probably be well used over the years, but not immediately—and especially not in the absence of strong will.*

We need time. Given the will and the funding, better programs are likely to be forthcoming with better results, whether or not they "solve the problem." But because of the nature of the case, this appears to be a task not for years but for decades, and it is well to remember that we are barely past the middle of the first one. In my judgment, the honeymoon is over, and donors and recipients alike need to settle down to the hard and difficult task of being partners over the longer run.

Where are we and where are we going? The advances of these few years appear to be novel for programs of this magnitude and delicacy, perhaps even unique, and are certainly not to be discounted. At the same time, we must recognize that they are largely, in themselves, the infrastructure—less the job itself than getting ready to do the job. It is a necessary step but not a sufficient result. We could end up, five to ten years hence, sharply ahead, moderately ahead, about where we now are, or moderately back, in a relative sense—probably not sharply back but quite possibly not really knowing. Where we end up depends on what we do now and in the interim.

The development of national family-planning programs was a truly historic innovation of the 1960s. The full outcome is still in the balance. As Francis Bacon wrote in *Of Innovations,*

> Surely every medicine is an innovation, and he that will not apply
> new remedies must expect new evils, for time is the greatest

* As a rough order of the magnitude involved, the averted births needed to cut the birth rate in half in the developing world (excluding mainland China), at a cost of $25 each, would come to about $1 billion a year. Today's allocation, both internal and external, is about $200 million.

innovator; and if time, of course, alter things to the worse, and wisdom and counsel shall not alter them to the better, what shall be the end?

Appendix

As noted in the footnote associated with Figure 2, Seltzer and Nortman estimated the personnel-years per thousand MWRA in each program by the procedure shown in Table 7.

The relationship of this measure of effort to achievement (users as a proportion of MWRA) is indicated in Figure 4, which is reasonably similar to Figure 2. The difference between Singapore on the one hand and India and Pakistan on the other, as the main countries off the trend, presumably reflects the disparity in their "readiness" for such an effort.

References

1. Dorothy Nortman. "Population and Family Planning Programs: A Factbook," *Reports on Population/Family Planning.* New York: Population Council and the International Institute for the Study of Human Reproduction, Columbia University, December 1969, Table 12.
2. Richmond K. Anderson, Director of the Technical Assistance Division, Population Council. Memorandum. January 1961.
3. Warren Robinson. *A Cost-Effectiveness Analysis of Selected National Family Planning Programs.* University Park: The Pennsylvania State University Press, December 1961.
4. George B. Simmons, "The Indian Investment in Family Planning." Unpublished doctoral dissertation, Department of Economics, University of California, Berkeley, June 1969.
5. Organisation of Economic Co-operation and Development, *The Development Centre Report on Population.* Paris, October 1969. Ch. IV.
6. Ronald Freedman et al. "Hong Kong: The Continuing Fertility Decline, 1967," *Studies in Family Planning,* No. 44 (August 1969).

Table 7. Estimate of personnel-years put into national family-planning programs by end of 1968

Country	Year program started (a)	Number of personnel (1968 or 1969) (b)	MWRA, 1969 (thousands) (c)	Personnel-years Factor (d)	Personnel-years Thousand (e)	Users (per cent of MWRA) (f)	Personnel-years (per thousand MWRA) (g)
Ceylon	1965	3,234	1,700	2	6.7	4.2	3.9
India	1964	513,000	96,000	2	1000.0	7.0	10.4
Indonesia	1968	691	20,000	½	0.3	0.1	0.02
Iran	1967	5,000	4,300	1	5.0	1.5	1.2
Kenya	1966	300	2,000	3½	0.5	0.6	0.3
Korea	1961	3,800	4,500	6	22.8	21.2	5.1
Malaysia	1966	230	1,600	3	0.69	3.4	0.4
Morocco	1965	173	2,600	2	0.35	0.4	0.1
Pakistan	1964	52,000	20,000	3	156.0	5.5	7.8
Singapore	1965	96	290	4	0.38	25.0	1.3
Taiwan	1964	1,400	1,700	4	5.6	17.0	3.3
Thailand	1967	1,300	4,400	1	1.3	4.1	0.3
Tunisia	1964	218	650	2	0.44	5.4	0.7
Turkey	1965	4,500	5,600	3½	6.8	1.7	1.2
U.A.R.	1965	8,500	4,600	5½	21.2	6.0	4.6

Column a: Source: (1, Table 6).
Column b: Source: (1, Table 7).
Column c: Source: (1, Table 4).
Column d: Based on columns a and b and judgmental value of trend in personnel build-up.
Column e: Column b multiplied by column d.
Column f: Source: (1, Table 12 except for Pakistan and Singapore, for which later data are available).

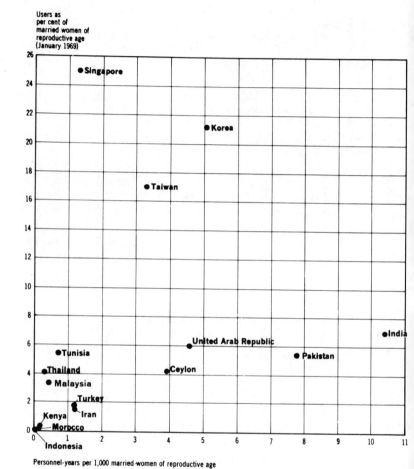

Figure 4. Relation of program personnel to achievement.

7. Hi Sup Chung. "The Korean Family Planning Program: Achievements, Problems, and Prospects." Paper prepared for Southeast Asia Development Advisory Group Population Seminar, New York, December 19–20, 1969.

8. John Ross. "Woman Years of Use, Cost-Effectiveness, and Births Prevented by the Korean National Program." Unpublished manuscript. New York: The Population Council, June 1968.

9. Ronald Freedman et al. *Family Planning in Taiwan.* Princeton, N.J.: Princeton University Press, 1969. Pp. 338–39.

10. L. P. Chow et al. "Demographic Impact of an IUD Program," *Studies in Family Planning,* No. 45 (September 1969).

11. Robert J. Lapham. "Family Planning and Fertility in Tunisia," *Demography,* Vol. 7 (May 1970).

12. Tomas Frejka. "Reflections on the Demographic Conditions Needed to Establish a U.S. Stationary Population Growth," *Population Studies,* Vol. 22 (November 1968), 379–97.

13. Christopher Tietze. "Mortality with Contraception and Induced Abortion," *Studies in Family Planning,* No. 45 (September 1969), 7–8.

14. Howard C. Taylor, Jr. and Bernard Berelson. "Comprehensive Family Planning Based on Maternal/Child Health Services: A Feasibility Study for a World Program," *Studies in Family Planning,* Vol. 2, No. 2 (February 1971).

15. Bernard Berelson. "Beyond Family Planning," *Studies in Family Planning,* No. 38 (February 1969).

16. Ronald G. Ridker. "Synopsis of a Proposal for a Family Planning Bond," *Studies in Family Planning,* No. 43 (June 1961).

17. Ismail Sirageldin and Samuel Hopkins. "Family Planning Programme: An Economic Approach." Unpublished paper. Lahore: West Pakistan Research and Evaluation Center, April 1969.

18. Joseph J. Spengler. "Population Problem: In Search of a Solution," *Science,* Vol. 166 (December 5, 1969), 1234–38.

19. Alfred Sollins and Raymond Belsky. "Commercial Production and Distribution of Contraceptives," *Reports on Population/ Family Planning.* New York: Population Council and the International Institute for the Study of Human Reproduction, Columbia University, December 1969.

20. Gavin W. Jones. "How Much Education Could Be Bought with

Family Planning Budgets?" Memorandum. New York: The Population Council, July 1969.

21. Morrie K. Blumberg. "Indian Family Planning Progress and Potential: The 1968–1969 Program." Mimeograph. New York: Population Council, January 1970.

22. Dudley Kirk. "Natality in the Developing Countries: Recent Trends and Prospects," *Fertility and Family Planning: A World View,* S. J. Behman et al., eds. Ann Arbor, Mich.: University of Michigan Press, 1969. P. 85.

23. Dudley Kirk and Warren Sanderson, "The Accelerating Decline of Fertility in the Demographic Transition." Unpublished MS., 1970.

Discussion of Dr. Berelson's Paper

R. T. RAVENHOLT

R. T. Ravenholt is Director of the Office of Population, Agency for International Development, United States Department of State.

As usual, Dr. Berelson has provided rich intellectual fare for our consideration. In fact, he has covered many important points so well that I need respond to only a few.

I am impressed with the usual similarity of our views on matters of broad strategy in the population field. Dealing with similar problems, and having responsibility for allocation of substantial funds toward the solution of those problems, imposes a common discipline upon us.

Whereas persons without key responsibility for development of large action programs can devote their time and energies to picking holes in every strategy and program, we must do our best to develop strategies and programs that are effective even if imperfect. When directing far-flung action programs that encompass the developing world and take years to implement, one must hold steady to a few well-chosen goals and avoid turning and churning every time someone picks at a program action because of this or that imperfection, real or imagined.

Dr. Berelson spoke of some of the difficulties that have had to be overcome to develop population programs, and indeed the Population Council provided leadership in this field for more than a decade before the U.S. government became forthrightly involved.

We have learned from the experience of others and have sought to improve the efficiency of programs by providing many kinds of support, particularly by making oral contraceptives more fully available. This new emphasis is needed in many programs because of the demonstrated limitations of intra-uterine devices and other methods. It is well that the Population Council and a number of countries gave the IUD a thorough test so that its performance potential could be estimated. We now know what can be accomplished with intensive program effort, as in Korea and Taiwan. Clearly the family-planning programs that place main emphasis on the IUD develop less favorably than those that also make oral contraceptives available.

We now have enough experience to choose a strategy that is more effective than one chosen on an intuitive basis a decade or even five years ago. We now know that for a family-planning program to be most efficient it must offer *what women want*. One can emphasize the theoretical advantages of inexpensive and long-lasting ways, but in the end it is really what the customer wants that determines whether the gains are efficient and durable. The evidence of the last decade now indicates that the *majority of women prefer the pill* to other methods of fertility control, in spite of all that is said about the daily decisions that have to be made. Somehow, they seem to do it. And I am not really convinced of the argument that if a woman chooses an IUD she only has one decision to make, because it seems to me that on countless days thereafter, whenever there is a little spotting or bleeding or discomfort, real or imagined, she has a decision to make: Does she wish to keep this bothersome object in her or does she not? I think the difference is not nearly so great as was initially thought between the demands of pill and IUD use upon the intellectual and memory resources of the woman.

The potential of the Lippes Loop has been fairly well tested in Korea and Taiwan. True, there have been some deficiencies in these programs; they have not been perfect. Yet I do not believe there will ever be a better Lippes Loop program in India or Africa than there already has been in Taiwan and Korea. These programs have measured the potential of this IUD and have demonstrated that although it can make a valuable contribution, it is not by itself sufficient. It is readily accepted by older women with a considerable number of children, but the very fact that it is aimed at the termination of childbearing, rather than at the delay and spacing of reproduction, limits its efficacy. In country after country there has been initial rapid acceptance, with a rise, then a plateau, and often a decrease in the number of users. Its impact upon fertility has been perceptible, but the experience of Korea and Taiwan indicates that it is difficult, even under good circumstances, to bring the annual crude birth rate much below 30 per thousand per year with a program based mainly on the IUD. To reduce the birth rate below 25, and certainly to reduce it below 20, other methods must be used—methods aimed at the threshold of reproduction so that young women can delay their first, as well as subsequent, pregnancies.

In a number of countries—small countries it is true, such as Hong Kong and Singapore—that switched more readily to the pill in 1966 or 1967, the birth rate has dropped rapidly to 20. Korea and Taiwan have recently made pills available, first to women unable to retain loops, and then to all women. It seems unnecessarily restrictive to limit pill use to women unable to retain IUDs. Surely the birth rates in Korea and Taiwan would now be lower if pills had been made more generally available earlier. In countries that have gone forward mainly with the pill, on the other hand, programs have generally developed more favorably. The trends of use of this method in various societies differs from IUD trends in that there is ordinarily a continuous increase in the number of pill users whenever they have been made generally available.

This consistently rising curve of acceptance has been only slightly disturbed by the recent wave of alarm about the hazards of pills. Judging from the requests we are receiving from many countries and organizations, the use of the pill continues to increase. At present there are probably about the same number of women in the developing countries using oral contraceptives as IUDs to control fertility—about 6 or 7 million women in each case. This is only a small fraction of the women who should be using this most effective means of contraception. We anticipate the numbers of users will double and redouble during the next several years as no-cost and low-cost supplies become more abundantly available to women previously unable to purchase them. The U.S. Agency for International Development is now providing about a million cycles of oral contraceptives per month to family-planning programs in more than forty countries.

Dr. Berelson has popularized the term "beyond family planning" and has carefully analyzed the many peripheral variables that probably do influence fertility patterns. He has emphasized the fact that these variables operate *through* family planning, and therefore that the development and improvement of family planning is of central importance to any program aimed at improved constraint on fertility.

Others have used the term "beyond family planning" to denigrate the central role of family planning in resolving the population crisis. They imply that the current intense concern with the provision of information, means, and services for family planning is a transient phenomenon—that there are more effective actions, not only *beyond* family planning, but *instead of* family planning that could be implemented to achieve needed fertility control.

Incentives for not having children are often suggested as a likely way to increase motivation for family planning in India and other exotic lands where the population crisis is particularly intense. Indeed, this concept is at first glance seductive. But further study and reflection limits one's optimism that fiscal incentives for not having children will ever make an important contribution to fertility control. If there were validity to the concept of paying women incentives for not having children, why does the United States not move to solve simultaneously its twin problems—poverty and high fertility—by this means? Surely, in a rich country it should be feasible to transfer funds from the provident to the improvident to motivate them to constrain their fertility. But even if it could be shown that it is effective, this action would be politically unfeasible in the United States. In less developed countries with meager resources and weak governments, it is basically impossible to modify fertility practices substantially by giving incentives for not having children: This would necessitate transferring fiscal resources from families with more children (usually poorer) to families with fewer children (usually richer). It would be like trying to make water flow uphill.

The women of the world have demonstrated very thoroughly by now, in many countries, that they have a great interest in the control of their fertility. They *do* recognize that this is fundamental to their well-being, and, when given the information and the means, a large proportion of them choose to limit their fertility. We need to get on with the very arduous and time-consuming task of extending adequate information and services for family planning throughout the world.

Dr. Berelson has stated that he would be happy if we get to a general annual birth rate of 20 per thousand in twenty years. I am more optimistic than this. I believe we will get there somewhat before twenty years. I believe this because as I look at the world picture, at the action that is now going forward in many countries—such as the activities of the programs of the Population Council, the International Planned Parenthood Federation, the United Nations, and the bilateral assistance programs—I realize that family-planning activities are accelerating rapidly. The problem is yielding perceptibly to the concerted attack. Naturally, it has yielded first in the smaller countries, but we see it beginning to yield even in the somewhat larger countries. And it is yielding despite the fact that the programs are still far from perfect. Many of them are only modestly funded and myriad weaknesses are still evident.

The family-planning methods used so far in this battle are still only our light artillery. Lately, and increasingly, we are finally able to bring to bear the heavy artillery that we were unable to use during the last decade—namely, access to postconceptive means of fertility control. This, in the 1970s, will become the most important element in family-planning programs in most countries. And the experience of other countries, as Dr. Berelson indicated, has demonstrated that all of the abortion programs have had remarkable demographic effect. This has been true even in situations in which surgical abortion is readily available but without much contraception. When available along with a strong contraceptive program—oral contraceptives for young women, IUDs for somewhat older women, as well as sterilization for all who wish to terminate their fertility—these programs will become remarkably more effective. The birth rate will drop rapidly in every country where women can choose to reproduce only if and when they please.

8

Population Control in India

JOHN P. LEWIS

John P. Lewis is Dean of the Woodrow Wilson School of International Relations, Princeton University.

My assignment is to discuss the implementation of India's commitment to population control, not to recite first principles, and I would be happy to comply without delay—were it not for one thing. Let me at the outset warn that a sequence of circumstances, particularly involving India as it happens, may tempt the U.S. government to relax its newly found concern about population control in the less developed countries.

After decades of political inhibition, the Washington enthusiasts for positive population policy rushed in with a vengeance in the mid-1960s. In their scramble to make up for lost time, they injected a shrillness into the United States' approaches to the problem of population growth in developing countries that was unlikely to wear well in any case. But they also made a tactical blunder. In 1966 (the phenomenon can be quite precisely dated) they tied the developing countries' population problem very tightly to their food problem.

At that time most Western observers had become deeply pessimistic about the food outlook in less developed countries. There had been significant and accumulating reasons for such pessimism; the near panic that suddenly ensued was triggered by a natural accident in India. In the crop year 1965–66 India was afflicted by the worst drought of this century, and then, to a degree for which there was no recorded meteorological precedent, in 1966–67 it was hit by a second bad drought. On the face of it, such freakish weather was a strange base from which to extrapolate secular disaster, but from all quarters, sage and otherwise, we were overwhelmed with "Famine-1975" forecasts—and the advocates within the U.S. government of strong population control in the less developed countries bound their case almost exclusively to the food issue.

Although the one-to-one food-population linkage underscored the population problem, it also narrowed it dangerously. It mixed together two problems that had quite different time frames for operational and policy purposes. Some of us who were uneasy about the linkage were bràsh enough to believe that the new agricultural strategies that were being undertaken in such Asian countries as India and Pakistan before the first Indian drought hit (but whose implementation was given added impetus by the droughts) might succeed in making the "Famine-1975" forecast look pretty silly rather soon.

We seem now to have been right. The last thing to suggest is that the so-called Green Revolution can be casually or complacently regarded as a *fait accompli*. The agricultural breakthrough has only fairly begun, and it will keep going only if it continues to enjoy the same revised national priorities, the same improved policies, and the same rapidly improving supplies of inputs that have gotten it well started. To hail the Green Revolution as easily the most important recent economic change in these countries is in no sense to sweep aside the problems of inequity and of social and political tension, which the very emerging success in agriculture may heighten.

Yet it does appear that during the past three or four years the food-production trends in India and some other Asian countries have moved upward. With appropriate policies the new trends should be able to maintain momentum for some years. Accordingly, the specter of famine is receding, and we are in danger of relaxing on the population front—because the food-population linkage has conditioned us to do just that.

In my judgment, however, the occasion for official skepticism about the basic need for population control is long since past. Certainly it is past as far as India is concerned. It is not that the Indian population crisis exclusively or even primarily is a food crisis. It never should have been billed as such. It is not that the population problem is peculiar to India. From the world's viewpoint India is a crucial case because it is such a large jurisdiction; but the present Indian population growth rate is somewhat lower than in a number of other countries, and from the Indian viewpoint the need for restraint is no greater than that of many other equally poor countries.

The urgency that nevertheless attaches to population restraint in India stems in part from the fact that the country is indeed poor. Because it is poor and because of the development stage it has reached, its longer-term growth prospects as well as the quality and hopefulness of life in the meantime will be profoundly affected by the pace at which its gross national product (GNP) per capita moves in the medium term of the next ten or fifteen years. And there is no real question in India that, at least for this medium term, the growths of per capita GNP and of the birth rate will be inversely related: the lower the birth rate, the higher the per capita GNP will tend to be.

Ultimately population growth must stop in India for the same reason it must worldwide: because of the sheer constraints of space. There was a time when the hypothesis that the surface of the world is flat was perfectly serviceable for policy purposes. By now the hypothesis that the surface of a sphere is infinite is equally outmoded.

There is only one other matter of first principles that requires comment. Sometimes it is suggested that the need for purposive population control may be obviated by the intervention of the "natural" or inadvertent checks that growing incomes and improving educational standards may place upon population growth. In a country like India it is, of course, to be hoped that these reinforcing factors will help. But it is too late in the world's timetable to wait for them. In the interaction between income and educational standards on the one hand, and birth rates on the other, the causation must flow in both directions. This is essential to India's escape from poverty. It is essential not only that improvements in income and education reinforce the downward pressures on birth rates but also that positive constraints on the birth rate widen the slices of the resources pie that individual consumer-investors and individual students can claim.

For these reasons I start this analysis of efforts to retard India's population growth with the premise that the cause is not only just but urgent.

Population Strategy Since 1965

The subject of India's population strategy is surprisingly complicated. To arrive at a sensible view of the present situation, prospects, and possibilities, it does little good to dwell on only one or more facets of the problem, whether they be contraceptive technology, organization, demography, motivation, delivery systems, or whatever. What is needed is a total-systems approach. But to deal with the subject in that manner, and in some conceptual detail, in a paper of this scope will exact some costs: I shall have little space to assemble supporting evidence for points made or inferences drawn, and my historical account of the effort in India will be highly selective.

My first historical ellipsis is to assume, almost, that the Indian government's population-control effort began in 1965. India was one of the first countries to adopt positive restraint of the birth rate as a formal national-policy goal. By 1965 the official family-planning program had been under way for almost fifteen years and had acquired a fairly sizable clinical, administrative, and budgetary apparatus, especially in urban areas. But it was only in 1965 that the program embarked on its present radically ambitious course.

Two forces actuated the new departure in 1965. The first was an accumulating set of administrative and leadership pressures brought to bear in behalf of an accelerated effort. The second force was a technical development, and I shall return to it later.

The pressures to which I refer could be called "political" except that they did not feature the normal party or interest-group pressures of domestic politics. Rather, they included, first, concern accumulating at various points in the range of public and private Indian organizations already engaged in family planning. This collection of organizations did not yet add up to anything like a dynamic array, but they had their strong units. In particular, certain state governments like Madras and the Punjab were running well ahead and had become articulate exemplars of more vigorous approaches. They were actively seconded by those foreign technical assistance units, notably those of the Ford Foundation, already locally active in the field.

Second, and more important, in the winter of 1964–65 population control for the first time acquired a strong political lead from near the top of the Indian government. This was somewhat curious since Prime Minister Lal Bahadur Shastri was not a "self-starter" on the subject and the Minister of Health, Dr. Sushila Nayar, within whose portfolio family planning fell, was a Gandhian physician who never quite overcame her prejudice in favor of continence as the only really wholesome mode for curbing fertility. However, two of the intellectually strongest members of the government (the same two largely responsible for formulating India's new agricultural and general economic strategies during the government's remarkably innovative 1965–66 period), C. Subramaniam, Minister of Food and Agriculture, and Asoka Mehta, Deputy Chairman of the Planning Commission and later Minister of Planning, activated the moribund Cabinet Committee on Family Planning. These two men sold their colleagues on the urgent need to curb India's rapid population growth. Moreover, in 1965 the government of India found official aid donors for the first time taking a lively, pointed interest in population control. During the first half of that year the United Nations, the World Bank, and the U.S. Agency for International Development (AID) each sent in teams of family-planning experts to reconnoiter the situation, preach more activist approaches, and offer assistance; in effect, strengthening the hand of the Subramaniam-Mehta initiative.

The technical breakthrough—the other major factor actuating the 1965 family-planning takeoff—solved an old problem. Indian family planners long had felt hampered by the lack of a contraceptive technique that was effective, safe, reversible, and, above all, cheap. The new "loop," or intra-uterine device (IUD), looked like an ideal response to these specifications. The early results on trials in Taiwan and Korea were encouraging; the visiting expert teams strongly favored it; and it was approved for general use by the Indian Council of Medical Research in January 1965. Although other contraceptive techniques, notably sterilization, were not officially abandoned, the loop was made the chief vehicle of the radically stepped-up effort launched in July 1965.

The new effort had the air of a crash program. Although it was lodged in the Ministry of Health under Dr. Nayar, who, some felt, still lacked passion for the cause, it was given new, more vigorous administrative and technical (medical) leadership and was backed by a ramifying multimedia propaganda effort. The government projected very rapidly rising training and manpower requirements and a massive expansion in delivery units, equipment, and budgetary support.

The goals of the new program were rough-hewn. India had a fair number of trained demographers; but its demographic analysis was not well focused, and its demographic data were weak. This was especially true of the detailed, regionally specific, intercensal data needed for evaluating particular experiments and projects. Nevertheless, bold targets were duly, if arbitrarily, adopted to give the enterprise sufficient drive. It was decided that the birth rate, then estimated to be in excess of 40 per thousand per annum, should be reduced to 25 by 1975. Despite the further reductions in the death rate that would occur during the same interval, it was thought that this should reduce the net population-growth rate from the official estimate of 2.5 per cent to about 1 per cent in 1975. Subsequently, the nation's fourth Five-Year Plan, originally scheduled to end in 1975–76, was postponed three years, and the Family Planning Programme's official birth-rate target also was backed off three years. Adjusted downward to avoid a lowering of objectives, the goal became a birth rate of 22 per thousand by 1978.*

Very quickly after its launching, the program began to focus on subtargets. This was done to communicate urgency and to create incentive within the proliferating administrative structure that was being built. New goals were created for particular contraceptive techniques and for individual regions, states, subdivisions, and in some cases, individual villages. As these subtargets were passed down through the system and the quantitative returns were gathered month by month and set against them, there developed an almost manic focus on near-term achievement. In the latter months of 1965 the data being reported were heartening. Many observers remarked on the parallels to the new crash effort being attempted in agriculture, and although the organization being shaped was racked with growing pains, there was great hopefulness in the family-planning enterprise.

India's 1965 family-planning decisions were crucially important not simply because they launched the accelerated effort that has since continued but because they fixed a *pattern* of policy. This particular model solution still dominates Indian population policy. Before we go on to consider the post-1965 experience, we will do well to make explicit the implicit hypotheses of the 1965 decisions.

The Bureaucratic-Clinical Delivery System

First, it was assumed that the principal contraceptive technology for India was a *clinical technology,* requiring a clinical delivery system. At the time this was expected to be the loop, but even when the loop faltered, emphasis shifted to another clinical technique, sterilization. Although the Indian program

* Independent demographers have found this target, typically, unrealistically ambitious. Yet there has been little disposition to alter it—probably because no one has wanted to scale down the immensity of India's problem. Ultimately, even the reduction of the net population-growth rate to 1 per cent per annum will not be good enough, and yet this inadequate goal would permit an average of no more than three surviving children per couple.

has not precluded such nonclinical (or less clinical) technologies as the condom and the pill, it has stressed techniques
that require the heavy, case-by-case involvement of medical
and paramedical personnel. Moreover, the needed technology
—the loop and the vasectomy—was thought to be in hand;
thus there was less attention paid to research into further improvements in technology than there was, for example, in
agriculture.

Second, the country decided to place its bets on a *public
bureaucratic-clinical delivery system* that, with a public-interest
motivation, would undertake eventually to deliver specific
family-planning services from tens of thousands of outlets to
tens of millions of families. Given the clinical hypothesis together with the poverty of most Indians and the spottiness of
private health services, especially in the countryside, this was
an inevitable decision. And yet it tended from the beginning to
minimize involvement of private organizations, of profit-moti-
vated private medical practitioners (modern or traditional),
and of commercial and market mechanisms. It placed maximum
reliance on the quick, successful building of an enormously large
and complicated, conceptually centralized bureaucracy that
nevertheless would operate a vast number of delivery points and
the training and other structures to support them and would
solve all of the problems of clearance and logistics in between.

Third, this massive administration was left within the *established public-health bureaucracy* and was therefore also
subject to the full administrative rigors of federalism. Health, as
the saying goes in India, is a "state subject," over which the
several states, even when they are predominantly or wholly
funded from the central government, exercise heavy control.
The decision to stay within the public-health bureaucracy was
not an inevitable one. At about the same time, the opposite
choice was made in Pakistan. There, family planning was administratively divorced from health and given a single-purpose
function and an active, centralized organization mandated to
operate nationwide. In India, strong substantive arguments

were and still are made against separating family planning from public health. For example, a 1969 U.N. review team strongly advised, for motivational and other reasons, keeping family planning joined as closely as possible to the public-health program of maternal and child care (1). However, there were also political reasons for the decision, both within the central government structure and vis-à-vis the states. It left family planning lodged in one of the weakest functional cadres in the Indian administrative system—the cadre most hesitant in effecting expeditious bureaucratic clearances, most subservient to the Finance Ministry overlords who preaudit its operations—and one in which enervating frictions between (generalist) administrative and technical (medical) personnel already were a long-standing tradition.

Fourth, the policy design chosen relied heavily on certain *motivational* hypotheses. Not only was the accelerated effort preoccupied initially with reaching the market of ready and willing acceptors for which contraceptive coverage was only a problem of logistics; more fundamentally, the program assumed that there was no hard-to-bridge gap between private self-interest and public self-interest in the population field. The need was only to awaken individuals to their own best interests and then to make the services for implementing these interests available. Hence the motivational campaign became mainly an attention-getting exercise. The program developed a rather pronounced bias against "bribing" acceptors to participate—even though some traces of the opposite approach that had been tried in Madras and elsewhere recurred from time to time, usually in tentative, disguised, or almost frivolous form.

Fifth—since the policy design specified an administratively ambitious, massive crash program to be executed in a context of especially difficult federal-state relations, under a reluctant minister, with one of the most infirm official cadres in the Indian system—the policy design assumed that *strong unflagging leadership from the top of the government* would continue to accent, dramatize, drive, and pull the whole enterprise along.

At the time of adoption, this was not implausible. Subramaniam and Mehta had every reason to expect that they would continue to collaborate in this role.

The last point is especially interesting, particularly because no close observer, at least no Westerner to my knowledge, remarked on the point at the time. The policy design implicitly assumed that population control was a *politically neutral* issue in India. Statesmanship could be exercised without great cost. There was pride in the fact that formal, doctrinal religious opposition was minimal. There was little concern over the needs of good Hindus for sons to light their funeral pyres or over the population implications of the rivalries between religions. The predictable opposition of such directly disadvantaged groups as the traditional purveyors of abortions was dismissed as inconsequential (perhaps too casually dismissed in the light of some of the organized rumormongering about IUDs that such groups subsequently contrived). There was also little thought about the pressures that intergroup rivalries (not just between religious communities; but between caste, class, and occupational groups; between subregions within states; and between the states themslves) might begin to put on political leaders who became identified as all-out promotors of this new massive, busy, bureaucratic intervention into personal affairs.

When they are added up in retrospect, these underlying premises of the 1965 policy scarcely sound like those of a winning strategy. How has the strategy fared in fact?

Evaluations of the Policy

The first point to be emphasized is that the effort has fared quite well. The government of India has something of a genius for inept public relations abroad, and therefore it is not surprising that many distant observers have acquired the impression that nothing much has really happened in family planning in India. On the contrary, there has been an enormous step-up in the program since 1965. Despite its frequent turnovers, the top civil-servant leadership has been strong. Training and other supporting activities have been rapidly expanded and deployed; staffing, although encountering bottlenecks, has moved forward.* Family-planning operations are under way in some measure in over five thousand rural primary health centers at the sub-district, development-block level, and there are more than 19,000 subcenters. The number of mobile clinical units touring the countryside has more than doubled. Urban operations also have expanded sharply. During a period of tightened fiscal circum-stances for government programs in general, expenditures on family planning by 1968–69 had expanded more than five-fold since 1964–65, and sixteen-fold since 1963–64, the year pre-ceding the launch of the accelerated effort. According to the fourth Five-Year Plan, they are due to double again, achieving a level of something like 750 million rupees annually by 1973–74. In 1968–69, the *per capita* outlay on family planning in India already was as large as or larger than it was in those countries, notably South Korea, Taiwan, and Pakistan, usually regarded as front runners in the field.

Moreover, India's rapidly swelling clinical delivery system has been pressing for performance and, in absolute terms, has achieved striking gains. In the four years ending in 1968–69, for example, five million sterilizations were recorded—six times the cumulative total theretofore.

When one compares over-all performance to targets, how-ever, and in particular considers the experiences with different contraceptive technologies, the record starts presenting problems. In the first place the IUDs were a grave disappointment. In-sertions started with a rush: 813,000 were made in 1965–66 and an even larger number the following year. But then, despite the continuing expansion of the delivery system, the curve started reversing. It already had fallen to 480,000 in 1968–69, and in many areas removals of loops were outpacing new insertions so that the net stock of couples protected by this means had de-clined.

* Documentation of the quantities mentioned in the next several para-graphs is to be found in (1, 2), in other Indian government documents, and in various unclassified documents of the U.S. AID Mission to India, 1968 through 1970.

In part the IUD "failure" was a case of excessively high expectations. Although there are nutritional reasons for women in India to have higher rejection rates than do women in countries like Korea and Taiwan, in fact the rates were not much higher. Rather, the principal problem was failure to provide acceptors with adequate advanced instruction and, in particular, adequate and accessible follow-up facilities for dealing with complications. As a result, fears, suspicions, and bad experiences with the loop, aggravated by hostile rumor campaigns, were allowed to gather psychological momentum. Undoubtedly the IUD is capable of some rehabilitation in India. But it will remain only one of the items in the "cafeteria" of devices and techniques that the program offered once IUD use began to fall off.

"Cafeteria" or not, the program actually fell back mainly on sterilizations. Despite some limited AID-sponsored experimentation with pills, birth-control pills have had very little play in the mass government program. Neither, the 1965–69 figures would suggest, have condoms (this is a particularly interesting matter to which I shall return later), and the government, despite a fair amount of talk, has been timid about pushing the abortion-legalizing legislation that would have augmented this widespread form of traditional birth prevention. Sterilizations (in which India is the world leader in per capita as well as absolute terms) did a yeoman job of taking up the performance slack when IUD progress first began falling off, notably in 1967–68 when almost 2 million volunteers were sterilized. But then that performance also leveled off, and the 1969 U.N. team (deploring the backlash that the overemphasis on targets had induced by pushing sterilization too aggressively, especially on disadvantaged and illiterate groups in some areas) concluded that the uptrend was unlikely to resume.

At the suggestion of the World Bank and the invitation of the Indian government, the U.N. dispatched a team to review the program early in 1969. The report of this skilled group of experts of diverse nationalities is highly illuminating (2). Not only are its factual findings informative, but it demonstrated the ambivalence that Indian family planning can engender in those who study it closely.

The U.N. Report

The report issued by the U.N. team compliments India on the ambitiousness and progress of its efforts. It took a stance on an issue that had been inflaming certain Washington quarters at that time—namely, whether or not the Planning Commission was curbing the maximum feasible expansion of the family-planning effort in its fourth Five-Year Plan allocations. The members of the U.N. team found that the program's rapidly expanding allocations had consistently been running ahead of the system's capacity to absorb the funds. In other words, the bottlenecks were managerial, including those of financial management. They reflected no insufficiency in the aggregate financial allocations to family planning.

On the particulars of management the team had a number of useful suggestions. Specifically they centered on improving the flexibility of financial administration and strengthening the program's evaluative processes. But they suggested no magic that would engineer a quantum jump in the rapidly expanding bureaucratic clinical system's rate of growth or in its capacity to use resources. Generally the report indicates that the program is ambitious; it is doing pretty well; and it would be foolish to press it unreasonably. The team was explicit in expressing distaste for the high targets and crash programs that had characterized the post-1965 effort.

And yet on the same pages with these various notes of reassurance, the team reverts time and again to its major finding: The Indian program as it is now constituted, given its record to date but extrapolating as hopefully as one can, is not making it. Virtually every careful appraiser has come to the same conclusion. The U.N. team notes that, even with optimal planned expansion, the Indian delivery system can cover no more than one-third of the 100 million Indian couples of reproductive ages by the end of the present Five-Year Plan. In this vein, the team seemed at times to suggest an immediate trebling of the whole effort—despite the side-by-side points about administrative absorptive capacity. The team explicitly asked for a substantial increase in the foreign aid earmarked for family planning, even though there is no evidence that foreign exchange had been or would become a real constraint on the family-planning system.

Given its rather remarkable ambivalence about a system that was doing rather well within its own terms of reference but was also in process of missing its mark by a mile, the even more remarkable thing about the U.N. team is that it remained overwhelmingly congenial to the theory of the Indian program. Although it would have the Indians reweight their emphases on IUDs and sterilizations and even though it put in what by now has become the *pro forma* plea for more and better research into contraceptive technology, the team did not quarrel seriously with the operative scope of the Indian technological spectrum. It thoroughly approved of the merger of public-health and family-planning activities, and it reinforced the official Indian distaste for financial incentives.

In short, although the U.N. report contains much useful information and a variety of helpful specific recommendations and although it is likely to leave the managers of the Indian program relatively unruffled, it is very likely to leave any objective reader thoroughly puzzled.

The U.N. team let itself be captured by the Indians' 1965 policy model. Whether because of the convictions with which team members arrived or of on-the-spot conversions, they essentially accepted the hypotheses on which the Indian commitment to an overwhelmingly bureaucratic clinical family-planning system rests. Therefore they were not much inclined to consider alternatives that range beyond the constraints of that model. This conveys the gist of my own estimates. But before I try to pull them together, I must introduce one other dimension of the performance record on which the U.N. reviewers remain notably silent and on which my own thinking has shifted.

In the spring of 1969 in Delhi when the preliminary report

of the U.N. team became available, some of us were deeply disappointed because we felt they had totally ducked the key issue —the issue that could reconcile the apparent inconsistency in their findings between administrative-absorptive capacity and over-all inadequacy. That issue, we thought, was the quality and strength of the program's leadership from the top down. In the opinion of many Western observers, from the time in 1967 when both Subramaniam and Mehta lost their connection with the program (the former by loss of his Parliamentary seat, the latter by a change of portfolio), Indian family planning lost the kind of totally committed, all-out, senior-Cabinet-level leadership that was so plainly required if the massive, creaking system was to perform up to anything like the 1965 expectations.

The particulars of an analysis of this situation were arguable, but they reduced in large measure to the proposition that Prime Minister Indira Gandhi had not exhibited a sufficiently constant, dynamic sense of urgency in behalf of family planning. It was usually remarked that she had nothing like the same record on this subject as, for example, President Ayub had in Pakistan. If only this variable could be changed, many of us felt in 1969, then a quantum jump in the absorptive capacity of the system might indeed be possible. We thought the U.N. team had better credentials than any other official foreign donor or adviser for bringing out this ultimate issue, and we were disappointed when its report failed to say word one about top leadership.

I do not know whether the U.N. team was being wise or only circumspect in this regard, but now I have more respect for its silence. For meanwhile I have come to believe that prominent advocacy of family planning may indeed *not* be a politically neutral venture in India. More and more of the intergroup suspicions and rivalries mentioned earlier are encountered by the program. One hears of Muslims who fear that their numerical strength is being whittled away vis-à-vis Hindus, and vice versa, of untouchables or rural labor castes who suspect there is a scheme to do them in. of situations such as that in Telangana where intrastate regions are jousting for long-term position.

Thus far the seventeen Indian states have varied widely in the diligence and success with which they have taken up the program. In November 1968, as the U.N. team reports, official estimates of the percentage of eligible couples covered by the IUD and sterilization programs varied all the way from 28 per cent of the potential in the Punjab to a mere 5 per cent next door in the state of Rajasthan.

Today, as a means of developing federalism further, the government of India is increasing its large disbursement of general-purpose funds to the states. For purposes of equity and to avoid charges of political favoritism, it is basing disbursements on formulas which invariably include population as one of their prime variables. Thus those states which perform best in family planning face the prospect of being increasingly penalized in the sharing of federal resources.

To recognize these accumulating political clouds is not to suggest that the family-planning program should reduce its goals. The cause deserves all of the investment of statesmanship that Indian leaders can afford. But seen in the context of Indian politics in the 1970s, the opportunity costs of taking an activist-interventionist position in this area may be greater than many of us earlier realized. It may be, if the lead that Mrs. Gandhi has given the program in recent years has been insufficient, that she is exhibiting the political sixth sense for which she is well known. Reports of a backlash against Pakistani family planning in the post-Ayub period may have increased the concern of Indian leaders.

Recommendations

Let me offer one final piece of evidence—a truncated case study—for my emerging thesis that the Indian family-planning effort has been confined excessively to the bureaucratic-clinical model of operations and that success in the future will require major supplementation of, if not escape from, that model.

The case is that of condoms. Among the items on the Indian technological "cafeteria," the poorest showing to date unquestionably has been that of this most venerable contraceptive device. Compared with Pakistan a year or so ago, for example, India was doing better with sterilizations and not too much worse with IUDs, but its use of condoms per capita was only about one-twentieth of that in Pakistan in 1969. I was struck by the U.N. team's near dismissal of this factor in their evaluation. They made almost no reference either to the need for better distribution of condoms or to the new "commercial condom distribution scheme." The latter is undoubtedly the most imaginative potential innovation in Indian family planning in the past three or four years.

Condoms either have been given away free at public-health clinics, where few men have gone to the trouble or embarrassment of picking them up, or have been sold in some drugstores at prices few Indians can afford. The mass commercial distribution scheme would create an intriguing amalgam of the public and private sectors. A Ford Foundation marketing specialist conceived the plan which was worked out with the co-operation of some of his Indian government and business colleagues and some A. D. Little consultants. The top leaders of the Family Planning Ministry adopted the plan in principle, and AID underwrote the initial supply of condoms. The planners reasoned that condom use might rise radically if a standard brand-name condom, actively promoted by advertising, was made easily available at a highly subsidized price. Condoms would not necessarily be associated with the clinics but with the hundreds of thousands of outlets of the country's larger retail marketing firms whose channels reach farthest into the countryside. Accordingly, six mass distributors—two soap companies, two tea companies, a cigarette firm, and a flashlight-battery manufacturer—were enlisted in the effort, essentially on a public-service basis. The brand name was established. The government agreed to make available a sufficient free supply of condoms (the AID initial stocks) to start the program. The condoms would be sold over the counters of the tobacco, tea, soap, and flashlight shops for a price of three for two cents. The proceeds would compensate the retailer, cover the distributors' out-of-pocket costs, and pay the advertising agencies that would be hired by the composite enterprise that would run the whole undertaking. A modified version of the plan was adopted in mid-1968.

There is, I think, every possibility that this scheme is an excellent piece of social engineering. It could well lead to a larger family-planning contribution by the simple condom than has yet been achieved in any developing country. But to date we do not know the potential of the plan because at every turn its implementation has been victimized by the habits and pre-occupations of the bureaucracy. The family-planning administrators objected to the management as an autonomous, commercial-style corporation. They insisted upon keeping the project under their own wing. Then they found themselves unable or unwilling to recruit the few key business executives needed to run the project because of the conflict with the civil-servant salary standards. They were more interested in getting promotion done cheaply by government publicity units than in hiring advertisers. They proved totally impervious to the scheme's requirement for constant, intensive market research.

This experiment urgently needs to be resuscitated and pursued. But meanwhile it illustrates the limited interest that the bureaucratic-clinical system has in a market-oriented, nonclinical family-planning strategy.

Off and on for five and a half years now, I have been studying the complexity and elusiveness of population control in India, and there is no particular reason to think that my present reading of the situation will remain constant. For what they are worth, however, I have cast my current impressions in the form of needed policy for the 1970s.

First, to rise above the constraints of the 1965 policy model, two lines of action should be taken:

1. *Promotion of far more research in reproductive biology and contraceptive technology.* The resources of Indian science are such that a substantial amount of this research can be done within India itself, especially in conjunction with internationally coordinated research programs. The major obligation rests never-

theless on the affluent countries. The biology is essentially the same and most of the technology is transferrable. Compared with the new Green Revolution technology, the world's present array of contraceptive technology is faltering and primitive. Investment in research and development in this area, although it has been rising recently, is paltry.

2. *Improvement of demographic data and analysis.* Here, too, agriculture has the advantage. Like most countries, India keeps far more detailed, reliable, and informative records of how it grows crops than of how it grows people. The country needs better population data from stronger demographic research centers. It needs advanced training in order to refine its long-term population targets. But more urgently it needs competent, frequent sample censuses and a variety of area-specific data on fertility and population characteristics for purposes of evaluating specific experiments and projects and for the close monitoring of new elements in the population-control strategy.

Second, every political effort must be made to improve the workings of the present bureaucratic-clinical system. A firm lead from the top can do much to post able administrators, to encourage delegation of authority and shortened clearances, to improve the system's financial flexibility, and to experiment with management consultants. In the past the avoidance of error and the adherence to administrative rules have been rewarded. Now the breaking of bottlenecks must be stressed. With the help of these managerial improvements, problems such as the rehabilitation of the IUD, the recruitment of women doctors, and the more effective linkage of family planning with maternal and child-care services and with nutrition programs should be zealously pursued.

Third, the Indian population-control program must range well beyond its existing boundaries to succeed. I have two specific suggestions in mind. There should be more active encouragement of private, service-motivated organizations and efforts—social welfare groups, industrial firms, labor unions, cooperatives, and others.

More important as supplements to the existing system, however, are likely to be nonclinical, commercial innovations. Here again one can take a leaf from the agricultural experience. One of its most striking features is its dependence on commercial markets, not on bureaucracies, as organizing mechanisms. I have already cited one outstanding illustration of a nonclinical commercial possibility—the subsidized condom scheme. It should be cut loose from the government and urgently pursued along the lines originally intended. Subsidized distribution of birth-control pills through private medical channels may warrant similar consideration. Likewise under this heading I would certainly include legalization of abortion which, although obviously clinical, would place an additional burden mainly on private health delivery systems.

There is a third supplement to the present program that, it seems to me, has every prospect of being more important than either of these first two but would augment both of them. Financial incentives for family-planning acceptors should be experimented with intensively with an eye to their eventual adoption.

The hypothesis that there is or can quickly be an adequate convergence between individual and societal preferences on population limitations in India is, on the face of it, implausible. I readily agree with those observors who say it would be useful to know more about the relevant motivational patterns and that research in that area should proceed apace with technological research. But meanwhile the issue is much too vital to be left hanging on an amiable assumption. Whatever we have learned about the motivations of Indian families confirms, as far as I know, the common impression that the average Indian couple wants at least two surviving sons. This may be for ritual Hindu purposes or for what, from a Western, industrialized perspective, we would call old-age-and-survivors insurance.

As we have noted, even the interim goals of Indian population control leave room for an average of no more than three surviving children per married couple. It takes little technical competence in demography to recognize that it is going to be difficult (at least as long as sex determination remains infeasible) to get an average of no more than three children out of the self-interested behavior of a population desiring an average of two sons. The only safe course, I suspect, is to use financial incentives (positive or negative) to pull private preferences into line with public needs. In principle it should be possible to find a set of incentives that will induce couples to increase the spacing of their earlier children enough, or otherwise limit their total outturn sufficiently, to conform with social objectives.

Obviously the ultimate design of such a set of incentives would have to be the subject of extensive study. Some of the issues this study must consider are whether the incentives should incline toward the carrot or the stick (most who have discussed them have favored the former), what their scope should be, how they should be calibrated to family-planning performance, what forms the benefits should take, whether they should be immediate or deferred, and how the children of "overproducing" families should be shielded from the "disincentives" levied upon their parents. However, enough has already been done to explore some of these issues in India to suggest that administrable schemes probably can be contrived. As for their fiscal feasibility, there is no a priori reason to assume that a workable set of taxes and transfers could not be contrived. This is so if the purpose is important, if by its impact on income per capita the innovation itself over time could yield a significant development dividend, and if it is possible that it might take only a moderate scale of incentives to bring average private preferences into line with public needs. And the fiscal feasibility would be that much easier if, as seems likely, most of the benefits that the arrangement would provide could be of a deferred nature.

In my remarks about the political clouds that now hang over the family-planning program, I anticipated my final argument in favor of the incentives approach. The present population-control system, still largely faithful to the 1965 model, requires a massive administrative structure, preferably driven by top political leaders, constantly engaged in selling the family-planning product to a passive, if not reluctant, public. This may not be a viable political formula for the 1970s. It may be far more feasible for the central government, standing more nearly at arm's length from the administrative and clinical conduct of family planning in the states and districts of India, to introduce a set of financial incentives sufficiently powerful to induce tens of millions of couples to *pull* services from a variety of delivery points. This would include an efficient public clinical system as well as various private agencies, private practitioners, and commercial suppliers. My guess is that the government of India is going to have to rely heavily on the indirect, impersonal style of the incentives approach.

That an ex-AID Mission Director has written at some length on this subject without significantly referring to the role of foreign aid cannot, I suppose, escape notice. My allocation of space reveals my sense of priorities. I confess to the opinion that what foreign-aid donors can contribute to population control in India is usually overrated by the donors. Foreign exchange has not been and is unlikely to be a significant constraint on this problem. Technical assistance projects of the traditional kind have a very limited future. Flexible, sophisticated, multidisciplinary staffs in the field missions of donor agencies can be helpful to their Indian counterparts in the kind of rethinking I have been discussing. But now we are reducing our field missions generally.

It will remain appropriate for the major donors to take the liveliest interest in population policy as a vital dimension of the Indian development effort. But the government of India repeatedly has shown that it is not very receptive to donor "leverage" on its policy choices in this complex and sensitive field. And the mandate the U.S. Congress has given AID to press funds on the government of India whether it wants them or not can be positively counterproductive in its impact on Indian program management.

Population control is probably the most important development problem India faces. It is also about the farthest from being solved. But the solution, good or bad, will be over-whelmingly Indian.

References

1. "An Evaluation of the Family Planning Programme of the Government of India," Report of a United Nations Advisory Mission. Mimeograph. New York: United Nations, dated November 24, 1969, released January 28, 1970.
2. *The Fourth Five-Year Plan.* New Delhi: Government of India, 1970.

9

Changing Public Attitudes toward Population Growth in Japan

MINORU MURAMATSU

Dr. Minoru Muramatsu is Chief, Section of Demography, the Department of Public Health Demography, Institute of Public Health, Tokyo.

This brief presentation of the attitudes toward family planning of the general public in Japan centers particularly on the postwar years. Consideration is also given to certain efforts to support and strengthen the basic motivation toward the small family and the practice of family planning—both the official government programs and private, voluntary activities.

The decline in fertility after the war in Japan was precipitous indeed. According to the official statistics the number of live births per thousand was 34 in 1947. In 1957 the number was reduced to 17, a 50 per cent decrease in ten years. To compare these two years is probably not very fair, since the birth rates immediately after the war reflected abnormal demographic conditions (the so-called baby boom). However, if we take 1920 as a starting point, the year in which Japanese birth rates began to move down along with the modernization of society, we still note that the demographic transition was completed within a relatively short span of time, less than 40 years. This transition has usually taken a century or so in Western countries. Japan, then, is a latecomer in the demographic transition, but has gone through the entire process with unprecedented rapidity. (See Figure 1.)

Nowadays the general pattern of two or three children per family has become an established norm among Japanese

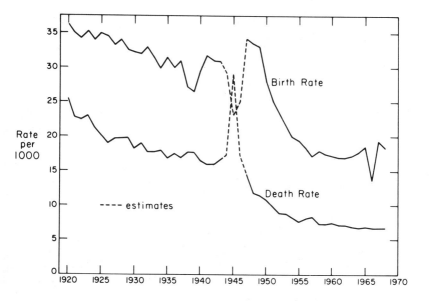

Figure 1. Birth and death rates, Japan, 1920–68. Source: (1).

couples. According to the Mainichi Newspapers' opinion surveys summarized in Table 1, a large majority of those couples with two children do not want to have any more, although a significant minority want one more child. (However, there has been a slight change in this connection in more recent years.) Also, of all the live births registered in 1966, as many as 85

Table 1. Number of additional children wanted,
couples with two children, Japan, 1950–67

	No more (*per cent*)	One more (*per cent*)	Two more (*per cent*)	More than two more (*per cent*)	No answer (*per cent*)
1950	29.8	32.8	19.2	6.9	11.3
1955	42.7	32.3	15.8	3.2	6.0
1959	57.7	25.5	7.2	1.4	8.2
1963	71.7	22.3	3.2	0.6	2.2
1965	70.5	23.5	2.4	0.4	3.2
1967	71.1	20.0	3.1	0.8	5.0

Source: (2).

per cent were the births of first or second children. The Ministry of Health and Welfare's 1964 nationwide survey on birth-control practice found that, of those couples who had ever practiced some form of contraception, more than 80 per cent had begun to do so after the arrival of their second child at the latest (3).

The two- or three-child family has now become almost universal throughout the country. There are differences in this family-size norm between urban and rural districts and between different educational and occupational classes, but the degree of such differences has markedly diminished. Today one seldom sees families with half a dozen children. In addition, the traditional desire to have at least one son seems to be disappearing steadily in favor of smaller families regardless of the sex distribution among the children.

Japan's postwar fertility decline obviously did not result from a "natural" change in the physiological capacity for reproduction. It certainly indicates that there have been wide-scale attempts to control fertility intentionally. Four factors are usually listed to explain this phenomenon: the advancement of the age at marriage, induced abortion, sterilization, and contraception.

The significance of the first of these four, the change in the age at marriage, was investigated by the Institute of Population Problems several years ago. Although there was a postponement of marriage by a little more than one year among Japanese women in the first postwar decade, its role in the over-all decrease in the birth rate was almost negligible (4). The other three factors, therefore, are of primary importance.

A considerable amount of academic interest and practical discussion have centered on roles played by each of the three factors in the decline of fertility in Japan. No unobjectionable conclusions can be drawn, however, because of the technical difficulties of assessment. At this point we can only assume that up until 1960 or so induced abortion was the most influential factor and that contraception has gradually gained dominance over induced abortion since that time.

In 1948 a bill now known as the Eugenic Protection Law was introduced in the Diet. It met no particular opposition and was passed the same year. The legal basis for the performance of abortion by specifically qualified medical practitioners under broadly interpreted conditions was thus established. Even today some doubt exists as to the real purpose of this liberalization of abortion laws. Opinions are divided on whether it was put forward mainly for population control or whether it was primarily a medical and public-health measure to minimize the harmful effects of criminal abortion. In all likelihood, both these considerations were included, but in any case the law was not intended to introduce a new method of fertility limitation to the public. Its intention was merely to provide a safer and easier channel to procure induced abortion, which was already being practiced fairly extensively.

In 1952 the national government, through its Ministry of Health and Welfare, launched a nationwide program for the promotion of family planning. The main goal was to bring about a change from induced abortion to contraception as a means of voluntarily regulating fertility. The whole network of the public-health system was brought into the operation of the program, and administrative responsibilities were allocated so that official agencies could, where appropriate, provide general education in family planning for the masses and technical instruction for individual couples. For personal instruction in the techniques of conception control, a large group of midwives were called upon. A few years later, another measure entitled the poor to receive instruction and contraceptives through the financial assistance of public agencies.

The essential point we should notice in relation to these government family-planning programs is that they were implemented to meet the people's needs and desires. A high motivation toward planned parenthood already existed at the grassroots level. The position of the government was to provide the ways and means for easier, more rational fulfillment of such basic motivation.

There has been considerable activity among a number of private organizations too. The Mainichi Newspapers Agency, for example, has long been interested in population and family planning and has conducted a series of opinion surveys on the subject. Its newspapers publicize new developments in the fields of population and contraceptive techniques, both in Japan and abroad. The Family-Planning Federation of Japan, a coordinating body of all the private family-planning organizations, has likewise done a great deal in general education.

In opinion surveys one group of publications repeatedly emerges as the most influential source of information on family planning and contraception. As shown in Table 2, all mass communications media have been important, especially among city dwellers, but by far the most important have been the women's magazines. Several major women's magazines with a combined circulation of a few millions repeatedly carry articles with detailed accounts of contraception, induced abortion, and sterilization. These accounts are often so detailed that one might think they were addressed to a professional medical audience. The contribution made by women's magazines has been undeniable, but the reason these publications put so much emphasis on this subject is that it increases sales. They are satisfying the demands of their audience. It was not the magazines

Table 2. Sources of information about contraception, Japan, 1965

	Close relatives (e.g., husband, parent) (per cent)	Friends (per cent)	Doctors, drugstores, health centers (per cent)	Public-health nurses, midwives (per cent)	Mass communications media (per cent)	Lecture meetings, women's meetings (per cent)
Large cities	17.7	10.0	19.6	10.8	37.2	4.6
Medium-sized cities	19.9	9.1	14.6	13.4	36.4	6.6
Small cities	14.9	7.2	16.0	16.3	33.0	12.4
Towns and villages	12.6	6.3	14.1	22.6	27.2	16.7

Source: (2, 1965 issue).

that created basic interest; it was the people's attitudes that influenced the selection of articles in the magazines.

Most crucial in the postwar development of family planning in Japan was the pre-existence of basic motivation toward the small family size, a motivation strong enough to induce couples to limit fertility, even though it could involve personal, psychological, or economic inconveniences. This leads us to pose a very fundamental question: Why were Japanese people so highly motivated and predisposed toward family planning even before the government's intervention?

There is no single answer to this question. It can be answered only by enumerating multiple contributing factors.

1. For generations the Japanese people have placed an exceptionally high value on education. The 1867 Meiji Restoration initiated a modern system of general education for the entire population. But even before this, education had been highly appreciated as a personal asset. Many small communities had established private institutions in which one tutor taught several pupils to read and write.

An immediate effect of education in relation to family planning is obvious: People can easily be informed of the subject through leaflets, pamphlets, magazines, and the like. But a more important effect of education is that it makes people more receptive to new ideas and practices. The Japanese people in general are characterized by their openness to innovation. Even peasants living in traditional villages are fairly quick to learn from the ways of their city friends. Universal education must have played a significant role in creating such eagerness to absorb new ideas and modern concepts.

2. The Japanese national character has historically displayed a quality of ready adaptability. The people have traditionally made changes easily whenever a changing environment has demanded it. In a sense the Japanese people are so practical and realistic that they sometimes go to the extreme of what they believe to be uncommendable conduct. For example, practical considerations will often outweigh reluctance toward induced abortion. For the wide acceptance the concept of family plan-

ning has received, this characteristic must have been quite an instrumental factor.

3. The average Japanese does not hold deep religious beliefs. One function of religion is to impose absolute norms on behavior. Being free from religious censure, an average Japanese may well feel he can make many moral decisions on his own. Widespread use of various methods of contraception and induced abortion in particular may seem more understandable given this aspect of Japanese character.

4. Perhaps a characteristic social conformity has also strengthened the family-planning movement. Once family planning found its place in the practices of a certain proportion of local inhabitants, then the idea spread quickly within that area. Once the pattern of the two- or three-child family had been accepted by the educated classes, then the same decision was easily followed by the rest of society. Admittedly, conformity is not unique to the Japanese, but the strength of its effect in Japan is worth mentioning.

5. In any discussion of birth control in postwar Japan, induced abortion is mentioned. As stated earlier, induced abortion was a significant factor in the reduction of births shortly after the war. But it was not a phenomenon that appeared suddenly at that time. A few centuries ago, Japanese peasants resorted to induced abortion during crises, such as crop failure or economic distress. Even infanticide is said to have been practiced. Harsh and drastic as it is, induced abortion has deep roots in the Japanese tradition.

6. The psychological effect of the defeat in the last war was tremendous. Among other things it caused a sharp drop in the standard of living for the general public. According to some statistics, the immediate postwar standard of living dropped to half the level of the prewar average. This sudden deterioration of living styles among people who had been striving all along to better their daily life was a shocking experience. In addition, Japanese couples witnessed with their own eyes the sharply contrasting affluence enjoyed by Americans stationed in Japan after the war. This gave them an unusually strong impetus first

to restore and then to further improve their living standards. Thus, many Japanese couples undoubtedly began a vigorous practice of birth control well before the organized family-planning campaigns urged them to do so.

7. Japan's land area is small. Population pressure certainly has maintained a psychological influence toward limiting fertility. However, the smallness of land area has also facilitated the rapid development of transportation and communication, which, in turn, has facilitated quick dissemination of information to people living in the most remote areas.

8. About a century ago the social class system preserved from ancient Japan was completely abolished. Since then the "revolution of rising expectations" has become reality. One hears countless stories of individuals born to a low social status who successfully climbed up the social ladder, once they had acquired a certain degree of education. A knowledge that doors to opportunity are open to anyone naturally encourages people toward more intensive planning for the future.

9. With the Diet's introduction of the Eugenic Protection Law in 1948 and the government's initiation of the family-planning program in 1952, the Japanese public recognized that the government not only provided technical help but also officially supported and encouraged family planning. Although the dignity or authority of the government was lessened in the minds of Japanese people after the war, the knowledge that birth control had official endorsement could have been of considerable significance in certain sectors.

The main theme of this paper so far has been the significance of a basic motivation toward the small family at the grass-roots level as a prerequisite to widespread acceptance of family planning. This theme has been related to the Japanese experience after the end of the war. About this point of view, there seems to be a consensus among Japanese scholars interested in population and family planning.

However, these observations do not necessarily mean that we give no credit at all to the specific family-planning programs carried out by the government and private organizations. On the contrary, a fair treatment of the subject requires a few words about the possible roles played by the family-planning programs.

What would the postwar birth rates have been in Japan if there had been no organized efforts to promote family planning? If we somehow find an answer to this question, we may be able to distinguish the contribution that the family-planning programs made apart from the declining trend in fertility already in motion.

No one can repeat past experience with some change in parts of its components, once it has taken place in a human history. The following analysis, therefore, should be regarded as representing only one kind of attempt, using theoretical reasoning as its basis.

On the basis of three-year moving averages of the recorded birth rates in Japan for the period 1921–37, the author made an effort to apply a logistic curve that would best fit the past course of events. Its graphic representation and the mathematic equation are given in Figure 2. The extrapolation of the curve beyond 1937 thus gives expected values of birth rates after that year if there had been neither the war nor the postwar family-planning programs.

Against this expected curve, the actually observed birth rates after the war were plotted, placing the actually observed 1950s value on 1939 of the logistic curve. The year 1950 could reasonably be regarded as the time by which postwar demographic abnormalities had been almost liquidated; also the birth-rate values for these two years coincided completely.

On this assumption, it is interesting to note that the actually registered birth rates come well below the expected trend for the period 1951–64. The difference is most pronounced for 1954, 1955, 1956, 1957, and 1958, the ratio of the observed rate to the expected being 0.80, 0.80, 0.78, 0.76, and 0.82 respectively. This observation agrees very well with our recollection that the government and private family-planning programs were generally at their height during these years.

In short, the hatched area in Figure 2 reflects, at least in part, the role played by the government and private family-planning movements. The psychological effects of the defeat in the war are also thought to be reflected here, but it is difficult to isolate them. In any event, it is safe to say that the govern-

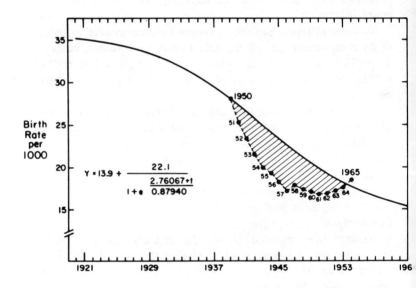

Figure 2. Actual versus expected crude birth rates, Japan, 1950–65. Source: (1).

ment and private organizations did exert considerable influence in further lowering the birth rates from what could have been anticipated as a "natural" downward trend and in accelerating the whole process of fertility decline if we accept the reasoning presented here. Even in the absence of organized efforts to promote family planning, however, the fertility of the Japanese people would have fallen to the same low level, but the number of years required for it to do so might have been greater—possibly ten years or so.

In addition to such quantitative speculation as the above, it is possible to make certain qualitative observations about methods of limiting fertility. If it had not been for the family-planning teaching campaigns, birth limitation probably would have been achieved by even more numerous induced abortions. Movements to urge the general population not to resort to abortion have, by and large, not been as successful as hoped, but it does not necessarily follow that they have borne no fruits at all.

In summary, the real basis of the postwar fertility decline in Japan was the aspiration, motivation, and action of the people themselves. Governmental and private family-planning programs were significant in that they supported, facilitated, and accelerated this enormous social transition in the history of Japan.

References

1. The Health and Welfare Statistics Association, *Trends in Nation's Health*. Tokyo, 1970.
2. The Population Problem Research Council, Public Opinion Surveys on Family Planning. Tokyo: The Mainichi Newspapers, 1950, 1955, 1959, 1963, 1965, 1967, 1969.
3. Government of Japan, Ministry of Health and Welfare, *Public Opinion Survey on Family Planning*. Tokyo, 1964.
4. S. Kono. "Effects of Age and Marital Status Composition upon the Decline in the Birth Rate," *Japan's Experience in Family Planning—Past and Present*. Tokyo: Family Planning Federation of Japan, 1967. Pp. 27–28.

10

The United Nations System and Population Problems

CHARLES F. GALLAGHER

Charles F. Gallagher is Director of Studies of the American Universities Field Staff and Consultant on International Programs, University of Hawaii.

United Nations activities in the field of population are complex and of long standing.* They have dealt with a wide spectrum of directly and indirectly related problems, and they have produced numerous useful detailed studies, statistical materials, and advanced methodological procedures. Yet, ironically, the United Nations and its extended family of specialized agencies, which were pioneers in drawing attention to world population problems, are considered by some observers to have proceeded at a disappointing pace and to be even now reluctant to assume their full responsibilities. At a time when United Nations agencies are still deciding exactly how far current mandates go with respect to policies and programs that might fulfill these responsibilities and what specific actions should be undertaken by which bodies, many outsiders are doubtful about the future of United Nations work.

It is the basic premise of this paper that United Nations in-

* This chapter on United Nations activities in the field of population is not intended to be a comprehensive survey of work by all agencies in the system. Nor is it a study of the work in the field at country or regional level. It is a commentary on the work and role of certain bodies within the system, and especially of those agencies in Europe with whose headquarters the writer is familiar.

278

volvement in population problems is by now broadly assured at the functioning level on a self-sustaining basis and that it is increasingly essential to deepen this involvement. If the record so far leaves something to be desired, the long-range prospects are as promising as they are crucial. It would appear that the longer the range, the more necessary will be some kind of international population body that holds as universal an authority as possible, at least of a moral nature, in this sensitive field.

Today we see a broad trend toward diverting into multilateral channels many activities that previously were handled bilaterally. Individual governments have problems in divorcing the more selfish from the more altruistic strains in their foreign policies—to the extent they can indeed be separated—and in allaying the suspicions of others about their attitudes and actions. These problems point to future emphasis on multilateral action, even if the underlying motivations for the shift are not always wholly idealistic. There are hopeful signs in the heightened concern to find a basic framework for development on an all-inclusive, global level, to restructure the relations between rich and poor countries, and to approach the world's ecological problems cooperatively. In population matters too—because of their intimate relationship with all these problems—only a collective will that is impelled from within the world self and guided by its common intelligence will be able to come to serious grips with the problem.

History of United Nations Activities

The United Nations has been engaged in the study of population problems almost from its inception, but it is convenient to divide the record of its activities into two periods: first, a long span of nearly twenty years during which work consisted almost entirely of studies, meetings, reports, and research; second, a span beginning in the mid-1960s during which policies became firmer and programs more active. This second phase culminated in the organizing of direct assistance to governments on a wide scale and marks what may be the beginnings of a third period in the 1970s.

The United Nations Population Commission, a standing body of the United Nations consisting of representatives of member governments, normally meets every two years to discuss population questions and has done so for over two decades. It reports to the Economic and Social Council (ECOSOC), which in turn reports to the General Assembly. As early as its third session in 1949, the Population Commission began to consider seriously what the role of the United Nations should be with respect to population-planning measures. This discussion showed a deep split between member countries favoring an active role for the organization and those opposing it on moral, religious, and other grounds. It was clear that the United Nations still had to adopt a cautious, neutral stance in regard to population policy. In consequence, a compromise resolution adopted during the same session stated that every country should have a population policy but omitted any reference to United Nations help in implementing any such policies. In the early years, occasional discussion by the General Assembly followed much the same lines; responsibility lay with the government concerned, and United Nations agencies should not try to persuade any country to adopt a family-planning program. Despite a considerable change in the general atmosphere recently, this principle is still maintained in theory.

Nevertheless, the United Nations began responding to requests for technical assistance in population questions at an early date. The first request came in 1953 from India, which asked for help in studying different methods of family planning at the village level and for assistance in surveying receptivity to such methods. Other requests in that decade came from Indonesia, Trinidad, and Egypt, among others. In addition, during the 1950s the United Nations established three regional demographic research and training centers in Bombay, Cairo, and Santiago, Chile, to provide advisory services to governments within their respective regions. These centers are held to have had a major influence on government policies in some cases; in

Chile notably, the fertility study carried out by the Santiago center led directly to the establishment by the Chilean government of a population commission to advise on family planning.

In these early years, however, most United Nations effort was concentrated in the field of demographic statistics. In 1953 the Population Division of the Department of Economic and Social Affairs published a first major comprehensive study called *Determinants and Consequences of Population Trends,* later revised and brought up to date. The *Demographic Yearbook* was inaugurated and has become an invaluable tool for standardized statistical information. In 1958 and again in 1963 the United Nations published detailed long-term projections of future population growth according to various assumptions, appending to these works manuals on the methodology of such projections and life tables for use in developing countries. If statistics are the cornerstone of effective policy-making, particularly in developing countries, these pioneer contributions, which appeared when most major political and moral forces in the world were still majestically unconcerned with the problem, should not now be undervalued. The focus of the first World Population Conference in Rome in 1954 was symbolic of the temper of those times. The meeting limited itself almost completely to exchanging information about the collection and coordination of demographic statistics and to discussions of statistical research methods.

By the time of the second World Population Conference in Belgrade in 1965 much had changed. Probably the most important new factor was an awareness of the severity of population growth. The statistical work of the United Nations had borne its first significant fruit, for this feeling arose as the result of censuses taken with United Nations help in many developing countries in 1960–61, particularly in India. Partly because of this, attendance at the Belgrade conference was almost double that of the Rome conference eleven years before, and eighty-eight countries were represented compared to seventy-four on the previous occasion. More striking was the emphasis on the demographic aspects of such matters as educational development, labor supply and employment, agricultural development and food supply, savings and investment policies, and technological development and industrialization. The representative of the Secretary General at the closing session subtly broke new ground while repeating well-worn phrases by noting that:

> The full measure of the success of the Conference will be what it adds over a period of years in the future, to the strength and impetus of efforts devoted to the collection of basic demographic data, the extension of research frontiers, and the development of action programmes to cope with population problems. (1)

Other developments immediately preceding this conference —a number in Asia, where population problems were most acutely felt and where a consensus for action first developed— were setting the stage for later changes in attitude. In 1962 the United Nations General Assembly had held the first debate in its history devoted entirely to population matters. At its conclusion a resolution was adopted inviting member states to formulate their own population policies and calling for an intensified program of international cooperation in the field. More specifically, it asked the Secretary General to conduct an inquiry among member states concerning the relationship between economic development and population growth and the problems faced by them as a result (2).

The Asian Population Conference in December 1963 went further and invited governments "to take account of the urgency of adopting a positive population policy related to their individual needs and to the general needs of the region." It called on the Economic Commission for Asia and the Far East (ECAFE) to extend the scope of its technical assistance to regional governments, including assistance to family-planning programs, and ECAFE endorsed this recommendation at its next session the following spring.

It is impossible to fix a precise date for the breakthrough toward the attitudes that marked the second period of United Nations work in population, but a debate in ECOSOC the summer of 1965 was certainly crucial. In the resolution that came out of it the United Nations was for the first time given a specific mandate to provide technical assistance, advisory services, and training for action programs at the request of governments desiring assistance (3). It was still agreed, however, that the United Nations and its specialized agencies would refrain from recommending or promoting any particular policies to governments. A technical-assistance mission of population experts already in the field in India under terms of the ECAFE resolution of March 1964 and operating according to a quite liberal interpretation of its mandate fortunately had its legitimacy confirmed by this ECOSOC resolution.

The period beginning in 1965 and covering the following three or four years has been described as one of "resolutions affirming, endorsing, remembering and—sometimes—reaffirming the commitment of one or other of the agencies in this area of activity" (4, pp. 21–22). This severe and not wholly unjustified judgment fails to allow, however, for the period of adjustment necessary before a concert of nations in which many were still reluctant could begin to move forward. A General Assembly resolution in 1966 called on all United Nations bodies and agencies "to assist, when requested, in further developing and strengthening national and regional facilities for training, research, information, and advisory services in the field of population" (5). This marked the first time that a body representing the great majority of mankind engaged itself even vaguely in a commitment toward population problems. Its historical and psychological importance should not be underestimated.

At the end of 1966 the Secretary General was given a Declaration on Population Growth and Human Dignity and Welfare signed by the heads of state of twelve countries, and one year later in December 1967 on the occasion of Human Rights Day, a formal Declaration on Population by World Leaders was presented to the United Nations signed by the heads of state or prime ministers of thirty countries.* Shortly after that, popula-

* The signatories are Australia, Barbados, Colombia, Denmark, the Dominican Republic, Finland, Ghana, India, Indonesia, Iran, Japan, Jordan, (South) Korea, Malaysia, Morocco, Nepal, the Netherlands,

tion problems and basic human rights were linked, and the concept that "parents have a basic human right to determine freely and responsibly the number and spacing of their children and a right to adequate education and information in this respect" was enunciated in the Proclamation of Teheran issued unanimously by the International Conference on Human Rights sponsored by the United Nations in May 1968 (7, p. 5). Essentially, the transition that took place in the critical years 1966–68 was that proponents of family-planning measures were no longer a small, bold minority on the international scene, and those who upheld the status quo were put in a defensive position.

Perhaps the most noteworthy outgrowth of the General Assembly resolution was the establishment in 1967 of the United Nations Trust Fund for Population Activities. Bulwarked by the General Assembly action of the preceding year, Secretary General U Thant struck a distinctively more activist tone at that time, pointing out that

> Now that certain inhibitions have finally been lost, it is for us to establish the needed programming machinery in order to help governments in preparing projects, including the establishment of *bold projects in family planning.* [Emphasis added.] (8, p. 41)

Nothing of such a forthright nature had ever been said before by a secretary general, and the trust fund was the first United Nations step into autonomous programming and project planning.

The programming machinery is currently being developed in two major ways. In the field, ten population program officers were appointed in January 1969 with a mission to assist countries in their respective regions in preparing practical projects for technical cooperation in population matters. These officers are normally attached to the offices of the United Nations Development Program (UNDP) throughout the world, in Africa, Asia, the Middle East, and Central and South America. It is

New Zealand, Norway, Pakistan, the Philippines, Singapore, Sweden, Thailand, Trinidad and Tobago, Tunisia, the United Arab Republic, the United Kingdom, the United States, and Yugoslavia. For the text of the declaration, see (6).

anticipated that additional officers will be recruited as necessary. At headquarters, an office for population programs and projects was created, with responsibility for supporting and coordinating these field activities and for programming for the future. The fund budget, originally set at $1 million in 1968, has provisionally risen to $15 million in 1970. Half this sum was pledged by the United States on the condition that eight other contributing countries collectively make an equal pledge and with the implied understanding that more money from United States sources will be channeled through the United Nations in future years if effective work is carried out.

As a corollary to these activities, the United Nations is planning to extend the services of the three already existing regional demographic centers mentioned earlier to include family-planning activities, to establish two additional centers of the same kind in Africa, and to increase the number of fellowships available for study at all of them. Last but not least is the plan to establish an international population institute (probably in the United Kingdom) to deal with the interdisciplinary components of research, training, and advice on family planning.

Recent Developments in the Specialized Agencies

While the gradual evolution described above was getting under way in the United Nations parent organization, a similar intensification of attention to population questions was taking place in several of the specialized agencies. In some it may even have preceded general United Nations concern; in others it still lags behind. To understand why this is so, it is necessary to keep in mind the structure and primary concerns of the agencies, as well as their relationship with each other and with the United Nations as a whole.

The specialized agencies are autonomous bodies, each one having its own constitution, membership, and budget; they are not subject to direct control from United Nations headquarters as such. Moreover, each has developed its own style of action, partly determined by its interaction with its constituent membership and partly self-generated or shaped by the personality of its particular leadership and bureaucracy. Each has its own vast, accumulated body of expertise, its own rationale, its own self-justification, and its own view of its particular problems. An agency like the International Labor Organization (ILO), founded in 1919, long antedates the United Nations itself and shows a noticeably strong esprit de corps that often makes it unusually independent in approach and action. The importance of leadership is shown in the many early warnings given in the 1950s by Director-General Sen of the Food and Agricultural Organization (FAO), and to an equal degree somewhat later by Director-General David Morse of ILO and Director-General Rene Maheu of the United Nations Educational, Scientific, and Cultural Organization (UNESCO). The importance of politics here as in any organization is indicated by the recurrent rumors, which seem quite unfounded, that the successor to the head of FAO for a time deliberately downplayed population problems because his predecessor had so strongly insisted on their urgency. At any rate, through the very nature of its activities FAO was probably the first international organization to recognize and state clearly the dangers of population growth in the period before the Green Revolution of the 1960s, which gave a breathing spell in the battle against hunger.

For all their autonomy and their, at times, strong leadership, which might like to force the pace, the specialized agencies are by no means free agents. They are members of the United Nations family, and it is difficult to be too far out of step with their associates. They are also subject to supervision by their own national constituent members, many of which were for years as reluctant to move into active population work as were their counterparts at the General Assembly.

Thus the ECOSOC and General Assembly breakthroughs in 1965 and 1966 may be said to have stimulated and to have been simultaneously paralleled by resolutions adopted by several of the specialized agencies at about the same time. These in turn have gradually led to a more direct involvement in population matters by the agencies. Although that involvement is not exactly overwhelming, there are some noteworthy constants running through recent activities in almost all agencies of the United Nations system: a greater emphasis placed on action programs at regional and country levels as opposed to discussions at headquarters level; more weight given to projects and programs in technical cooperation; an attempt to limit research and technical proposals to those that can serve as practical tools for policy-making or for supporting field activities; and a tendency for separate agencies to converge upon similar policy objectives from different, but often complementary, angles of approach.

Food and Agricultural Organization

This agency has recently concentrated on policy-oriented research regarding the implications of population growth for not only agricultural development and its concomitants but also on rural employment and rural levels of living (9). Its work on the interrelationships of rapid population growth, agricultural productivity, and distribution of the labor force between agriculture and other occupations is felt by ILO officials to harmonize neatly with some of their own studies in employment and training prospects in developing countries. In addition to this kind of research work, FAO initiated field activities in 1968–69 for its Planning for Better Family Living Program with orientation seminars for regional officials and a pilot training course for women community leaders in Ceylon. In these courses, which touch on fields of interest to the World Health Organization (WHO) and UNESCO, the full cycle of family life is examined as a unit: planning for children; the cost of their education; the amount, kind, and cost of food needed during their childhood and growth; the expense for the mother in economic and energy terms as well as to her general health; and the effects of population growth in national socio-economic development. The overall purpose of the program in FAO words is "to develop a process whereby a nation can provide for all its people the opportunity to acquire the knowledge, skills, and attitudes that will enable them to make sound decisions with regard to all aspects of family life, including marriage, parenthood, and family size" (10, 11). The next pilot projects in the program are to be undertaken in 1970–71 in four countries in East Africa.

International Labor Organization

Despite the positive attitude of ILO leadership at the highest level, the agency was not empowered to put a specific emphasis on population questions until the resolution adopted in June 1967 by its International Labor Conference (12). The activities of ILO are highly specialized, and since then the agency has mainly been "grafting" population work and studies onto already established programs and areas of competence. This is done with special regard to (a) introducing family-planning information into workers' education, labor-welfare, and cooperative programs; (b) doing policy-oriented research on the demographic aspects of social-security schemes; and (c) integrating family-planning activities into health and medical programs for workers at the job site.

The targets are both employers and employees: the former are often more receptive than might be thought. The principal means are educational seminars, trade-union information conferences, and on-the-spot advisory services. Trial projects, under which family-planning counseling has been provided by factory-level health services, have already been carried out in Indonesia and Thailand and are planned for Taiwan and South Korea. In research terms the major ongoing contribution of ILO is the manpower studies for the World Employment Program, an integrated project designed to provide projections of labor-force statistics for over-all social development planning on a national, regional, and global basis. The agency appears to believe it must concentrate on its areas of specialization, in which it claims to be years ahead of any other organization, while steadily expanding whatever activities will contribute to slowing the rate of population growth in developing countries through the various devices outlined earlier. Where it cannot directly support family-planning activities, in those countries that have not adopted national programs, it seeks to stimulate informally an

awareness among planners, employers, and trade-union leaders
in particular, of the serious obstacles placed by rapid population
growth in the path of developmental goals such as raising real
wages and insuring social security.

United Nations Educational, Scientific, and Cultural Organization

The executive board of UNESCO gave mandates to the
organization in November 1967, and the general conference
reinforced them in the autumn of 1968. However, UNESCO
activity has been lagging behind that of several other agencies
—both in content and in elan (13). A coordinated program
within which UNESCO was held to be competent to act, according to its general conference resolution of November 1968,
included the fields of education (developing teaching materials
and curricula; working in adult, women's, and community education: and studying the possibility of including family-planning
materials in experimental literacy programs); the social sciences
(studying the complexity of family planning in the context of
different cultures); and communications (studying ways for
the establishment and operation of efficient programs and providing relevant information and documentation).

The preliminary and rather abstract nature of this commitment has been matched by the scanty results so far attained. Of
the studies reported in 1968–69, all five were still in process at
last report and were being discussed in the future tense. The
work of UNESCO in projecting such things as school enroll-
ments and teacher-recruitment problems and costs is certainly
useful and has a meaningful parallel relationship to ILO labor-
force projections, FAO urban-rural migration data, and the like;
taken in conjunction with these kinds of studies by sister agencies, it is among the most important of the activities now engaged in by UNESCO.

In practical terms, advisory missions were sent to Tunisia in
late 1968 for consultation on its national family-planning program and to Indonesia in 1969 as part of a mission for assistance
in educational development with reference to population ques-

tions. Of possible future interest are consultations with countries that have asked for advisory missions, especially with respect to including family-planning counseling in functional literacy projects. But all in all, the UNESCO record of action to date is meager. Even granting that the nature of UNESCO and its basic interests are such that it may never be able to play a primary role in population studies and work at the functional level, it appears that a considerable sharpening of its efforts will be required if it is to keep up with the progress registered by some other agencies.

United Nations Children's Fund (UNICEF)

The executive board of UNICEF approved assistance in family-planning programs as part of maternal and child health services for the first time also in 1967 (14). This agency works closely with WHO (see following section), and this decision was the result of recommendations made by the UNICEF-WHO Joint Committee on Health Policy. Somewhat like WHO, UNICEF moved gingerly into the population field while stressing, more strongly than did some of its colleagues like FAO and ILO, its nonadvocacy of any specific way of handling population-control programs. Nonetheless, in the past two years more than $3 million has been allotted for maternal and child health (MCH) assistance projects that encompass family-planning aspects in which UNICEF has given technical advice and training in the use of contraceptives and supplied transport and other auxiliary services, although it has not yet given contraceptives directly. The countries assisted so far are India, Pakistan, Singapore, Thailand, and the United Arab Republic, and the potential for expanding UNICEF services seems good.

The agency claims that its allocations for family planning within its MCH service programs understate its over-all impact because all MCH programs contribute indirectly to increasing understanding of childbearing and child-care problems. It further points out that in 1968 the family-planning aspects of MCH services were increased in countries like Pakistan and Indonesia and that for the first time requests for such integrated programs were now coming from a number of countries that previously had no official policies on family planning, including such Latin American nations as Jamaica, Trinidad, and Barbados. In sum, the impression given at UNICEF is one of slowly gathering momentum and a more positive attitude compared to the situation three years ago. To what extent this represents a new concern with the quality of children's lives instead of its previous concentration on preventive health measures in conjunction with WHO is a question that needs further observation.

World Health Organization

Along with the four agencies already discussed, WHO is the fifth member on a permanent basis of the Working Group on Population, a subcommittee of the Administrative Committee on Coordination (ACC), which groups together these five agencies, the International Bank for Reconstruction and Development (IBRD), UNDP, and the other divisions of the United Nations concerned with population questions. It is also one of the most autonomous of the specialized agencies, probably the most prestigious and the most ponderously conservative, and certainly the one about which the greatest amount of controversy has revolved with respect to its role in the field of population studies. The quality and quantity of the work it has done in a number of specialized subfields—including basic statistical work on morbidity and mortality figures; the biological, clinical, and epidemiological aspects of reproduction; and various areas of public health—are widely appreciated. The amount of data at least indirectly related to population problems turned out by it far exceeds that of any other specialized agency (15). Yet, as the National Policy Panel of the United Nations Association of the United States on World Population has pointed out:

> WHO is an organization which has massive prestige and commands almost universal respect, especially for its work in malaria and smallpox eradication. However, the organization has not taken the lead in family planning as it has in other fields. (4, p. 45)

This forthright criticism—which some credit as having done much to spur greater WHO involvement—has been seconded by and partly explained in a statement of the Special Assistant to the United States Secretary of State for Population Matters:

> Surprisingly, very few medical people have any formal training in the physiology of human reproduction, birth control practices, or the relation of population growth to economic and social growth. These things simply were not part of the curriculum when all but a few of the most recent graduates went to college and medical school. It may not be surprising, therefore, that when two years ago the World Health Organization approved the provision of requested advice on family planning it included the provision that such services should not interfere with the regular duties of WHO to provide help in preventive and curative medicine. (8, p. 216)

Clearly the weighty mechanism of WHO is moving today, but it is still true that its disclaimers about endorsement or promotion of "any particular population policy" are more strictly laid down than with any of the other agencies considered here. Balanced against this is the gradual shift in attitude reflected in the successive resolutions of the World Health Assembly (all entitled Health Aspects of Population Dynamics) in 1967, 1968, and 1969. In the first one, no mention is made of family planning and the emphasis is put on the threat to public health stemming from "abortions and the high maternal and child mortality rates . . . in many countries" (16). In the 1968 resolution, the phrase "the health aspects of human reproduction" was changed to "the health aspects of human reproduction, of family planning, and of population dynamics." Also new in the 1968 resolution was "the concept that this programme requires the consideration of economic, social, cultural, psychological and health factors in their proper perspective . . ." (17).

Finally, in the 1969 resolution the wording evolved into "emphasizing the primary importance of social and economic factors for the solution of these problems [i.e., human reproduction, family planning, and population dynamics]" (18). On two other occasions in the same document, the qualifying phrase "including family planning" had been added to a description of health needs and health services.

Although these promising changes in key phrases are only verbal commitments, they nevertheless reflect the change slowly but surely taking place at WHO, which is for the first time joining its confreres at FAO and ILO in looking at the gamut of population problems within a framework of total societal development. Programs to advise member governments on sterility problems are being carried out—in Gabon and the Central African Republic, for example—but the amount of work that is beginning to incorporate family-planning components into ongoing national health services and MCH services far outweighs that kind of activity and has increased rapidly in the past two years.

So far, WHO has tentatively identified forty-two countries where existing WHO projects are considered appropriate for including family-planning components. Apart from extending its services in this direction and meeting additional requests from other countries, the agency expects to concentrate on health statistics projections for the coming five years, and on short-term training programs for public-health physicians, nurses, midwives, and auxiliaries. Perhaps the best testimony to the new spirit abroad at WHO is the statement in the 1969 resolution that family planning and population dynamics are now to be "considered as a normal part of in-service training programmes."

International Bank for Reconstruction and Development

A word should also be said about the important but anomalous position in the population field occupied by IBRD, or the World Bank (19). The bank became active only in 1968, when Robert McNamara became president. In his first meeting with the board of governors in September 1968 McNamara proposed that emphasis be put on three fields of action, which were essentially (a) gathering information regarding the developmental consequences of rapid population growth, (b) financing family-planning programs, and (c) collaborating on research with other organizations on family-planning methods and population-control programs at the national level. In November 1968 a department for population projects was established to carry out the second of these areas of action. In 1969 the president's speech at the annual meeting of the World Bank and the International Monetary Fund, timed to coincide with the release of the so-called Pearson Report (20) on economic development strategy, was a remarkably forthright sociological address devoted to the long-range problems of population and poverty; and its candor caused some stir among the assembled bankers of the world.

As with other United Nations agencies, limitations of staff and recruiting difficulties have limited IBRD activities so far. A technical mission has been sent to Jamaica, but no projects in family planning have yet been financed separately by the bank. Preparations are going forward in four countries, however, and joint arrangements with WHO have been made for missions in six others. What is noteworthy at the bank today is the clear priority that has been given to population concerns and the feeling of urgency and dynamism engendered there in a relatively short time. The drawback is that the World Bank, almost alone of all United Nations organizations, is regarded with suspicion by many developing countries as a kind of disguised rich countries' club. The very commitment of McNamara himself is likewise viewed with some restraint by a number of public officials from nations in the developing world where his connections with the Pentagon and the war in Vietnam—despite what are known to be the subtleties of his personal position—cause him to be still much mistrusted at bottom by public opinion. In the IBRD one sees the paradox that the agency perhaps best suited to provide new leadership in population problems is at the same time the one facing the greatest psychological obstacles in proving its sincerity and disinterestedness in pursuing these new directions.

Conclusions

In turning to a consideration of various recommendations for future action by the United Nations and possible changes within the system, significant differences in point of view can be seen in the proposals advanced by outside critics and those put forward by workers within the framework of the organization.

Outside observers have centered their critiques on four main areas in which they feel restructuring and upgrading is desirable. The first involves setting up a strongly centralized control post for population activities in the form of a population commissioner's office to be located within the United Nations Development Program (UNDP; 4, pp. 29–36). The population commissioner, as envisaged, would have the main role in planning all United Nations assistance to the population programs of member governments, would be in charge of the population trust fund, and would serve as the principal representative of the United Nations in intergovernmental gatherings dealing with population policies and programs, thus allowing the United Nations to speak with one voice.

The second area has to do with strengthening UNDP itself, by integrating its activities in technical assistance and general development programs with specific work in population matters. This recommendation, made by, among others, the United Nations Association of the United States National Policy Panel, confirms the sharp criticism addressed recently to the United Nations generally and to the UNDP specifically by Sir Robert Jackson in his report on United Nations work in development as seen over the past twenty-five years (21).

A third area concerns the population trust fund, which, under the kind of leadership envisioned above, should have its financing increased as quickly as possible to a minimum of $100 million by 1972, a sum viewed by most observers as impracticable. The fourth and final area concerns problems of coordinating the various activities of United Nations agencies, and it has been suggested that the population trust fund would be in a

position to streamline the present state of intrasystem cooperation and division of labor.

In contrast, discussions of the future among United Nations
officials, to the extent that they are publicly revealed, have
tended to back away from the concept of an over-all population
commissioner. The most recent major statements by the Secretary General and the Director of the Population Division down-
grade centralization and stress a "coordinated and integrated
approach" in which "greater emphasis should be placed on
action programmes at the regional and country level" (7, p. 7).
The Director of the Population Division for his part has emphasized the importance of the role played by the subcommittee
on population of ACC composed of the several United Nations
agencies working on population. Nonetheless, at the meeting
of the United Nations Population Commission in Geneva in
November 1969, some of the delegates most active in the field
criticized the complications of ACC coordination procedures.

My own view, based on conversations with some of the ACC
members and a degree of personal familiarity with the workings
of the group, is that its membership, small in numbers and
made up of experts well known to each other, is a potentially
useful catalyst for more active coordination, but that the principal problem lies in translating its joint decisions to the upper-
to-medium level of the bureaucracy in each cooperating agency,
a level made up largely of specialists who in some cases prefer
to go their own way.

Most ACC members profess no opposition to setting up an
office of population commissioner, but also show little real
enthusiasm for such a move. Their ambivalent feelings appear
to be rooted not so much in bureaucratic resistance and inertia
as in a genuine understanding that this step by itself would not
solve the complex problems of interagency coordination.

Whether or not such an office is soon established, the pressures of history appear to be moving toward linking population
problems with development in general. For example, FAO has
already shifted its focus from population-hunger to population-
development. More recently WHO, as noted earlier, has broad-

ened its view as well. As other agencies fall into line, the kind and degree of cooperation required in this over-all framework will inevitably grow and be reflected in the work of a body like the ACC, as to a large extent it already is.

This cursory survey of United Nations activities in the field of population has been held generally to the operational level rather than the philosophical or ethical side of the question. On philosophy there is certainly enough evidence available to show that a sustained and serious effort is now in the process of being shaped by the United Nations, and one need not pursue that point here. Ethics should on no account be neglected if one wishes to capture the imagination of mankind; therefore, a few words in summary might be in order.

The United Nations stands today, twenty-five years after its formation, on the threshold of an unprecedented opportunity with respect to population. The breadth and depth of its many kinds of expertise can, under the proper direction, be harnessed into the over-all work on development that is getting under way at the beginning of the Second Development Decade and for which groundwork was laid in the first difficult, but nonetheless pioneer, sessions of the United Nations Commission on Trade and Development (UNCTAD). A true *prise de conscience* has taken place in the most recent years, and the growing move to incorporate population work and studies into current and projected development programming is perhaps the key step. It is hard to foresee how population programs can independently acquire a sufficient momentum to be viable on a sustained basis in all societies; but if one regards development or modernization as an unceasing process of improving the quality of life, then population planning, to the extent that it is successfully integrated in that process, will hopefully become as routine in operation as the other concomitants of development—health and welfare measures, education, labor, and the like (22). This eventual "de-politicalization" of population problems within a universalized development program would appear to be the only way to achieve the necessary sustained tension. In the end such a program can be carried out only by the United Nations, which today successfully manages without fanfare the few existing examples of nonpolitical, standardized, cooperative internationalism in the fields of postal communications, weather watches, international health standards, and certain international legal conventions.

In considering the over-all role of the United Nations in population questions in the 1970s, three points of importance stand out. The first of these interrelated issues is that a clear national will to implement population policies must exist within a given society and spring from internal sources. To the extent that this will is evident, or even latent, the United Nations may be best placed to nurture and encourage it as it emerges and grows, both by setting up a broad technical infrastructure and by purveying information and specialized services to governments, especially in the case of smaller countries where they are not available, or in larger countries like India, in counseling, evaluating, and generally acting as an amicus curae.

The second point concerns the currently sharp division in the attitudes, expectations, and interaction between "donor countries" and "recipient governments." United Nations work in this domain might well help blur the unhealthy division now often made between "us" and "them," by bringing together the "advanced" practitioners and the more recent learners and by encouraging cross-learning and cross-teaching among recipients, especially on a regional, shared-information basis.

The third major fact is the increasingly general realization that outsiders cannot themselves induce a society to examine its population problems in cold candor and take remedial action. Here, too, the United Nations at its best can perhaps provide a psychological booster that no single government or group of governments can give by suggesting that "outsiders" are "insiders" as well and that we are all together in the same boat, facing continuing population problems regardless of the level of development or the population measures already taken in the "advanced" countries, as part of the movement toward the ever receding frontier of modernization.

The term "United Nations" stands for a collective "we." The

strong desire to make it universally representative underlines our feelings of innerness in this respect, and the organization stands, with all its recognized defects, as the most ambitious effort this "we" has yet made to organize ourselves—first our political conduct, then our economic activities, and now, hesitantly for the first time, some of our more sensitive patterns of social behavior in human rights, racial equality, the use of narcotics, the position of women and children, and many other areas. If it turns out that the United Nations is finally unable to handle urgent population issues as part of this ever expanding effort at organization, it will not be the fault of that body. It will simply mean that "we" have shown ourselves not to be really serious about the problem.

References

1. Second United Nations World Population Conference, Belgrade. "Summary Report." Vol. I. New York, 1966. P. 318.
2. General Assembly Resolution 1838 (XVII). *Official Records of the General Assembly,* Seventeenth Session, Annexes (Agenda Item 38).
3. Economic and Social Council Resolution 1084 (XXXIX).
4. United Nations Association of the United States of America, "World Population: A Challenge to the United Nations and Its System of Agencies." May 1969.
5. General Assembly Resolution 2211 (XXI). *Official Records of the General Assembly,* Twenty-first Session, Supplement No. 16. December 7, 1966.
6. United Nations, *Population Newsletter,* No. 1 (April 1968).
7. United Nations Population Commission, Fifteenth Session, November 1969. *Report on the Progress of Work* (Report of the Secretary General). E/CN. 9/230.
8. Development Centre of the Organisation for Economic Co-operation and Development. *Population: International Assistance and Research.* Paris, 1969.
9. K. C. Abercrombie. "Population Growth and Agricultural Development," Food and Agriculture Organization of the United

Nations. Economics Department *Monthly Bulletin of Agricultural Economics and Statistics,* Vol. 18, No. 4 (April 1969), 1–9.

10. Food and Agricultural Organization Nutrition Division, "Planning for Better Family Living," NU:Misc/69/28. Rome: November 1969.

11. United Nations Population Commission, Fifteenth Session, November 1969. *Five-Year and Two-Year Programmes of Work: Activities and Programmes of the Food and Agricultural Organisation of the United Nations in the Field of Population and Closely Related Fields.* E/CN. 9/234/Add. 1.

12. United Nations Population Commission, Fifteenth Session, November 1969. *Five-Year and Two-Year Programmes of Work in the Field of Population: Activities and Programmes of the International Labour Organisation in the Field of Population and Closely Related Fields.* E/CN. 9/234/Add. 5.

13. United Nations Population Commission, Fifteenth Session, November 1969. *Five-Year and Two-Year Programmes of Work: Activities and Programmes of the United Nations Educational, Scientific and Cultural Organisation in the Field of Population and Closely Related Fields.* E/CN. 9/234/Add. 2.

14. United Nations Population Commission, Fifteenth Session, November 1969. *Five-Year and Two-Year Programmes of Work in the Field of Population: Activities and Programmes of the United Nations Children's Fund in the Field of Population and Closely Related Fields.* E/CN. 9/234/Add. 4.

15. United Nations Population Commission, Fifteenth Session, November 1969. *Five-Year and Two-Year Programmes of Work in the Field of Population: Activities and Programmes of the World Health Organisation in the Field of Population and Closely Related Fields.* E/CN. 9/234/Add. 6.

16. Resolution of the World Health Assembly, WHA 20.41. May 25, 1967.

17. Resolution of the World Health Assembly, WHA 2143. May 23, 1968.

18. Resolution of the World Health Assembly, WHA 22.32. July 23, 1969.

19. United Nations Population Commission, Fifteenth Session, November 1969. *Five-Year and Two-Year Programmes of the International Bank for Reconstruction and Development in the*

Field of Population and Closely Related Fields. E/CN. 9/234/ Add. 3.

20. Commission on International Development, Lester B. Pearson, Chairman. *Partners in Development.* New York: Frederick A. Praeger, Inc. 1969.

21. Sir Robert Jackson. "A Study of the Capacity of the United Nations Development System." Vols. I, II, DP/5. E.70.I.10. United Nations: New York, 1970.

22. Charles F. Gallagher. *Lessons from the Modernization of Japan, Part I: The Role of Ideology.* Fieldstaff Reports, East Asia Series, Vol. XV, No. 2. January 1968.

Discussion of Mr. Gallagher's Paper

D E N N I S O N R U S I N O W

Dennison Rusinow is an Associate of the American Universities Field Staff, Hanover, New Hampshire.

As a nonspecialist only recently involved in population research, it has struck me that among the contributors to this study—a very impressive "in" group in the field of population concerns—are perhaps too many preachers preaching to other preachers and other converted, reaffirming the magnitude and the urgency of population problems. Perhaps I have been living too long in the socialist countries of eastern Europe, but it seemed to me that it was only when we got down to the Leninist question "What is to be done?" that we arrived at the crux of what a population conference ought to be about. And so we arrived at Mr. Gallagher's very succinct and admirable summary and critique of the role of the United Nations and its specialized agencies in this field. Despite all the qualifications carefully inserted into that paper, I think this was still one of the most optimistic views presented here.

Two messages seem to me to emerge from this paper. The first is that the role of the United Nations and its specialized agencies, so far and relatively, is not to be disdained and is developing somewhat more rapidly than the pessimistic authors in this volume would have led us to expect. The second— implicit if not explicit in the paper—is that if the United Nations and its agencies did not exist in this field and to this end, we would have to invent them. It seems to me that the role of the international agency becomes so important precisely because of a dilemma or a contradiction, which has emerged over and over again in several papers and in the course of discussion. The parameters of this dilemma or contradiction are the following.

First, for a variety of reasons that we have heard a good deal about, technical innovations in fertility-control techniques—and, hence, the initial push for their wider use—must come largely from the technologically advanced countries in general and from the United States in particular. At the same time the developed countries in general and the United States in particular are in fact politically inopportune agents for the propagation of these techniques and for arguments concerning the urgency of the problem. The motives of the United States are frequently and understandably suspect. Therefore, an international agency would be more opportune and a world agency the most opportune to work in this field.

I am somewhat familiar with Yugoslavia—a case in point here. As the Communist rulers of a socialist country with special pretensions in the nonaligned world, Yugoslav leaders obviously cannot appear as accomplices in a conspiracy of the "haves" to keep the "have-nots" in their place, demographically or otherwise. But they could appear, and did, as hosts to that 1965 World Population Conference and, significantly, as the only Communist signatory among the thirty who signed that December 1967 declaration on population presented to the United Nations.

How capable are the United Nations and its specialized organizations? Why are they not more so? Mr. Gallagher referred several times to criticisms of U.N. agencies in general and of WHO in particular, many of which he found justified. The validity and the rationale of these criticisms are really based on an assumption that Mr. Gallagher made in his introduction —the disappointing pace of the United Nations and its reluctance to assume its full responsibilities in this field. What full responsibilities? Defined by whom? Delegated by whom and why and to what end? Now, Mr. Gallagher later in his paper makes clear that this has never been made clear and that this is part of the problem. Why? Because in a sensitive area no consensus has emerged for a concert of nations with its reluctant hangers-back; therefore, international agencies have to go slowly and respond only to national needs and requests that have already been articulated. This may be the reason for the significant emphasis in the paper on the role of individual personalities in making one U.N. agency rather than another particularly activist in this field. This is presumably the reason he suggests that the World Bank is the agency perhaps best suited to provide new leadership in population problems. In the light of the emphasis in this volume on population control as an aspect of public health and preventive medicine, it would seem to me that WHO should be the agency best suited to provide leadership in population problems, and I would like to hear more about WHO and its role and ambivalences.

Mr. Gallagher speaks, finally and with justified optimism, of the evolution of United Nations' attitudes and functions since 1965 and the turning point in that year. But he goes on to look forward to "eventual 'de-politicalization' of population problems within a universalized development program [as] the only way to achieve the necessary sustained tension." Now, do we really believe that "de-politicalization" is achievable? In addition to the problems of arousing awareness and concern, of building a consensus about the need to act in this field—in the face of social, cultural, and religious obstacles—we also face, particularly in terms of international action, what seem almost intractable political obstacles at the international level. Is it feasible to "de-politicize" this kind of a problem? Berelson's paper noted that Rumania recently reversed its abortion policy, in alarm at its rapid approach to zero population growth. Are there any reasons other than "tribal" for this particular policy reversal? I do not know and have not heard of any others. That Latin island in a Slavic sea on a nationalist binge—thumbing its collective nose at the Russians in particular—simply got worried about being flooded by the rising tide of ethnic neighbors with higher birth rates.

How do we get around, if we cannot go through, this particular kind of problem? Are the United Nations and its specialized agencies to play a Fabian or a revolutionary role for us in this field? Are they to be merely responsive, supporting the general will as it emerges, or provocative in the formation of that will?

And is the latter socially possible? I have had the impression from the more pessimistic papers that it may not be possible and that the most that any population program or any institution concerned with population problems can do is to play a modestly active but basically responsive role, quickening the movement in the right direction when a will has already developed to move in that direction.

This is all part of the question: "What is to be done?"

11

Population Planning
and Belief Systems:
The Catholic Church
in Latin America

THOMAS G. SANDERS

Thomas G. Sanders is an Associate of the American Universities Field Staff, Rio de Janeiro.

It is commonly believed in the United States that the principal obstacle to family planning in Latin America is the Roman Catholic Church. In part this opinion stems from the Church's official position, which in the form of Pope Paul VI's encyclical *Humanae Vitae* (1) was opposed to the most effective methods of contraception; and in part from the assumption that the Latin American branch of the Church is the world's most docile, characterized by intellectual backwardness, social conservatism, and manipulation of the populace. Observers have drawn a simple causal line between Latin America's rate of population increase, the highest of any of the world's regions, and the overwhelming adherence of its population to the Catholic faith.*

To those really acquainted with family planning in Latin America, however, the charge against the Church appears in practice to be grossly exaggerated. The Catholic position is

---

* The chief explanation of Latin America's high rate of population increase is its absorption of medical and sanitary advances that have reduced mortality rates while high natality rates continued. This reflects the region's status as the most developed part of the less developed world.

certainly a cultural factor that must be taken into consideration, but any serious analysis becomes an explanation of why the Church is not as formidable an impediment as it appears on the surface. Such an enterprise is not intended for apologetic reasons, but rather to clarify what are the real problems in Latin American family planning and what are not. Understanding Catholicism as a set of values and the Catholic Church as an institution are indispensable for understanding Latin America, but both are too complex to blame or praise facilely for a similarly complex phenomenon like the status of family planning.

One approach to this question will involve an analysis of several levels of Catholic thought and action, beginning at the top with the papal *magisterium* (teaching) and proceeding through the bishops, theologians, and priests to the laity. It should be clear from this confrontation with the ideology or theology of normative Catholicism that the Church, despite a certain unity of thought, allows for extensive diversity in the practices of its faithful. A second approach will focus on "popular" Catholicism. We are still at too early a stage in empirical studies to provide a complete sociological interpretation of Latin American Catholicism, but we should not assume that religious institutions, any more than other institutions, can be interpreted only by examining their ideals or ideology. We must try to understand, insofar as possible, how Latin Americans as individuals subject to a variety of cultural pressures really think and practice their Catholicism.

Normative Catholicism

Papal Teaching

The chief source of the image of the Catholic position on family planning comes from the highest teaching authority of the Church; it is the widely publicized encyclical of Pope Paul VI *Humanae Vitae*. In the controversy over its position on contraception, three aspects of the encyclical were obscured, each of which we should examine dispassionately: its authority, its central themes, and the background of its position on contraception.

1. Although educated people know that the Pope can speak infallibly on faith and morals, they usually do not understand the difference between infallible and ordinary teaching. If we take seriously the restricted conditions for infallibility defined by the First Vatican Council (1870), only one statement in this century (in 1950, on the Assumption of the Virgin Mary) is acknowledged by theologians to be unquestionably infallible. Ordinary papal teaching like that in *Humanae Vitae* is *authoritative* for Catholics in the sense that they should seriously examine it, respect it as the voice of the Church's supreme pastor, and conform their behavior to it. Certain circumstances, nevertheless, may lead individual Catholics to demur from the official teaching—when, for example, major thinkers within the Church hold a different opinion or when they themselves after a conscientious evaluation of their convictions and circumstances arrive at a contrary view. Whereas the faithful Catholic will usually find his moral outlook in harmony with the teaching of the Church, classic theology always recognized the existence of situations of genuine doubt and divergent conviction—in which case, one's individual conscience is the final authority, even though it contradicts the position of the Church.

2. Although its condemnation of artificial methods of contraception received the principal attention, *Humanae Vitae* had as its central message the exposition of two themes, conjugal love and responsible parenthood. Although these themes may seem obvious dimensions of an appropriate relationship between spouses and between parents and children, they represent a revolution in Catholic thought. The traditional moralists, drawing from St. Paul and St. Augustine, discussed marriage largely in legalistic and negative terms, regarding it as an instrument for procreation and a remedy for sexual sins. Its chief positive feature was as a sacramental vehicle for transmitting saving grace and motivating moral action. What the Catholic theologians now call the "humanistic" or "personalistic" side of marriage, about which statements began to appear only in

the late 1920s,* was ignored. The best way to grasp the shift in the Church's outlook is by contrasting Pope Pius XI's *Casti Conubii* (1930) (2), the definitive statement on sex and marriage before the Second Vatican Council (1962), with the themes common today. By the time of the council the deficiencies of the traditional outlook and the consistency of themes like conjugal love and responsible parenthood with the current Catholic theological renewal made a great impression on the assembled bishops. *Humanae Vitae* has importance in Catholic theology, then, not simply because Pope Paul VI adopted a position on contraception based on traditional modes of thought, but because he sanctioned treating marriage in interpersonal terms. The contradiction between his thinking on contraception and his affirmation of the centrality of conjugal love and responsible paternity underlie the consternation which *Humanae Vitae* provoked among many bishops, priests, and laity.

3. The period of gestation that *Humanae Vitae* underwent gave Catholic couples time and justification for adopting modern contraceptive methods. Leading moral theologians in the early 1960s began to argue that it was licit for women to take estrogen and progesterone pills; and at the Vatican Council a number of bishops urged a decision on this matter. When the Pope himself decided to review the subject, the slow process of selecting a commission, expanding it, and rejecting its recommendation in favor of a personal decision produced a lengthy period of uncertainty during which Catholics throughout the world began using oral contraceptives. They had the willing support of priests who considered effective contraception a logical adjunct of the new matrimonial theology.

These three points apply universally to the Church and help explain the well-publicized insistence of many lay persons in Europe and North America on continued use of oral contraceptives. In Latin America also, the years of delay coincided with extensive discussion of contraception in newspapers and maga-

* The leaders of the new marital theology are generally acknowledged to have been Dietrich von Hildebrand, H. Doms, and Bernardin Krempel.

zines and with the initiation of private and public family-planning programs in most countries. Many urban, educated middle- and upper-class Latin Americans, the minority of the population able to understand and care about the position of the Church, began using contraceptives on the advice of private doctors and continue to do so now. The "demonstration effect" is very strong in Latin America and extends to all articles of consumption, including oral contraceptives. Educated Latin Americans do not differ significantly in their response to such problems from educated Europeans or North Americans, even though they live in an underdeveloped part of the world. Nor, as we shall see, is their Church backward in its attitudes.

The Role of the Bishops

The position of bishops is important for understanding what the Church thinks in a given geographical area, but we should recognize the conformist role they play, in contrast with priests or laymen. In their dioceses they have a special responsibility to unify and defend the positions of the Church. They must bring together and meet the needs of a flock that comes from many levels of life and has sharply differing views. Obviously bishops have their own opinions, and some have become spokesmen for controversial positions; but they ordinarily do not act on their own authority. They see themselves as interpreters of the Church's teaching within their jurisdiction, although that teaching is sufficiently ambiguous to give them considerable leeway. The bishop, however, does not go around saying that he disagrees with the Pope. If he does disagree, he says nothing.

Before *Humanae Vitae* many Latin American bishops had an open attitude to contraceptives for several reasons. The Latin American Church was never as concerned with the use of artificial means of contraception as, for example, the North American Church. Before 1960, the bishops apparently did not know that contraception was used; or if they did, it represented no great problem for them. When the issue became a reality and entered the stage of discussion, the extreme conservatives took a hard line in opposition, but the rest adopted a tolerant attitude of wait-and-see. Often they retreated by saying that the matter was under study, but many genuinely felt that effective contraception was morally significant on the personal level or that it represented an alternative to the far more serious problem of abortion. It became popular among Latin American bishops by the mid-1960s to argue that, given the unsettled state of the question, the decision should be left to the conscience of the people involved. Eighteen of twenty Chilean bishops with whom I discussed the matter shortly before *Humanae Vitae* permitted conscientious couples to use oral contraceptives or sent them to a Catholic doctor, assuming that he would probably prescribe oral contraceptives (3). Thoughtful Latin American bishops are not insensitive to the problems of women with many children; on this personal level of clear need, especially, they discerned nonegoistic reasons for contraception.

As private and public family-planning programs appeared, many bishops expressed fear that doctors were using psychological pressure in favor of the pill and the intra-uterine device (IUD) rather than rhythm. Confronted with the obvious receptivity of "Catholic" patients to a simple and effective method, however, the bishops usually faced facts and fell back to a position of rejecting abortion and sterilization and insisting that patients not be coerced into violating their consciences. In Colombia the bishops have sporadically criticized the family-planning programs, which prescribe artificial methods and which were conducted with the sympathy of the nation's last three presidents. In part, however, this stems from the special position accorded to the Church as guardian of public morality by the constitution of Colombia. That this criticism has not moved beyond the spoken and written level may be partly ascribed to a more dominant interest of the Church: to maintain its privileges through good relations with the government.

Many Latin American bishops, while sympathizing with the desire of individuals to plan their families effectively, have opposed institutional programs because of their foreign influence and financing. This point of view has great strength among the radical wing of the Brazilian episcopate, which is probably the most influential group of bishops in Latin America. They believe that any program with United States government support should be resisted because it must aim in some way at furthering North American and undermining Latin American interests. According to Monsignor Hélder Câmara, Archbishop of Recife, and the symbolic leader of this group,

> I will never forget the words of President Lyndon Johnson—five dollars applied to birth control is a better investment than a hundred dollars used in development. I still retain that impertinence in my hearing, and I thank the Pope for taking a position although it creates problems for the underdeveloped countries (4).

> There is a certain temptation in the developed countries to regard development as a matter of birth control, and when this control is directed from abroad, it causes repugnance in me (5).

Dom Hélder and his associates, who are noted for their sensitive social consciences, have yet to resolve the anomaly of not supporting institutional means by which the lower class, which needs it most, can get effective information on contraception.

The introduction of family-planning clinics and the empirical studies accompanying them caused a profound awakening among Latin America's more thoughtful bishops to the fragility of the Church's sexual ethic in practice and led them to doubt the Church's strength in their supposedly Catholic societies. High rates of illegitimacy and abortion, as well as the readiness with which people were using contraceptive methods forbidden by the Church, led them to rethink their criticisms. Did not the Church have more pressing concerns, such as developing a more profound Christian consciousness in the people and promoting a more meaningful family life?

With the appearance of *Humanae Vitae,* many Latin American bishops, like those in other parts of the world, were surprised and disappointed. I was in Chile at the time. After a hasty meeting of the bishops of the central part of the country, Raúl Cardinal Silva Henríquez of Santiago expressed their consensus in a brief television message: The chief emphasis of the encyclical was on "responsible parenthood," and no Catholic need ever feel alienated from the Church because he cannot fulfill all of its demands. Cardinal Silva did not mention the prohibition of artificial methods of contraception.

Cardinal Silva was typical of many prelates who now found themselves in a dilemma. Their openness to contraception on both the personal and policy level was now contradicted by the Pope. Fortunately, they could derive from the encyclical a justification for continuing in practice what they were already doing. The emphasis in *Humanae Vitae* on the extraordinary discipline, even heroism, necessary to fulfill the norms of the Church enabled bishops along with priests to take a tolerant view toward the frailties of most Christians. Pope Paul comforted persons who continued to use unacceptable contraceptives by telling them "not to be discouraged, but rather have recourse with humble perseverance to the mercy of God, which is poured forth in the sacrament of Penance." And he called on priests to be "intransigent with evil, but merciful toward individuals. . . . Teach married couples the indispensable way of prayer, prepare them to have recourse often and with faith to the sacraments of the Eucharist and of Penance, without ever allowing themselves to be discouraged by their weakness." On the public level, the Pope acknowledged the existence of a problem of "rapid demographic growth" and the consequent strain on the resources of underdeveloped countries. Moreover, he admitted the right of public authorities, as he had in his previous encyclical *Populorum Progressio* (6), to provide couples with information on acceptable methods for limiting and spacing children, consistent with the natural law.

The chief effect of *Humanae Vitae* on the bishops has been to instill in them a sense of obligation to give lip service to the Pope's position, even when they personally do not agree with some aspects of it. As unifiers and transmitters the bishops have scrupulously avoided criticizing the encyclical publicly.* On the other hand, practical considerations and disagreements over

* One exception is Monsignor Koop, Bishop of Lins, São Paulo, Brazil (7).

policy in national and regional episcopal meetings have led them to emphasize the acceptable and tone down the controversial in their pastoral letters. In most cases their private comments to clergy have stressed the escapes available in individual pastoral situations.

When national hierarchies criticize family-planning programs, conservatives act from strong conviction, but in many cases the more open bishops are merely conforming to the expectations of *Humanae Vitae* and the pressure of papal nuncios. Nowhere in Latin America does a hierarchy have more than a verbal campaign against family planning, and in most countries the Church is quietly focusing on other matters. The Chilean episcopate, which initially supported contraceptive programs as an alternative to abortion, issued the following statement in August 1969:

> We manifest ourselves to be clearly in disagreement with the anticonception campaign which the National Health Service is developing. We reiterate our unconditioned agreement with him who fulfills the supreme *magisterium* in the Church and who in the encyclical *Humanae Vitae* reminded us of the Christian sense of marriage and the demands of the natural law, reproving the use of artificial contraceptive methods. (8)

However, the Chilean bishops, whose dominant characteristic for decades has been realism, will certainly not provoke the sophisticated middle-class and contraceptive-using lay Catholic elites in their secularized country. Bishops in Colombia, both individually and collectively, have continued their criticism of government cooperation with family-planning programs. Despite this, a recent analysis of that country's social problems (the most extensive ever produced by the episcopate) emphasizes conjugal love and responsible parenthood, referring briefly to *Humanae Vitae* "for a correct formation of the conscience of the Christian" (9). In this case, the bishops oppose the program, but lack a consensus on the proper policy to follow. The Peruvian episcopate, which denounced family-planning largely on nationalistic grounds in January 1968 (before *Humanae*

Vitae) (10), has remained silent since, but there is an absence of large-scale public and private family-planning programs in that country. The huge and divided Brazilian hierarchy, with over two hundred bishops, responded to *Humanae Vitae* with a brief pastoral (11) but has also been quiet since. Several bishops, though, have attended as observers the national seminars of the Brazilian Society of Family Welfare (Bemfam), the International Planned Parenthood Federation affiliate, which operates over seventy clinics.

The nearest thing to a consensus of the Latin American bishops may be found in the document (12) produced by the Latin American Bishops Conference (CELAM) at Medellìn, Colombia, shortly after and somewhat under the pressure of *Humanae Vitae*. The document treats two themes:

1. On the demographic problem in general, it acknowledges a dilemma because "our countries suffer from underpopulation and need demographic growth as a factor of development. But it is also certain that our excessively low social, economic, and cultural conditions are adverse to a pronounced demographic growth." A "unilateral" or "simplist" approach is "incomplete and therefore wrong," and an "antinatalist policy that tends to supplant, substitute, or lead to forgetting a policy of development" is "especially damaging." The document praises Pope Paul VI for insisting on "an integral policy focused on development" as the answer to population increase, for disowning policies of birth control as a condition for economic aid, and for defending the rights of persons, especially the poor and marginal members of society.

2. On the personal level, the bishops describe the teaching of *Humanae Vitae* as "clear and unequivocal," but to those couples with difficulties and anxieties they offer "our support without distinction."

The relatively negative attitude of the Medellín document toward family-planning programs does not, however, exhaust the Church's response. A more positive outlook typified by a pastoral of the Venezuelan bishops in 1969 may also be considered part of the consensus (because at no time since the renovation of the Latin American Church began in the 1950s has anyone ever suggested that the Venezuelan bishops might be innovative or advanced). The Venezuelan bishops condemn "birth control" as a program *obliging* couples to reduce the number of children wanted, but they support "family planning" as a human right and responsibility, in the sense that parents produce only as many children as they can give such decencies as food, clothing, and education. The bishops argue that the state has a role in educating and providing the means of achieving responsible paternity, as well as in combating abortion and other criminal and immoral actions against human dignity. They conclude:

> The state ought . . . to concern itself that the population receive convenient information and education about the methods approved by Christian morality for a responsible regulation of natality, especially the poorer population. Lack of economic power cannot be a motive for discrimination in this matter. Nevertheless, in a pluralistic society, with non-Catholics and non-believers, it is not forbidden to the institutions of the state to give information on other methods to those persons who may decide to use them according to their own consciences. (13)

It would be a mistake to assume that in individual dioceses the problem of contraception continues to agitate the bishop, his priests, and the laity. They determined their response to this issue before *Humanae Vitae*. The encyclical merely provided an occasion to review the practical procedures to follow, which in the end usually represented a reaffirmation of what was being done. A bishop is known for either a rigid or lenient policy toward forbidden contraceptive methods; priests have worked out their pastoral approaches; and the more sophisticated laity by and large have settled the matter with their consciences.

New developments could certainly lead to action by national hierarchies. For example, the initiation of publicly financed programs would undoubtedly provoke some response from the bishops of Brazil or Peru. A major factor in the nature of such a response is the consciousness of power by the episcopates.

In countries like Colombia, Church leaders still believe that they exercise great influence politically and in the people's minds, but those in Brazil and Chile have no such illusions.

The Response of Theologians and Priests

Descending in the Church structure we come to the intellectual expression—the theologians who interpret the *magisterium*. Few bishops are well versed in theology and usually depend on the advice of clerical, and sometimes lay, experts.

Nearly all Latin American theologians studied in Europe and, consequently, their attitudes in response to *Humanae Vitae* were similar to those of their European mentors; but in most of Latin America, they have agreed not to criticize the encyclical publicly. Brazil is a notable exception. There every major Church writer on marriage and population problems and the leading journals *Revista Ecclesiástica Brasileira* (for priests) and *Vozes* (for laymen) have openly questioned it. Both journals, which are edited by Frei Clarêncio Neotti, O.F.M., one of the priests most active in Bemfam, have a tradition since about 1962 of mediating the new marriage theology from Europe to Brazil. Since the encyclical, articles in the *Revista Ecclesiástica Brasileira* and *Vozes* have consistently disagreed with Pope Paul VI, chiefly over his "biological" view of human nature.* Against it they contend that a more diversified concept of human expression—involving reason, the capacity for relationship and responsibility, and the dedication of marriage as a whole to God's intention—entails genuinely effective contraception.

The practical justification for contraception most commonly

---

* For typical examples, see statements by Snoek (14), dos Santos (15). The leading Brazilian writers on the theology of matrimony are dos Santos (16) and, especially, Charbonneau (17), both critical of *Humanae Vitae*.

A major Brazilian Catholic demographer, also professor of demography at the Gregorian University in Rome, is Pedro Calderon Beltrão, S.J. In a country with vast unsettled regions and little official interest in population programs, Father Beltrão has written, "There is no doubt that our rate of demographic growth exceeds the optimal point and consequently, for good macro-social reasons, a policy of reduction of natality imposes itself as one of the essential elements of the national project of development and social welfare" (18).

followed in Brazil has been presented annually at the seminars of Bemfam by Dom Jerônimo de Sá Cavalcante, prior of the Benedictine monastery in Salvador, Bahia. In this view, "responsible parenthood" as defined by the Pope requires a decision on the number and spacing of children. The only method the Pope permitted, however, is rhythm, which has proven notably unreliable; and the Pope recognized this by calling on scientists to perfect methods acceptable to Catholic morality. *Until this occurs,* the Catholic couple should select one of the existing effective methods available to plan responsibly their family. According to Dom Jerônimo:

> Personally I do not make a distinction between artificial and natural methods, because what is artificial is created by man and therefore is a human method. . . . As long as medical science says that the method is not sterilizing or prejudicial to the health of the couple, and it is not imposed by any authority or power, then this method can be perfectly accepted. (19)

In Chile, the theological issue was handled by a statement of theology professors at the Catholic University of Santiago. After pointing out that the encyclical was not infallible and citing the principal themes, they confessed that on the question of contraception they were divided. The majority felt that the Pope's position was "reformable" because the matter required further study, especially of the conditioning factors in human nature for making such a decision. The minority, on the other hand, believed that the force of the encyclical and its consistency with tradition made it essentially infallible. The document closes with a paragraph recognizing that Catholics might "adhere, after serious study and consultation, to one or other of the theological opinions mentioned" (20). The document thus clearly gives more emphasis than the encyclical itself to the debatable nature of its authority and provides a green light for individuals to make their own decisions.

It is not surprising, then, that all over Latin America priests in their pastoral work have agreed to encourage couples to make their own "responsible decision" and are granting absolution to those who confess use of "artificial" methods. We cannot determine what percentage this involves. Two Brazilian priests who often lead retreats and seminars on *Humanae Vitae* for clergy found about 80 per cent of these priests "open" on the matter. One of them has written what being "open" means:

> Personally I found three attitudes (among couples) toward the encyclical. One couple said to me: The encyclical is right and we are going to return to using the charts. Another couple said: The encyclical is nice, but we are not in a situation to observe it now. Here then would be a place for the "law of growth." The third attitude is of those who reflected and studied it with honesty and did not convince themselves. They disagree respectfully. In my opinion, all these attitudes are valid according to the case. (14, p. 145)

Other priests are more blunt. In the wake of *Humanae Vitae,* the Carmelite fathers of the city of Belo Horizonte issued a statement complaining that the Pope did not take into consideration the opinions of the conciliar bishops and his own commission in reaffirming the traditional doctrine.

> The attitude of Pope Paul VI caused a profound sense of frustration among not a few couples wanting to maintain fidelity to the ecclesiastical authority within the demands of modern life. To ease the drama of conscience which this event brought, we should recall that each one of us will be judged by God in accordance with his own conscience. And the criterion of judgment of conscience is the Evangelical Message of the Total Liberation of man in Christ, through which we express in ourselves the image of God. To express in ourselves the image of God, everything, even the Natural Law and the Authority of the Pope, serve as instruments. (21)

In Latin America, as in other parts of the world, priests from the same religious order and diocese have met to agree on pastoral strategy. Prominent Jesuits in Colombia and Franciscans in Brazil told me that their orders had agreed in such meetings to be "open." In Latin America today the younger priests especially are in close touch with the economic problems and aspirations of the lower and middle classes. Frequently in talking with priests who work in slums, for example, I find that they do not even question the morality of contraception in a context in which women struggle to support children on their husbands' minimal salaries and what they themselves can eke out from part-time work. Admittedly, my contacts tend to be with the more liberal clergy, but I have yet to discuss this matter with a priest in Latin America who did not in counseling leave the contraceptive method up to the individual conscience.

Popular Catholicism—the Culture Religion

Although we may assume that the "ideology" of the Church plays an important role in whether some Catholics use contraception or not, it is extremely doubtful that this is so for most Latin Americans. One of the curious discoveries of researchers on the use of contraceptives among women in major Latin American cities was that there were no significant differences between Catholics and non-Catholics or between Catholics of greater and lesser devotion.* In a recent study of slum-dwelling women in Santiago, Chile, the author concludes: "The results of the study of religious influence serve to confirm that neither the type of religious creed, nor its greater or lesser practice, are factors of real weight in the decision to use contraceptives" (23). Personnel working in family planning in many countries insist that the religious issue rarely comes up in their conversations with patients.

Facts like these have received wide publicity among students of population problems, but a meaningful explanation has not. The answer seems to be that most Latin Americans adhere to various forms of culture religion that lack a close linkage to sexual morality and accept practices contradicting normative Catholicism.

The origins of this culture religion go back to the Spanish and Portuguese conquest and to the introduction of slavery.

* See, for example, (22).

In this clash between two sharply divergent ways of life, the Iberian conquerors tried to impose their culture, including religion, on the native Indians and subsequently on African slaves. The persistence of pre-Colombian religions among Andean and Central American Indians and of African religion in Brazil reveals the relative superficiality of the process of cultural imposition in those regions; but in most parts of Latin America the Iberians were more effective, at least in imparting a Catholic façade to popular religion. New symbols (Jesus, the Virgin Mary, the saints) replaced the Indian and African deities, and customary religious practice assumed a Catholic form as sacramentals, saints' feasts, and pilgrimages to shrines.

> We live in a country in which the effort of the first centuries of civilization and evangelization produced a culture with a Catholic base. In those first centuries, the Church baptized many rites, signs, and cults, succeeding in showing in this way to people that they could encounter God through them. . . . It is true that later the rites which were christianized came to lose their clear reference to Christianity, and on the other hand, the same Christian rites, like sacraments and sacramentals, have been distorted, becoming converted into elements more cultural and folkloric than Christian. (24)

The "conversion" of Latin America failed to communicate a strong internal perspective conforming to normative Catholicism. It is doubtful that the peasants of Spain and Portugal in the sixteenth and seventeenth centuries were very different because normative Catholicism demands a sophistication that neither they nor the Latin Americans could achieve.

Sociologists working in Latin America are now moving toward a consensus on the nature of "popular" Catholicism. Many of the most perceptive are priests who have the advantage of close contact with the beliefs and practices of the people and who readily admit that up to 80 per cent of Latin American Catholics adhere to popular Catholicism.

To sharpen the distinction between the two types of religion it is useful to postulate certain criteria of normative Catholicism and to contrast them with the popular outlook. Normative Catholicism involves at least the following characteristics:*

1. Adherence to a set of basic beliefs, such as the classical creeds and further dogmatic definitions that distinguish Roman Catholic Christianity from other forms of religion.

2. A strong sense of identification with the institutional Church as the chief center of religious life.

3. Participation in the sacraments administered by the Church as the basic instrument of salvation.

4. Conformity to ethical teachings communicated by the Church and which in some instances are distinctive.

Beliefs

In generalizing about Latin American popular beliefs, based on studies in a number of countries, Father Segundo Galilea, director of CELAM's Pastoral Institute, notes that although belief in God is deeply rooted in the masses, only 80 per cent believe that Jesus is God, 40 per cent that he is the Savior, and only 55 per cent believe Mary to be the Mother of God. The Trinity, the basic doctrine of Christianity, he describes as "unknown." "In any case, the most important beliefs are saints and sanctuaries, where they appear to believe in a plurality of 'virgins' " (26). If Jesus is not the Savior, what is he? According to an analysis of Brazilian Catholicism,

> Jesus is associated with Mary. Above all he is the Son of Mary, the Good Jesus, the Jesus of Sufferings, of the Cross, of Calvary, of Passion, the Jesus whose look makes his mother suffer. He is also in the center of the religion of suffering, of piety, of resignation. Jesus is pardon, sweetness, patience. He is the rescuer in adversities and catastrophes. (27)

Essentially, popular Latin American Catholicism conforms to peasant religions in many cultures, involving a sense of kinship with a nature rich in mana and symbolized by a multiplicity of mediators who are like members of the extended family.

* For this schema, I am indebted to Thales de Azevedo (25).

The Church as Institution

The average Latin American has little consciousness of himself as belonging to a universal institution, and his cultic acts are centered in the community and family rather than in the church edifice. In his home are the images of the saints before which he prays. The local church has exceptional sacred (as against profane) qualities. He crosses himself as he passes it, and often he will stop to light a candle at the altar of his favorite saint or to get some holy water for the good luck it brings. The priest is often also a respected person because he blesses things and thus wards off evil.

The Sacraments

In Latin America participation in the sacraments varies from country to country but is lower than most people realize. The sacraments that serve as *rites de passage* have strong cultural, though not necessarily religious significance. Perhaps 90 per cent of the people are baptized (ranging from 95 to 98 per cent in Mexico and Central America to 70 per cent in Cuba), and 30 to 70 per cent participate in First Communion and Marriage (though in countries like the Dominican Republic and Panama over 60 per cent of the children are illegitimate). However, attendance at mass, the central cultic act of the Church, is low, with about 20 per cent in the region going regularly. Variation is great among countries and even within countries. For example, Colombia as a whole registers 15 per cent, but the departments of Caldas and Antioquia register 60 per cent. In Mexico and Central America attendance at mass is greater in the lower classes, but in Argentina, Uruguay, and Chile greatest among the upper-middle class. Throughout Latin America women participate disproportionately. Use of the sacraments of Penance (confession) and the Eucharist is very low; usually a small minority of those attending mass take communion (24, pp. 11–22).

What kind of cult makes sense to most Latin Americans? Basically a relationship with the charismatic beings of the

Church (God, Jesus, the Virgin Mary, the saints) who bring blessings, good luck, benefits. Saints' days, pilgrimages, processions, candles lit at grottos—all reflect the quest of needy people for health and prosperity and protection from evil forces. Funeral rites, visits to cemeteries, devotion to the *animitas* (small shrines where people have died violently) guarantee the benevolence of the dead and reflect a belief in many spirits.

Religion and Morality

The average Latin American does not determine his moral behavior by the teaching of the Church. Father Galilea correctly describes the situation as follows:

> At first glance it may appear, especially to the foreign or superficial observer that the people . . . have no moral principles. This is not correct. The people have a morality, though often it is based on other norms . . . than ours. In the popular classes, for example, fornication and adultery are rather common in the men, although it is demanded that the women be faithful. The antinatural control of births and abortion has wide acceptance. . . . We should call attention . . . to the separation between morality and religious belief. It is normal to see in houses, buses, and so forth, stamps of saints next to pornography. . . . Among the moral values, friendship, affection, hospitality are more important than efficiency and economic values. The abnegation of women in home and work is extraordinary. . . . (26, p. 13)

The separation between religion and morality is central for understanding the role of Catholicism in Latin American family planning. An able interpreter of Brazilian culture who recognizes that the popular religion of his country differs from that of Hispanic America describes it as "a Catholicism deprived of its dogmatic and *moral* content" (28, italics added). In effect, the same Latin American woman who says, *"Soy muy católica,"* may not use contraception for a number of reasons, but religion is rarely among them. Rather, practical consideration and availability of means become decisive. In many Latin American countries, it was the staggering incidence of abortion, a more serious violation of Catholic teaching than artificial contraception, which persuaded family planners that they could push ahead without religious or moral resistance in the popular classes.

Culture Catholicism is not limited to the lower classes, though in educated and privileged people it assumes a more complex and, up to this point, unresearched form. Participation in the Church is a matter of habit and respectability, and religion is regarded as a bulwark for preserving female virginity and the existing political and social order. The Church is honored as a pillar of the established system (although many Church leaders are desperately trying to escape this onus), but its teaching on contraception is ignored if large numbers of children stand in the way of greater material comfort and status.

Conclusions

The role of Catholicism in Latin America, like religion in other cultures, is ambiguous. Although a religion sometimes stands in judgment on the values of a culture, it is easy for individuals to find in it what they want. This is especially so with Catholicism, which has made so many different pronouncements over many years, often with ambivalence and affirmations hedged with reservations. Moreover, the Church has changed so rapidly in the past decade that, on social thought especially, the older generation received a training almost the opposite of that their children get today. Catholicism is more often used in the Latin American privileged classes to justify personal or class interests than the Church is able to use these same groups to further its social ethical concerns.

Despite the smaller amount of attention devoted to the effect of culture religion on contraceptive practices, it is a far more important factor than the lenient interpretations of *Humanae Vitae* within the formal structure of the Church. The dominant Irish Catholicism and the Calvinist-sectarian Protestant tradition of the United States always linked religious conviction with a strict sexual ethic. Because North Americans usually draw their impressions of Latin America from Mexico, which projects a splashy religious symbolism not found in the secularized region from Brazil through Uruguay and Argentina to Chile, it is hard for them to believe that this omnipresent Catholic religiosity is not reflected in opposition to "artificial" contraception. But it is not.

Family planning does face many obstacles in Latin America. Low educational levels, subjugation of women, rural isolation, recalcitrant traditions, and lack of medical facilities will prevent many people from adopting contraception in this century. National aspirations in the region's large and relatively unpopulated countries will continue to make leaders in government and public opinion reticent. Anti-United States and antiforeign attitudes among intellectuals and students will provide the strongest theoretical opposition. Nevertheless, the specter of a Church galvanizing millions of Latin American Catholics against family planning lacks theological or sociological reality.

Church leaders will undoubtedly want to contribute to the dialogue as family planning progresses in the future. The cooperation and mutual esteem between Brazil's Bemfam and the theologians and bishops is one example. The Medical School of Colombia's Javerian University and Peru's Christian Family Movement are currently providing women with progesterone pills for two years after childbearing, followed by the rhythm method, in experimental programs respected by family-planning leaders in both countries. Chile's Latin American Center of Population (CELAP) does research on population problems, trains leaders, and tries to clarify the Catholic position in a program with continental outreach. These efforts will probably increase, but at the same time, leading Catholics will join other Latin Americans in pointing to anomalies in family planning, such as (a) the desire of international and national elites for the masses to plan their families, but the unwillingness to allow them political and social participation commensurate with their numbers; (b) Americans who talk ominously of the economic consequences of demographic growth in Latin America, but spend a very large part of their national budget on a war against an underdeveloped country and trips to the moon; (c) the unwillingness of the developed countries to devote a small percentage of their national product to development of the less developed world; (d) the ignorance and indifference about Latin America in other parts of the world (for example, few appear to know that Uruguay and Argentina have very low and satisfactory rates of population increase).

It is regrettable that the ambivalence of the Church's position prevents it from taking a major role in the promotion of family planning in Latin America because the Church today is producing some of the most sophisticated and socially conscious elites in the region. However, those elites seem likely to prevent the Church from assuming an inhumane attitude of opposition. The whole controversy over contraception has had an important role in stimulating self-criticism within the Latin American Church and has given it an excuse to turn its attention quietly to other, graver problems, such as doing something about the unstable and tragic family life of many people.

References

1. Pope Paul VI. *Humanae Vitae—On the Regulation of Birth.* Washington, D. C.: U.S. Catholic Conference, July 25, 1968.
2. Pope Pius XI. *Casti Conubii,* in *The Church and the Reconstruction of the Modern World,* Terence P. McLaughlin, ed. Garden City: Doubleday & Company, Inc., 1957. Pp. 115–70.
3. Thomas G. Sanders. *The Chilean Episcopate,* Fieldstaff Reports, West Coast South America Series, March 1968. Vol. XV, No. 3, p. 16.
4. *Jornal do Brasil,* Rio de Janeiro, September 28, 1968.
5. *Diário de Notícias,* Rio de Janeiro, September 20, 1966.
6. Pope Paul VI. *Populorum Progressio—On the Development of Peoples.* Washington, D. C.: U.S. Catholic Conference, March 26, 1967.
7. Pedro Paulo Koop, Huberto Rademaker, and José Oscar Beozzo. "A Encíclica *Humanae Vitae*: Análise dos Argumentos," *Vozes,* Vol. LXII (November 1968), 987–95.
8. *Noticia Aliadas.* Lima: Centro de Información Católica, Apartado 5594, 1969.

9. Conferencia Episcopal (de Colombia). *La Iglesia ante el Cambio.* Bogota, 1969. P. 80.

10. *Noticias Aliadas,* No. 10. Lima: Centro de Información Católica, February 3, 1968.

11. "Declaração da Comissão Central da CNBB," *SEDOC,* Vol. I (February 1969), 1025–29.

12. CELAM (Latin American Bishops Conference). *La Iglesia en la Actual Transformación de América Latina a la Luz del Concilio,* Vol. II. Bogota, 1969. Pp. 77–88.

13. "Episcopado Venezuelano Favorável ao Planejamento Familiar," *Boletim da Bemfam* (December 1969).

14. Jaime Snoek, C.SS.R. "Meditando sôbre uma Encíclica," *REB* (Rensta Ecclesiastica Brasileiro), Vol. XXIX (March 1969), 138–45.

15. Beni dos Santos. "A Concepção Personalista do Matrimônio e a *Humanae Vitae,*" *Vozes,* Vol. LXII (November 1968), 976–86.

16. Beni dos Santos. *O Sentido Personalista do Matrimônio.* Petrópolis: *Vozes,* 1969.

17. Paul-Eugène Charbonneau. *Humanae Vitae e Liberdade da Consciência.* São Paulo: Herder, 1969.

18. Pedro Calderon Beltrão, S.J. "A transiçao demográfica," *Vozes,* Vol. LXIII (May 1969), 387–95.

19. Jerônimo de Sá Cavalcante, O.S.B. "Aspectos Religiosos do Planejamento Familiar," *I Seminário de Planejamento Familiar,* Vol. II. Mimeograph. Rio de Janeiro: Bemfam, 1968. P. 49.

Annals of meetings have been published in a revised form as *Anais do Primeiro Seminário Brasileiro de Planejamento Familiar.* Petrópolis: *Vozes,* n.d.

20. "Declaração de Professôres de Teologia da Universidade Católica de Chile," *SEDOC,* Vol. I (February 1969), 1071–75.

21. "Declaração dos Padres Carmelitas de Belo Horizonte," *SEDOC,* Vol. I (February 1969), 1061.

22. Carmen A. Miró and Ferdinand Rath. "Preliminary Findings of Comparative Fertility Surveys in Three Latin American Cities," *The Milbank Memorial Fund Quarterly,* XLIII, Part II (October 1965), 36–62.

Carmen A. Miró. *Un Programa de Encuestas Comparativas de*

Fecundidad en la America Latina: Refutación de Algunos Conceptos Erroneos. Santiago: Celade, 1970.

23. Josefina Lozada de Majuan. *Comportamientos Anticonceptivos en la Familia Marginal.* Santiago: DESAL/CELAP, 1968. P. 68.

24. Renato Poblete, S.J. "Aspectos Sociológicos de la Religiosidad Popular, II," *Mensaje Iberoamericano,* 2a época, No. 52 (February 1970), 14.

25. Thales de Azevedo. "Popular Catholicism in Brazil: Typology and Functions," *Portugal and Brazil in Transition,* Raymond S. Sayers, ed. Minneapolis: University of Minnesota Press, 1968. Pp. 175–78.

26. Segundo Galilea. "La Práctica Religiosa Popular," *Mensaje Iberoamercaino,* 2a época, No. 29 (March 1968), 12.

27. Emile Pin, S.J. *Elementos para uma Sociologia do Catolicismo Latinoamericano.* Petrópolis: *Vozes,* 1966. P. 70.

28. Thales de Azevedo. "Problemas Metodológicos da Sociologia do Catolicismo," *Cultura e Situação Social no Brasil.* Rio de Janeiro: Civilização Brasileira, 1967. P. 184.

Discussion of Dr. Sanders's Paper

NORMAN N. MILLER

Norman N. Miller is an Associate of the American Universities Field Staff, Hanover, New Hampshire.

I think Dr. Sanders has given this volume a badly needed refocus. He has brought our attention for the first time to the fact that belief systems do serve as barriers to the acceptance of family planning and to the control of population. Catholicism is, however, only one system of belief. If I may briefly compare Latin America to Africa, several interesting parallels are seen in authoritarian, hierarchical systems of thought. Africa has at least eight hundred ethnic groups, each with a slightly different belief system. These eight hundred systems are broadly related to ancestral worship, often overlaid by Islamic or Christian beliefs. Many are syncretistic, in that they intermingle with each other and produce interesting third forms of thought. For example, in East and Central Africa there are a great many separatist churches, messianic cults, and other breakaway religious groups that have admixtures of Christian and pagan beliefs. Cultural borrowing is commonplace, as seen in the substitution of a local leader's name for Christ's name in Christian hymns, prayers, and the like. Throughout Africa at least six thousand such movements are known.

My point is this: Until we begin to understand what the *local* beliefs of an individual or a group of individuals are regarding the acceptance of innovations and until we begin to understand how the belief systems dictate behavior, we shall be attempting to suggest social changes without basic information. It is at the grass-roots level that understanding must be gained. The village and the villager are the nerve endings of the entire process of diffusing ideas and innovations. Individuals locked into these systems of thought are quite willing and able to reject any innovation, including family planning, simply because it does not fit local beliefs.

In terms of such diffusion of beliefs, Dr. Sanders' paper could be described as follows: Ideas on family planning come from the Pope to the bishops to the people, in what we might call the P → B → P phenomenon. This is illustrated in Figure 1.

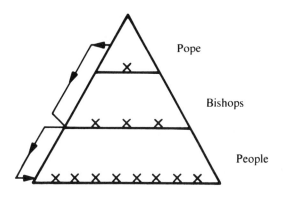

Figure 1. The P → B → P phenomenon.

I believe this treatment underemphasizes the basic problem: How does a hierarchical system of any kind, church, government, cult, or whatever, get its ideas down the organizational hierarchy to the people? In particular, how is acceptance of a new idea gained? Reception of ideas by the villager is the key to the entire success of any program.

To gain local acceptance of ideas, there are often three different types of village leaders who serve as gatekeepers and control the reception of ideas from the outside. First, the village administrative leader or local government official, who usually serves to pass on administrative or technical information and to pass on the demands of government. Second, the local political-party leader who is a propagandist for the new ideas.

In Africa these individuals are often alien to the village they work in, and although they have political legitimacy from the central government, they usually lack local acceptance. Third, traditional leaders such as chiefs, subchiefs, headmen, and religious and ritualistic leaders; this group is usually the key to the acceptance process. These people serve as translators of what the innovation means, as moderators, and as mediators of the entire process. This process of diffusion of innovations, such as a family-planning technique, for the rural peasant in many parts of the world is illustrated in Figures 2 and 3. The process can, of course, break down at any stage. Particularly, the views held by traditional leaders are crucial to the acceptance of the idea.

This is the reason an understanding of the traditional belief systems, that is, an understanding of what the traditional leaders are thinking and how they see their place in the system, dramatically affects the innovation. From the family-planning point of view the only sure answer to acceptance is highly detailed knowledge of the local area where the program is to be inaugurated. If we understand the local village and if we understand the attitudes and beliefs surrounding fertility, we can attack barriers to new ideas where they exist. It is important to emphasize that these beliefs are usually closed, self-encased systems. Like many other closed systems, these beliefs turn any attack on them into justification for their own existence. Such beliefs, in fact, stand as very important barriers to new ideas.

My over-all purpose is to call attention to the problems of rural acceptance of ideas, particularly problems related to belief and attitudinal barriers. We have begun to solve the technical and organizational problems surrounding the population problems. We have begun to understand the massive diversity of peoples. But we have not yet begun to understand the myriad of local beliefs held by the great majority of humanity. Particularly, we do not understand the potency of strongly entrenched belief systems that serve as barriers to such ideas as family planning. In short, the admirable analysis by Dr. Sanders

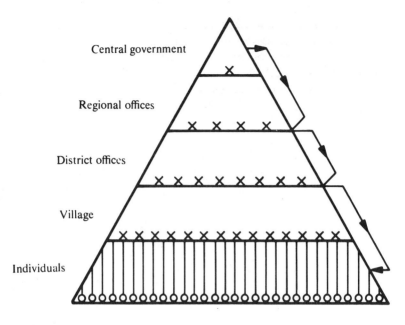

Figure 2. From central government to village.

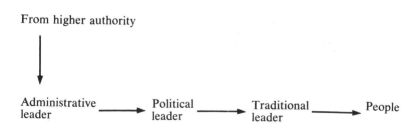

Figure 3. Within the village.

must be taken a few steps further. He has given us an excellent critique of the organizational hierarchy of religion as it relates to problems of family planning. What we need next is further analysis on how the demands of the Church are in fact received at the grass-roots level.

12
Belief Systems and Family Planning in Peasant Societies

L A I L A S H U K R Y E L - H A M A M S Y

Laila Shukry El-Hamamsy is Director of the Social Research Center, American University, Cairo.

Both "belief systems" and "peasant societies" are extremely broad and complex topics. To attempt to define and deal with them adequately, in addition to discussing their relationship to family planning, would be both overambitious and ingenuous, considering the present state of empirical knowledge. I propose, therefore, to concentrate on Middle Eastern peasant society, drawing upon insights and case materials from the society I know best—the Egyptian peasant society. Narrowing the topic will also be more appropriate to the particular approach I am advocating for the study of the complex relationship between belief systems and family planning. I believe that meaningful insights can be obtained only if we view the belief system as integrated with, and functionally related to, other basic aspects of the total way of life of a community.

Any discussion of the belief system of Middle Eastern peasants must deal with Islam, the predominant religion. Islam has been the object of study by humanists and historians of great renown. Unfortunately, most of these studies have been remote from the Islam of everyday life and particularly of everyday peasant life. What has been noted about writings on

335

Chinese thought, or on the great Indian traditions, is also true of most writings on Islam: Scholars have been largely concerned with the reflective ideas of the philosophers, theologians, and moralists and very little with what went on in the minds of peasants. To use such writings alone as a means of understanding the belief system of peasants would be invalid, since the teachings of the theologians finally filter through to the level of the peasant after much "diffraction and diffusion" (1, p. 80).

The concepts of "little traditions" and "great traditions" that Robert Redfield uses to describe the relationship between peasant culture and that of the larger society of which it is a subordinate part is useful in describing the relationship between Islamic theology and peasant belief systems. According to Redfield:

> In a civilization there is a great tradition of the reflective few, and there is a little tradition of the largely unreflective many. The great tradition is cultivated in schools or temples; the little tradition works itself out and keeps itself going in the lives of the unlettered in their village communities. The tradition of the philosopher, theologian and literary man is a tradition consciously cultivated and handed down; that of the little people is for the most part taken for granted and not submitted to much scrutiny or considered refinement and improvement. (1, p. 70)

In accordance with this concept, then, the relationship between the belief system of Moslem peasants and population planning needs to be studied, not only through an analysis of Islamic theology and doctrine, but also through an investigation of the living religion and "the little tradition," particularly those aspects of it that relate to the procreational behavior of individuals and families.

In fact, I would go beyond what Redfield is implying and say that even if we were to study the impact of belief on an urban, educated community, we cannot depend only on what the theologians and sacred writings say. We need to find out what the belief system is on the behavior level because even the belief system of the urban community represents a variant and not a replica of what Redfield calls "the great tradition."

Too many discussions of the relationship between Islam and population control begin with the assumption that Islam is one thing to all people, a uniformly defined and interpreted set of beliefs and doctrines. Dudley Kirk, for example, in his study of Moslem natality asserts that:

> Empirically Islam has been a more effective barrier to the dif-
> fusion of family planning than Catholicism. The monolithic
> character of Islam in this regard is overlooked because of its
> enormous territory, its linguistic diversity, its political atomiza-
> tion and the absence of a central religious hierarchy. (2, p. 66)

Yet, on looking at Moslem societies south of the Sahara, he finds natality being affected by cultural factors other than Islam and refers to the "greater variability in the natality of Moslems south of the Sahara, where the Moslem religion and way of life fuse with tropical African cultures and religions" (2, p. 70). Furthermore, in attempting to explain why Moslem countries have a high birth rate (from 40 to 60 per thousand), he finds it necessary to refer to factors other than religion:

> Moslem countries are all in the category of developing nations,
> and all have low indices of material development. These are
> usually lower than those of non-Moslem neighbors. High levels
> of education, industrialization and other aspects of modernization
> associated with declines in the birth rate have not made strong
> headway as yet in Moslem countries. In fact, class differentials
> in natality in the UAR, for example, suggest that a general rise
> in the level of living might at first tend to *raise* the birth rate,
> because of better nutrition, health, and other factors. (2, p. 72)

He adds that "Islam partakes of the pro-natalist social forces that exist generally in peasant and pastoral societies" and lists some factors such as high infant mortality, the importance of sons, and the larger family.

It is clear that, although investigators like Kirk find many other factors in Moslem societies to account for high fertility, they still talk of Islam as a monolithic force, the determining factor, and the "effective barrier to the diffusion of family planning."

People who hold such a view of Islam tend to interpret any changes in the attitudes of Moslems towards family planning as symptomatic of a weakening of religious faith instead of, as is often the case, a reinterpretation of belief.

My contention is that we must view Islam (as indeed we must view any religious system) as a religion that interacts with, affects, and is affected by the conditions and circumstances of the life of a group. A "fatalistic," family-oriented peasant who prays and fasts and has absolute faith in Allah as the Creator and provider of all things is a Moslem. So is an ambitious professional urbanite who also prays and fasts and has absolute faith in Allah. They may have very different world views and different interpretations of Islamic belief, but they both consider themselves among the faithful. The lack of a religious hierarchy in Islam, contrary to what Kirk asserts, gives individuals and groups leeway for interpretation of belief without risk of being forced out of the Moslem community.

What a particular Moslem society, consciously or unconsciously, selects, emphasizes, and reinterprets from the various possible strands of Islamic doctrine and thought depends largely on the life circumstances and exigencies of living with which it has to deal. The selected strands, once incorporated into the total fabric of belief, will reinforce and give powerful sanction to behavior patterns compatible with them.

This view of religion as a dynamic, interactive force underlies the topic of this paper, i.e., the relationship between population control and the belief system of the Moslem peasant—specifically the Egyptian peasant. To explore this relationship, the view of the jurists and the theologians of Islam on population control will be examined first. It will then be necessary to examine the conditions of Middle Eastern peasant life that emphasize, and are buttressed by, certain elements of Islamic belief; we need to explore the substratum of values and life orientations that have resulted from the interaction between basic peasant outlooks and selective Islamic values. Finally, we must examine the implications that these basic orientations and attitudes have for population control.

Islamic Doctrine and Family Planning

The relatively recent concern over the population problem in Moslem countries has occasioned some debate about the attitude of Islam towards family planning. A great deal of the argument has centered around what the sacred writings and other recognized authoritative sources of Islamic theology and jurisprudence have to say about birth control. The primary sources upon which any interpretation of Islamic law is based are the Koran and the Ḥadīth, or prophetic tradition. When no definite directive exists in either the Koran or Ḥadīth, Islamic jurists have had recourse to Ijtihād, which is the exercise of the faculty of reason for the formulating of an opinion. Clearly, the use of Ijtihād opens the way for a number of interpretations.

Dr. Muhammad Sallab Madkour, head of the Department of Islamic Law at Cairo University, has made a thorough survey of Islamic pronouncements on the subject of birth control and arrives at the following conclusion:

> There has been no Koranic text or definitive statement in the Ḥadīth that constitutes proof or evidence (on which to base a precise opinion). There have been only individual reports which were somewhat contradictory and the scholars have come out with different opinions. (3)

He affirms that the majority of the Moslem jurists have declared the use of contraceptives to be lawful, and only a few scholars have come out against it. All four orthodox schools of Islamic law, which form the basis for decisions relating to Sharī'a law, have allowed the practice of *coitus interruptus,* the method of contraception known to them. For example, the Mālikī and Hambalī schools have stated that the consent of the wife is a basic condition for such practice.

More recently, the muftis of different nations have made official pronouncements, or "fatwas," on the subject of birth control. The fatwas express differing opinions; some are un-qualified in their support of family planning; others are con-ditionally so. One main condition posed by most is the need for the consent of the wife. Another condition advanced by the Mufti of Malaysia, for example, is that contraception be practiced only for health reasons. To practice contraception "merely for the sake of preserving the beauty of the figure, or as a means of escape from the responsibility of bringing up children, is unanimously judged to be 'haram' or forbidden" (4). Most muftis oppose sterilization, but those who discuss abortion state that it is permissible up to four months of preg-nancy, on the grounds that the fetus is not a human being with a soul until then. The Egyptian fatwa declared that abortion is allowed only if the life of the mother is in danger.

A study of the opinion given by the Grand Mufti of Jordan, reported in the Population Council's collection of materials re-lating to Muslim attitude and family planning, is revealing in that it shows the kind of reasoning and the indirect evidence used to reach a conclusion favorable to family planning.

The fatwa emphasizes that the general viewpoint of Islamic law is that the law must accommodate itself to nature and to human conditions. The argument for family planning starts with the postulate that "one of the natural things inherent in human beings is marriage," the purpose of which is procreation and the perpetuation of the species. The fatwa presents the supporting evidence from the Koran in the following terms:

> God says: "God, too, has given you wives from among yourselves and has given you sons and grandsons from your wives, and supplied you with good things." Therefore, marriage has been one of the Islamic religious ways and procreation has been one of its desirable and gratifying aims. Even the lawgiver views multiplicity with favor, for multiplicity implies power, influence and invulnerability. This is why, in one of the traditions of the Prophet, marriage with an affectionate prolific woman is strongly urged. The tradition says: "Marry the affectionate prolific woman, for I shall be proud of you among the nations." (5, p. 3 f.)

But, the Grand Mufti argues further, God made marriage conditional upon the ability of the man to provide adequately for the children. "And let those who do not find a match," says the Koran, "live in continence until God makes them free from want out of his bounty." He goes on to quote the Ḥadīth: "O young men, whoever of you is capable financially let him marry, and whoever is not capable let him fast, for fasting dispels desire." The Mufti then concludes: "The definite inference is that 'restriction of procreation' is legal a fortiori, because to stop procreation altogether is more serious than to limit it. It is a cause for much wonder that those who urge celibacy should at the same time hesistate to allow family planning" (5, p. 3).

The Mufti also refers to the traditions that contain references to the practice of *coitus interruptus* during the lifetime of the Prophet, which he knew of and did not prohibit. One of the incidents most often referred to from the tradition, in support of birth control, is the following:

A man said to the Prophet: "I have a young wife, I hate that she be pregnant, and I want what men want; but the Jews claim that *coitus interruptus* is minor infanticide." The Prophet replied: "The Jews lie. If God wishes to create the child, you will not be able to divert him from that." (5, p. 4)

Although this last statement seems to be a reaffirmation of the supremacy of God's will, it is interpreted to mean that a human being should not entertain the fear that by using *coitus interruptus* he would be thwarting God's will. If *coitus interruptus* prevents the birth of a child, it is only because God also wills it so, and if God wishes a child to be born, it will be born.

Having reviewed the above evidence, the Grand Mufti concludes with the statement: "Accordingly we hereby give our judgement with confidence in favor of family planning" (5, p. 5).

Since Moslem theologians have pronounced it lawful—with or without conditions—for a Moslem to practice birth control, what impact are these pronouncements expected to have? First of all, a fatwa, or a respected Moslem opinion, naturally has much influence among the more reflective and pious Moslems; that is, among those who need to reconcile their behavior more consciously with what is acceptable to Islam. Even though a Moslem does not have to accept the opinion of the Mufti and is entitled to his own interpretation of the true belief, an official fatwa does give special weight and authority to the particular point of view it endorses. When a fatwa seems to express a liberal interpretation of a question, it usually means that educated public opinion is already aligned with this interpretation. For a national family-planning program the issuance of a fatwa giving religious support and sanction to birth control is very important. A government or a private group would have real difficulty in a Moslem country if they decided to establish a family-planning program in direct opposition to a fatwa categorically condemning the use of contraception.

What about the situation at the level of the peasant? Recently, a sheikh in an Egyptian Delta village was shouted down by the villagers and strongly reprimanded when he stood up, one Friday, and talked of the benefits to health and welfare of family planning. Obviously, so far as this group of peasants was concerned, the fact that official Moslem opinion considered birth control lawful did not crucially influence or alter their own thoughts and feelings about the matter. This does not, however, mean that religious belief is irrelevant. It simply means that the beliefs and values relating to procreation and childbirth among some Moslem peasants have less to do with the sinfulness or lawfulness of the practice of contraception than with other levels of their own belief system. What is really more pertinent, I believe, is their view of the world and the basic values and assumptions underlying their social system.

The Moslem Peasant World View and Its Relationship to Population Control

A world view is the way people perceive the realities around them, how they explain their relationship to these realities, and the characteristic attitudes and approaches they have developed to confront them. Many of the premises and values that underlie the world view operate on a subconscious level, even though they deeply color people's overt behavior. Descriptions of peasant cultures by such eminent anthropologists as Redfield, George M. Foster, and Oscar Lewis have shown that peasants in different parts of the world, because of circumstances, share many basic life orientations and values. Here I shall concentrate on the Moslem peasant but will make reference to Mexican peasants to point out some of these basic similarities.

The peasant's perception of his world is affected by the fact that he lives close to nature with its inexorable laws and unpredictable capriciousness. He understands some of its patterns, and uses and minipulates them to his advantage, but he does not basically transform nor completely control them.

Not only does the peasant feel he has little control over the natural world around him, on which his survival depends, but he also feels helpless in his relations to the larger world of men. Peasant societies are not self-contained independent units with all controls and sanctions emanating from within them. Peasant societies are, as A. L. Kroeber defines them, "part-societies with part cultures" (6). They are only one segment of the larger socioeconomic and political structure embracing the towns and the cities, as well as the peasant village. While peasant society receives ideas and material things from the town and the city, it supplies some of the basic needs of the town. The peasant community, however, stands in a subordinate relationship to the urban community, which exercises great authority and control over it.

Foster, discussing the Mexican peasants of Tzintzuntzan, says:

> The peripheral, dependent position of peasants seems to produce the conditions responsible for their view of life, and the behavior that, because they hold this view, they consider appropriate. Peasants have not understood, and they do not understand, the rules of the game of living that prevail in cities, to which they are bound, and for this ignorance they are at the mercy of personal and impersonal urban controls. . . . (7, p. 10)

> Peasants . . . can be thought of as classifying both the supernatural and the urban sides of life as equally unknowable and uncontrollable, places inhabited by beings with enormous powers for good and evil, whose motives and actions are exercised capriciously and unpredictably, against which man has no certain defenses. Magical spells or other positive acts of intervention are useless in the face of these conditions. Whether dealing with the saints or the city merchant or ruler, rural man must plead and supplicate, propitiate and fawn; if the heart of the power is moved to compassion, the peasant may achieve what he wishes. But the peasant will never know why the heart has been moved, or why compassion is forthcoming on one occasion and denied on the next. The knowable, by contrast, is limited to the tight little world which abuts the peasant and his village. (7, p. 11)

The Egyptian, like other Moslem peasants, sees all nature and all that happens to it and to himself as willed by the Creator, or God. He will plant his seeds, irrigate, weed, use pesticides, and rotate his crops knowing from experience and example that nature will respond better when thus maintained, but he believes that the eventual result of all this effort will, in reality, be what God wills.

Existing on the edge of survival, with little control over his livelihood, his health, life and death, or even over the actions of powerful men, the Egyptian peasant lives in constant fear of what is in store for him. Despite all care, the cotton worm may suddenly appear and wipe out the one crop that usually provides all family needs for the year; children and adults who are seemingly healthy may suddenly fall ill and possibly die. No one really knows what fortune or misfortunes a particular year may bring. Fear is a very real and basic syndrome in Egyptian peasant society. The same seems to be true of other peasant societies. Foster, in his description of a Mexican village, writes:

> Timidity and fear, of the known and of the unknown, of the real or only the suspected threat, mark everyone's behavior. People fear poverty, old age, the death of their spouses, of their

children, and above all their own deaths while still young, because this will leave their small children alone in a hostile world where no one will tend them the way parents would. Gossip is feared, eavesdropping is feared, envy is feared, anger is feared, fierce dogs are feared, and sleeping alone is feared. (7, p. 103)

There is even fear among Egyptian peasants when good fortune strikes. The evil eye, the result of envy or lack of humility, can readily change good fortune into misfortune: wealth can suddenly disappear; a promising son can turn bad; a wedding can turn into a funeral; and a beautiful healthy baby into a sick child. People need to conceal some of the good things with which they have been blessed to avert the evil eye. When a son is born, a blessing in peasant society, one declares it a girl; one does not say that a beautiful child is beautiful; and a woman will try to prolong childbirth in order not to be envied for having had an easy delivery. There are also evil spirits and jinn who can induce depressions or sickness in the mind and can possess a woman and make her sterile. This fear of spirits and the evil eye is, of course, common to other peasant societies.*

Charms, amulets, and ritualistic observances may be potent against these dangers, but above all God must be on your side. For example, the zar, an ancient curing ceremony in Egypt, in addition to incantations, drums, music, and dancing to exorcise evil spirits, also makes constant use of the name of God. One uses God's name again and again to bless every event. Any declaration of intent or wish should be followed by "if God wills," or "with God's permission." Any action must be initiated "in the name of God, the Bountiful, the Merciful." God's name must always be on the lips, for the use of His name is never in vain. He is the Omnipotent, the Decider, the Giver, the Affectionate, and all His ninety-nine names impress upon man that He is the source of all power and all bounty. Therefore, to stand up against the will of God would be a great sin and a terrible risk, when life's dangers can only be averted

* See, for example, Lewis (8, pp. 280, 282, 367).

and life's successes can only be attained *in shā ʻAllah,* "if God wills."

It is not surprising that the Moslem peasant, living so precariously, should decide that fate, as determined by Allah, is responsible not only for the pleasures and good things of life, but also for its misfortunes and pain. An old Moslem adage even goes so far as to say "God must be thanked even for misfortune." Surely life would be insupportable were the peasant to believe himself responsible, by his own deeds and efforts, for all that befalls him. It is, therefore, understandable that the Egyptian peasants should select from their Moslem traditions those injunctions that emphasize man's subordination to God and stress that all human successes can be achieved only if God wills it so. Misfortunes are more easily borne if one really believes that "what is written on the forehead must be seen by the eye"; that is, that all is determined and predestined by God.

This does not mean that the peasant believes that if all is determined by God, he can sit back and wait for what life has in store for him. The attitude, expressed by many, is: "We do our best, then the rest is up to God." The Egyptian peasant does work hard, and he does use better agricultural methods whenever their effectiveness is clearly demonstrated. There are limits to his ambitiousness because there are limits to possibilities of improvement; but when he can educate his children he does so, and when new opportunities seem real he tries to take advantage of them. One should also realize that God's will and fate are often used, consciously or unconsciously, to shift personal responsibility to outside forces. Very often, the peasant refuses responsibility or blame for negligence on the basis that he has done his best and that there was nothing he could do if God has willed that things go wrong. God's will is also often given as an explanation for behavior that the peasant himself follows for nonreligious, temporal reasons.

Clearly, with very limited scope for the improvement of one's lot, contentment becomes a very important virtue. Hamed Ammar, in *Growing Up in an Egyptian Village,* emphasizes the importance of contentment when describing how the accumulation of wealth is not included in the peasants' social incentives for work:

For contentment with what one possesses, as predestined by God, is the keynote of the villagers' happiness. In some dwellings and guest houses this ideal is written on the wall, "Contentment is an inexhaustible treasure." One should not amass wealth, but should spend it in pious acts, otherwise, according to the Koran, as Ali [the key informant] recited: "With the gold and silver a man accumulates he would be seared on the forehead, on the side, and on the back." He added that the prophetic tradition runs that if people are contented, God will look after them as He looks after the birds that leave their nests on feeling hungry and return to them well satisfied. Another prophetic tradition maintains that there are two types of people whose hunger is never satisfied: the searcher for knowledge and the searcher for wealth, and while the first is praised the second is condemned. This does not mean that the Koran or the prophetic tradition encourages apathy, as one can quote other statements conducive to hard work. But the mere fact that the statements, related by Ali and uttered by a great number of the literate villagers, are those exalting contentment, asceticism and submission to fate, to the exclusion of any others, shows a kind of selectivity in values entertained by the villagers. . . . Contentment thus actually means satisfaction with what one can get without the undue strain of striving to get ahead or the strenuous efforts for satisfying numerous material demands. It would be very difficult, with the fellah's simple tools and the sweat involved in his work, to convince him that his lot could be improved by more work. (9, p. 35)

Lewis also finds similar responses to life's insecurities among Mexican peasants:

Other traits, such as fatalism, stoicism in the face of misfortune, passivity, acceptance of things as they are and a general readiness to expect the worst, tend to lift from the individual the burden of personal responsibility for his fate, and perhaps help to explain the relative absence of guilt and self-blame. (8, p. 302)

Conservatism seems also to stem from the fact that the peasant needs to keep not only God but his fellow men on his side. God stays on one's side if one never angers Him; and one keeps one's fellow men on one's side by following the socially accepted and sanctioned behavior patterns of the group. In other words, conservatism spells security; safety lies in following all the rules of the game of society. This kind of conservatism has been observed elsewhere, as Foster writes:

> . . . Incapable of taking frontal action against the extra-village forces that control them, peasants have had to be content with local rules of the game of living—their cultures—which provide them with behavior norms which spell some defense in a world they see, quite rightly, as hostile and threatening. (7, pp. 300, 302)

A lack of foresight or concern about the future is another feature of the Egyptian peasant's attitude towards life. This is obviously congruent with the acceptance of God's transcendental will as controlling all things. However, both Lewis (8, p. 114) and Foster (7, p. 11) comment upon lack of foresight and relative unconcern about the future as a typical feature of other peasant societies.

The question of how the peasant's world view is related to family planning now needs to be explored. First, there is no special reason why the peasant, who takes his entire life for granted, should question so natural a process as procreation. He has little control over many of the forces around him, and least of all over birth and death. Second, as preliminary investigations have shown, when the possibility of control of procreation is presented to the Egyptian peasant, his world view as well as the positive value of children in his society—a topic to be discussed later—militate against its immediate acceptance. His hesitation is not due to any belief that the use of contraceptives is sinful, for as already noted, the religious leaders have pronounced it lawful, but rather to the fear of the consequences of attempting to challenge the will of God. Considering the fact that young children are constantly in danger of contracting illnesses, many of which turn out to be fatal, that infant mortality in peasant communities is 150 per thousand per year or above, and that 50 per cent or so of the children do not survive the first five years of life, it is understandable that fear and anxiety should underlie concern over children's welfare and survival.

Among Egyptian peasants these basic fears are projected in all kinds of behavior patterns. All types of charms and rituals are widely used to avoid illness and its consequences. One does not count one's children lest one endanger their lives. (Hence, questionnaires asking for the number of children are reluctantly answered.) It is like counting one's blessings; one may soon find oneself without them.

A peasant woman who for overriding reasons does not wish to have any more children will go ahead and use contraception, or even induce abortion. Thousands of peasant women currently use modern contraceptives offered in family-planning clinics when their health seems affected by numerous pregnancies or when they are assured as many or more surviving children as they want. But a contraceptive user may nevertheless harbor the anxiety that she may be pitting her will against God's and live in dread of consequences. The following incident shows how these underlying fears still operate even when birth control is practiced.

A peasant woman who had six grown-up children and who had decided to practice birth control refused to answer the question whether she intended to use contraception for spacing or in order not to have any more children. After much probing, her indirect answer was: "The Sheikh in the Mosque has been telling us, 'How dare you try and decide how many children you will have.' What if God turns around and takes away those you already have?" Obviously, she was not willing to state emphatically that she did not wish to have any more than the six children she already had for fear of losing them.*

The arguments used by one daya, or village midwife, to keep

---

* The examples used here and in the next three paragraphs are from field data collected by the author as part of the Population Project of the Social Research Center of the American University in Cairo.

women away from birth control are interesting for what they reveal about the level of belief to which she tries to appeal. Being herself part of the peasant culture, she keenly intuits what arguments would be effective. A woman worrying about her youngest boy's illness was told: "What do you expect? So long as you are using these pills, this child will not get well and that will be the cause of his death." As would be expected, the woman's answer was: "Then I will stop taking them."

The daya tries also to relate whatever misfortune hits the village to family planning, as when she propagated the following rumor about the census, which in people's minds is associated with family planning: "Once a questionnaire was circulated and people began to count the houses, then we had a terrible period in the village when both animals and people were dying by the dozen, and the village became frightened. The onions were not coming up, and the land did not produce any crops."

The daya's other pronatalist argument is that the number of children a woman will have is predestined and she can neither have more nor less than what "has been written." "Nothing can prevent conception," she declares, "for women are like chickens. They have a cluster which contains the number of children they will each have. One woman's cluster may have one child, another may have twenty." It is interesting that the same daya, after relaxing to the interviewer admitted: "I have not become pregnant during the last fourteen years. Many people have been urging me to go and seek treatment, but I refused because I had a son who died at nineteen years of age, and I grieved for him so much that I did not wish to have any more children. But, of course," she quickly added, "I feel that God will ask me to repay." In other words, having admitted that by her own action or inaction she had prevented pregnancy, she tried to be consistent with her pronatalist position by quickly shifting the argument and placing the emphasis not on the idea that one cannot prevent what is predetermined, but on the notion that one may anger God, whose will one is trying to oppose.

Another element in the basic orientation of peasants that obviously militates against family planning is the general acceptance of one's lot and the lack of foresight and planning. As would be expected, a large number of children are discovered to be a heavy burden only too late to do anything about the situation.

I would like to put in a cautionary word about taking religious arguments at their face value. Religious concerns may very well be the real basis for people's attitudes towards family planning, but investigators should remember that, in Moslem society, religious arguments are often used to explain behavior that is motivated by, or desirable for, other important reasons, such as the positive value of children. And in peasant society—particularly Moslem peasant society—there are many factors and conditions that make procreation and children positive values. I shall now consider some of these.

The Socioeconomic Structure and Attitudes toward Procreation

The great importance of the family for the welfare, and at times even the survival, of the individual in peasant society is stressed everywhere in the literature.

" 'To have no people' (that is, kin) is one of the greatest insults that could be directed to any person," comments Ammar about the attitude of the people in an upper Egyptian village (9, p. 56). Referring to the individualism of the Mexican peasant, Lewis says:

> Economic independence and individualism do not preclude certain loyalties, identification and reciprocities with others, but rather make these imperative for survival. Loyalty and cooperation within the biological family is a necessary adjunct to individual independence. Without a family to back him up, the individual stands unprotected and isolated, a prey to every form of aggression, exploitation, and humiliation known in Tepoztlan. The fate of lone widows and of orphaned or fatherless children is generally a sad one, even when the extended family offers help. (8, p. 296)

One of the big arguments for encouraging childbirth put forward by the village midwife is the importance of the large family. "The large family is better; a family of twenty, thirty, or forty is, of course, best. This is the difference between large and small, the difference between the river and the stream. A small family is very miserable indeed." The fact is that the number of adult males largely determines the economic and social security of the Egyptian peasant family. Economically, the more earners and workers there are in the family, the higher the income and the less traumatic and devastating to the whole family is the sickness or death of one of its important providers. In times of stress it is the kin on whom one depends for support, and the closer the kinship the greater the support. As the old Arab proverb goes: "My brother and I against my cousin; my cousin and I against the stranger." In areas of Egypt where a vendetta system exists that obligates the males of a family to seek revenge for any offenses committed against the family the ability of the family to counteract aggression or even avoid it is directly related to the available number of strong adult males.

Another factor that affects the birth rate is the importance of early marriage and the building of a family to a young male peasant. First, the wife is a valuable asset as a helper in all the activities necessary for obtaining a livelihood. Second, children are important for providing extra hands and, when they can be hired out, extra cash. Not only are children of paramount importance as nonsalaried labor to increase the family's productivity, but they also relieve their parents from part of the hard work and make it possible for them to enjoy some leisure time and to participate in the social life of the village. Boys are particularly important in helping their fathers in the field, and mothers wish to have girls also in order to get relief from the many chores allotted to a peasant woman, including taking care of younger children. Both boys and girls start carrying work responsibilities very early. A very small boy walking behind a loaded donkey or attending the water wheel or a tiny girl carrying a newborn infant are familiar sights in rural Egypt. Children can start contributing extra cash to the family income very early in life. Cotton, the main cash crop in Egypt, not only uses but requires child labor for certain operations, such as picking off the cotton worm and harvesting. Indeed, "children are the adornment of life," as the Koran says.

Sons, in particular, have a high premium in Middle Eastern peasant society; this is reflected in many popular sayings—"A boy is a joy even if he is stillborn" and "A boy who dies is better than seven girls" (9, p. 95). Their status is further reinforced by the Moslem Sharī'a law and by the stress laid by tradition on the responsibilities of boys toward their parents and sisters. In the Moslem patrilineal, patrilocal society, the son carries the name of the family and gives it continuity, whereas the girl is lost to the family if she marries outside the lineage. A son also preserves all inherited land and wealth within the family. Other aspects of Moslem inheritance laws put further premium on the boy—this is so beyond peasant society, and especially among the well-to-do. First, a boy inherits from his parents twice as much as a girl; second, in case a family has daughters and no sons, the girls inherit only half of the wealth and the rest goes outside the nuclear family to uncles, cousins, or other close kin.

A son is also the main security for his parents, and even his sisters, in illness and old age. The Sharī'a law makes it obligatory for the boy to provide for indigent parents. If he should fail to do so, the parents have a right to sue in court and force him to provide an alimony. Custom makes a boy also responsible for his sister and, as a maternal uncle, he has numerous responsibilities towards his sister's children. If she does not marry, he and other male members of the family are responsible for feeding and clothing her.

Because health conditions are poor there is high infant and child mortality in Egyptian villages, so a family needs to have a large number of children to insure the survival of more than one male child into adulthood. Thus, rural families will wait until a large number of children have survived beyond the earlier precarious years before the notion of family planning can be entertained.

The status and role of women within the peasant family is an additional factor that militates against population control. By and large, the status of the woman is subordinate to that of the man. All her important functions are performed within the family system and her status is derived from her family roles of wife and mother. In a Moslem peasant society with so much premium placed on children, particularly boys, the status of the married woman and her sense of security is intimately tied up to her procreational function.

A married woman is a low-status member of a household until she bears children, especially sons; then she is referred to as the "mother of the children" or "mother of the first-born son." There is no greater stress or insecurity than that which faces a sterile woman in Egyptian peasant society. The aim of marriage is to build a family, and the husband of a sterile wife is fully justified in the eyes of the society in taking a second wife or even divorcing her.

"A childless woman," says an Egyptian peasant, "is usually like a she-camel who does not conceive, puts on more and more flesh . . . but [is] not fruitful. . . . [She can never make her husband proud] amongst the menfolk. She is [like] a sore eye to her family. The proper woman is the one who is an 'envelope for conception.' "

If a husband should marry a second wife who bears boys, the sterile wife's lot is a very sorry one indeed. She is expected to work for her rival and to be content with very little attention from other members of the family. There is a feeling that she has to work for her keep and that it is good enough of the husband not to have sent her back to her family. The mother of the boys, on the other hand, is pampered, and her demands are readily met. It is not surprising that folk medicine abounds with prescriptions that are supposed to cure women of sterility, and that a majority of the clients at the zar curing ceremony are sterile women.

Polygamy and men's right to divorce at will add greatly to women's insecurity in a Moslem society. Some peasant women try to have as many children as possible in order to make it impossible for the husband to afford a second wife and to make it difficult for him to consider a divorce.

The existence of the extended-family pattern, in which a number of adults share the responsibility of taking care of young children, greatly lightens the burden of child rearing in a Moslem peasant society. Furthermore, the fact that peasant women do not play any significant roles outside the home that would conflict or place strains on their maternal roles also minimizes the burden of children.

In short, the perceived benefits and values derived from children in a Moslem peasant society greatly outweigh the perceived cost.

Conclusion

World view, basic beliefs, and life circumstances of the peasant all seem to be strongly conducive to high fertility. What hope is there, then, for population control? Not very much, I am afraid, where peasant life has undergone little transformation. It is my own belief that little can be done to change the attitudes of traditional peasant societies by merely setting up family-planning clinics or by repeating to people that religion does not oppose birth control.

Peasant society must develop economically and socially in such a way that the world begins to appear less threatening. It must appear to the peasant as a place where greater control is possible over the forces around him; where existence other than at a subsistence level seems feasible; where health and nutrition levels are higher and children have a greater chance of survival; where kin and children are no longer the only source of security; where women are given the opportunity to play other than family roles and to develop a new concept of self in which personal achievement has an important place and where motherhood is not viewed as the all-important goal and the only means to achieve status; where children demand more attention and greater economic, social, and psychological investment from parents so that they constitute both a cost and a benefit; and where education brings enlightenment and exciting new opportunities for individual effort to lead to achievement.

To bring about such changes will require rapid economic and social development in countries with large peasant populations—a development that they are incapable of achieving through their own efforts and resources. Both a greater and a changed awareness by the international community of the developmental needs of the poorer nations and of the relationship between such development and population control is necessary. Perhaps the emphasis that a dollar spent in family planning is more valuable than ten dollars in development was tenable as a propaganda slogan at a time when people refused to worry enough about population growth. We have reached the point, however, at which the need to do something about unchecked population growth is acknowledged in both developed and developing countries. In addition to expanding and improving family-planning services, efforts now should be directed toward discovering ways of bringing about those conditions that will ensure that the dollar spent on family planning is a dollar well spent. In that context, the dollar that is put into real development becomes a double investment.

References

1. Robert Redfield. *Peasant Society and Culture.* Chicago: University of Chicago Press, 1958.
2. Dudley Kirk. "Factors Affecting Moslem Natality," Paper presented to International Conference on Family Planning Programs, Geneva, August 23–27, 1965. Summarized in *Muslim Attitudes towards Family Planning.* New York: Population Council, 1967.
3. Muhammad Sallab Madkour. *Nazrat al-Islam ila tanzim al-nasl.* Cairo: Dar al-nahdat al-Arabiya, 1965. P. 26.

4. al-Syyid Yusef bin Ali al-Zawawi. "Fatwa: Ruling for Birth Control," *Muslim Attitudes toward Family Planning*. New York: Population Council, 1967. P. 9.
5. Sheidh Abdullah Al-Qalqili. "Fatwa: Family Planning in Islam," *Muslim Attitudes toward Family Planning*. New York: Population Council, 1967.
6. A. L. Kroeber. *Anthropology*. New York: Harcourt Brace Jovanovich, 1948. P. 284.
7. George M. Foster. *Tzintzuntzan*. Boston: Little Brown, and Company, 1967. P. 10.
8. Oscar Lewis. *Life in a Mexican Village*. Urbana, Ill.: University of Illinois Press, 1963.
9. Hamed Ammar. *Growing Up in an Egyptian Village*. London: Routledge & Kegan Paul, 1966.

Discussion of Dr. El-Hamamsy's Paper

ALAN W. HORTON

Alan W. Horton is Executive Director of the American Universities Field Staff.

Dr. El-Hamamsy's paper confirms several propositions that have been wandering about in search of approval throughout this volume. She has given us a clear exposition of the place of a belief system in a peasant society, with a heartening abundance of confirming material. Because Dr. El-Hamamsy's confirmations are largely evident, I shall confine myself to three remarks.

First, those who, like myself, have long been concerned with the Middle East will be intrigued to consider the position of this paper in the history of Middle East studies. Dr. El-Hamamsy's paper is something of a breakthrough. Samuel Zwemer, an American Protestant missionary living at the turn of the century, wrote *Studies in Popular Islam* (1) and other books in which he—like others of his era—saw Islam as a kind of great and grim disembodiment hanging over an otherwise pleasant part of the world. Even today students of the Middle East are not entirely free of this view. Now Dr. El-Hamamsy has made a clear statement on the place of Islam in Middle Eastern peasant culture and, by extension, on the place of other world religions in peasant cultures; and she has written the best statement to date on the relation of Islam to family planning. The similarities between her statements and those of Sanders about Latin America are striking.

Parenthetically, Dr. El-Hamamsy did not mention in support of her argument the beguiling fact that Egyptian Coptic Christian peasants—other things being equal—have precisely the same views about contraception as Egyptian Moslem peasants.

My second remark has to do with the relation of family-planning programs to general development, an underlying theme

358

throughout this volume. Dr. El-Hamamsy clearly implies that effective family planning is a function of proper development and over-all schemes for modernization. One of the fascinating arguments in this field is between this view (expressed by El-Hamamsy, Sanders, Lewis, and others) that effective family planning depends on the creation of new beliefs fostered by development and the other view (expressed carefully and with many qualifications) that a family-planning program can take root on its own merits, be self-sustaining, and survive effectively with infusions of elite or foreign energy. A discussion about these two different approaches would be helpful.

Third, the term "grass roots" has been used in reference to areas ranging from Africa to Japan. It was good to be reminded that in some areas of the world the rural-urban dichotomy remains a useful concept, and that in other areas it has outlived its usefulness.

The concept has meaning in the Middle East, providing one uses it with care. The dichotomy applies to westernized urbanites, on the one hand, and rural and urban poor, on the other. But this dichotomous relationship is not static. Two processes are at work, and neither of them is peculiar to the Middle East. One is a process whereby peasant mentalities are being urbanized; the other is a process whereby the mentalities of urban poor are being modernized. The two processes are in some ways similar and certainly evince a sameness of social direction. Although rural and urban poor may never completely develop the westernized urbanism found among modernized persons in Middle Eastern cities (a kind of urbanism that is in our day becoming universal), the road on which they are traveling is definable in those terms. ⸰

Let us take a rural case from northern Syria, a village some twenty miles from Aleppo where I did field work in the early 1950s. The village's rapid rate of change was fascinating. To oversimplify its history, the village in 1921 was almost totally out of communication with Aleppo. For at least two hundred years Ottoman power had been declining, and rural security was only occasional. When the French took over the mandate

for Syria in 1921, they established for the first time in centuries a complete rural security system. Peasants were suddenly
able to work in the fields alone instead of in groups, without
fear of losing lives as well as crops. Before that time a few
villagers in an armed group had made one annual trip to Aleppo
to trade their few cash crops for a very few necessities, but now
many villagers could go separately to Aleppo; the macadam
road near the village was built in 1927, and by 1933 all village
men and many village women made the trip to Aleppo by rural
bus many times a year. With rural security and all-weather roads,
there was a sudden interest in the growth of cash crops such
as fruit trees and cotton, and a whole series of new links between the village and Aleppo emerged. In short, a constantly
expanding communications network provided not only new
channels for economic activity but also channels for the spread
of modern urban attitudes. The mental make-up of villagers in
1921 had changed markedly by 1953—and at least as much
again, presumably, by 1970.

The contrast with Japan is instructive. There the rural-urban
dichotomy is no longer useful. A more apt concept has been
described by Leonard Reissman (2), namely, the concept of
a national urban society—one in which the mentality gap between rural and urban areas is minimal. A kind of "peasantry"
works Japanese land, but it is a peasantry with modern urban
values. An almost total communications network, including
schools and television, covers the country.

In terms of family planning, what are the implications of
these remarks? One of them is that effective communications
channels are a prerequisite to the total process of change that is
currently known as modernization. A small part of this process
involves changed attitudes on family planning and other social
and personal responsibilities—and downward population curves
depend on such changed attitudes.

References

1. Samuel M. Zwemer. *Studies in Popular Islam.* London: Sheldon Press; New York: The Macmillan Company, 1939.
2. Leonard Reissman. "Cities, Urbanization, and Change." Paper given at the American Universities Field Staff Conference, "Urbanization: Freedom and Diversity in the Modern City," December 12–13, 1968, University of Alabama.

Some Conclusions

HARRISON BROWN

The most important conclusion that has emerged from this volume is by no means a new one. Simply stated, we are confronted by a complex of interrelated problems, none of which can be divorced from the others. Rapid population growth is a very important element of that complex, but it cannot be isolated from the problems of technological change, economic development, the resource base, the environment, religion, politics, government, and the individual desires of $3\frac{1}{2}$ billion human beings. Our second important conclusion is that it is by no means clear that we are going to be able to extricate ourselves from the mess we are in.

The world is now fissioning into two quite separate cultures. The first, the culture of the rich, is made up of close to 1000 million persons having a per capita gross national product of about $2300. The second is the culture of the poor. This is made up of some 2500 million persons having a per capita GNP of about $180 or thirteen-fold less than that characteristic of the rich countries.*

From a monetary point of view the rich countries are getting richer; their per capita GNP is increasing 4 per cent yearly. Largely because of high rates of population growth, the lot of the average person in the poor countries is improving much more slowly—about 2 per cent per year. Thus the thirteen-fold gap between the per capita GNPs of the rich and the poor is increasing.

As an illustration of where this growing gap could lead us, if present rates continue, the poorer countries would reach the level of per capita income now characteristic of richer countries

* Source: The Statistical Abstract of the United States, 1970. Published by the U.S. Department of Commerce.

in 130 years. But by that time, at present rates of growth, the population of the poorer countries would be 130 billion persons! Also by that time the per capita GNPs of the richer countries would be about $860,000 or 370 times greater than that of the poorer countries today!

Clearly this fissioning process cannot continue indefinitely. Something has to give, and that "something," whatever it is, will probably "give" within the next two or three decades. This could take the form of a reversal of per capita economic growth in the poor countries and a more or less permanent division of the world into two groups: the affluent minority and the miserable majority. A more likely scenario is that the poor countries in their misery will erupt and that the rich countries in their stupidity will take sides. We see this happening today in Southeast Asia and in the Middle East. We may well see such developments become widespread in the years ahead and lead to all-out nuclear war, in which case the poor—if any population survives—shall inherit the earth.

Our discussions of the interrelationships between economic and social development and fertility have made it clear that rapid economic development of the poor countries is an essential element in reducing fertility and creating a world where people can lead lives free of the fear of starvation and free of the fear of nuclear holocaust. But most of us are convinced that they cannot do it by themselves. They need the help of the richer nations. Here we are faced with two primary questions: How much help can be given by the rich? How much help can be effectively absorbed by the poor?

At the present time, capital transfers for development from the richer countries to the poor (worldwide) comes to somewhat over $7 billion or less than one-third of 1 per cent of the collective GNPs of the richer countries. Although this is scarcely a burden and is grossly inadequate, it nevertheless represents some 1.5 per cent of the GNPs of the poorer countries. Here we must ask how high capital transfers should be if development is to take place at a rate that is truly commensurate with the need. Clearly, more money could be put to effective use to accelerate development, but on the basis of everything we think we know about the development process there is probably an upper limit to the level of capital transfers that could really be used to good advantage. That limit appears to be determined by the availability of the kinds of people who can make the decisions and carry out the necessary work of the development process.

If by some magic the flow of capital from the rich countries to the poor were suddenly to double, the additional funds might be absorbed effectively. If the flow were to increase much beyond that, however, there would almost certainly be a limit imposed by the scarcity of trained people. We must simply recognize that, in the long run, the time scale for development is the time scale for the training and education of people. There is no such thing as "instant development." We cannot expect to see dramatically rapid reductions in human fertility in the greater part of the developing world in the immediate future.

Nevertheless, there is a great deal that could be done to expedite the development process and to decrease fertility if the nations of the world would act forcefully and rapidly. For example, if the richer countries (those with above-average GNPs, including the U.S.S.R.) agreed to contribute approximately 1 per cent of their GNPs to a development fund, some $25 billion would be available annually for development purposes—an amount representing the respectable figure of 5 per cent of the GNPs of the poorer nations. Naturally such a high level of capital transfer would not be reached instantaneously. But within a few years it could be absorbed effectively if it were coupled properly with an expanded level of technical assistance.

To obtain from the richer nations an average of 1 per cent of their GNPs, one might wish to put the assessments on a sliding scale much like our income tax: The richer a country is on a per capita basis the greater would be its contribution as a proportion of its GNP. Similarly, the distribution of the collected funds among the developing countries should be placed on a priority basis depending upon the abilities of the individual countries to absorb capital effectively. Those countries that have almost no trained people would be very low on the priority list. Other countries that are able to absorb capital effectively would be high on the list.

Were the richer nations of the world to adopt the "1 per cent rule," the United States, whose GNP represents a sizable fraction of the total GNP of the donor nations, would be expected to make the largest single contribution, amounting to about $10 billion. This seems like a great deal until we compare it with the United States' military expenditures since World War II—which total no less that $1000 billion since 1946. Its military expenditures in 1969 alone amounted to some twenty times its expenditures for assistance to the developing countries.

We can obtain some perspective concerning the tremendous role of military expenditures in the richer and the poorer countries when we examine the table below, which gives expenditures for 1969 as compiled by the U.S. Arms Control and Disarmament Agency in its annual review of arms expenditures.

	Richer countries	*Poorer countries*
Military expenditures	$174 billion	$26 billion
Military expenditures as percentage of GNP	7.8 per cent	4.8 per cent
Public-education expenditures	$115 billion	$13 billion
Public-health expenditures	$54 billion	$5 billion
Rate of increase of military expenditures	7 per cent	15 per cent
Rate of increase of GNP	9 per cent	10 per cent

We see that in both the developed and developing countries military expenditures exceed expenditures for public education and public health combined. We see further that in the poorer countries military expenditures are climbing more rapidly than the GNPs. Although the poor countries spend a smaller proportion of their GNPs on military establishments than do the richer ones, the amount spent seriously impedes development. Further, the poor countries, stimulated in part by the polarizations created by the cold war, spend four times as much on military matters than they receive in foreign economic aid.

These figures suggest that arms expenditures of the developing countries over and above their needs for internal security should be subtracted from their allocations from the development fund. Those developing nations which insist upon maintaining large military establishments should receive little or no help.

What would the 1 per cent rule mean for the United States, whose assessment based on a sliding scale might be $10 billion? In 1970, U.S. foreign aid (including military aid) was some $4.1 billion, and U.S. military expenditures were about $80 billion, of which perhaps $25 billion were for Vietnam. Clearly an assessment of some $10 billion could come from cutbacks in military expenditures. There is plenty there if the United States could only get out from under.

It is essential that we in the United States turn outward and look at the problems of the world as a whole, yet we cannot ignore our slums, our own hungry and miserable, our system of medical services that is likely to fall apart at the seams, our cracking educational system, and our needs for housing and transportation. New cities are needed that will accommodate 20 million persons, but practically nothing is being done to plan these cities, let alone build them. A tremendous amount of research and development is needed on these problems. For years now America has been experiencing a process of technical, industrial, and human deterioration. Huge sums of money will be needed to reverse this trend and undo the damage already done.

If the United States could cut its military expenditures by a factor of 2, $40 billion would be released to help solve its foreign and domestic problems. Subtracting $10 billion for its share of international development would leave about $30 billion that could be applied to its own domestic problems. This is a very respectable figure.

Because the forces that support large military appropriations are strong, it will be difficult to achieve the liberation of such funds. But I am convinced that it can be done and that it can be done safely.

1. We must get out of Vietnam, where we should not have gone in the first place.

2. We must explore vigorously all possibilities for achieving a real measure of détente with the Soviet Union. I believe that this can be done partly by agreement and partly by small, but significant, unilateral actions. Examples of such an action would be a 5 per cent decrease in "standard" military budgets, which could be undertaken with no danger, and an announcement that if the Soviets follow suit, we will reduce expenditures by an additional 5 per cent the following year. In progressive steps our military expenditures would be down by a factor of 2 in about ten years.

3. There must be international agreements on conventional arms shipments to developing countries. It is unlikely that this can be brought about in the absence of a détente.

4. We should take the leadership in establishing truly effective peacekeeping mechanisms within the United Nations, including the establishment of more effective ways of resolving international disputes and the creation of permanent United Nations armed peacekeeping forces.

5. We should secure agreement by the richer nations to allocate 1 per cent of their GNPs to a United Nations fund for development within the framework of a carefully worked out series of guidelines for making allocations.

6. I seriously doubt that such sweeping changes can be brought about, including the resolution of our internal problems, unless the people of this country do something about Congress. As it is organized at present, Congress is an anachronism, run in large part by old men who do not understand the nature of the modern world. Every effort should be made through the political process to defeat at the polls those senators and representatives who block progress and to replace them with younger people who are in tune with the times, who will push Congressional reform, who will abolish the archaic seniority system which

prevents our taking a multiplicity of important actions. Certainly in this vast country there must be men of the quality of Jefferson, Hamilton, Madison, and Jay, who in their twenties, thirties and early forties helped develop our Constitution and then helped secure its adoption.

I believe that the most important single activity that young people can engage in today is to help weed from Congress the senile, the stupid, and the inflexible, and elect in their place men of intelligence and vigor who can help bring about the changes which are so badly needed.

In my opinion the most important single observation made during our lunar landings was not of the moon itself. The most important observation was that of the Earth, viewed from afar in its majesty as a single body with a single interconnected web of life and a single interconnected humanity. One world; one mankind. Viewed this way, ideological conflicts seem to pale into insignificance.

Yet the world is divided into some 130 nations, each of which likes to call itself sovereign. In short, it is a system of international anarchy that modern technology has rendered obsolete. This is a fact that people must come to grips with *very* soon. World anarchy must be replaced by a system of world law, so people and nations can live in peace.

Alexander Hamilton once asked himself—when he was still under 30—"Why was government instituted at all?" and he answered, "Because the passions of men will not conform to the dictates of reason and justice without constraint."

I believe it is appropriate to end this volume on technological change and population growth with a mention of world law, for it illustrates how the growth of the human population pervades every element of world society. Population growth, its causes, and its consequences represent a vast fabric of interrelated problems, none of which can be solved by itself and most of which must be solved at the world level.

Index

abortion, 29, 30, 123, 134, 141–43, 165–66, 170, 172, 192, 206, 212, 221–22, 241; and Islam, 340, 349; and Latin America, 221–22, 312, 324; and Roman Catholic Church, 311, 312, 314, 316, 324–25

Afghanistan: family planning in, lack of, 204

Africa: age structure in, 22; agriculture in, 66; belief systems in, 330, 332; birth control proposals in, 226; birth rate in, 27, 178, 183; death rate in, 183, 188; education in, 182, 183, 194–95; family planning in, 180, 191, 193, 194, 195, 198, 204–205; family size in, 193–95, 197–198; health in, 11, 188; KAP surveys, 181–82, 191–92, 195; population growth and social structure, 178–83, 187–200; resettlement, 193–94; UN assistance in, 284–85, 288

Agency for International Development: birth control and family planning, 2, 132, 180, 240, 247, 254, 259, 264

age-specific fertility, 27, 28, 29, 31, 39

age structure, 19; in Costa Rica and Denmark, comparison, 22, 23; in less developed countries, 21–22, 28, 29, 53

agricultural population, 3, 9–10, 11, 17, 19n

agriculture, 5–12; animals and livestock, 3–4, 5, 6, 9, 14; in developed countries, 11–12, 66; grains, high-yielding, 45, 70–71, 86–87, 95, 96, 97, 98; in less developed countries, 11, 45–47, 50, 66, 72–99 passim, 111, 186, 243, 244; new technology, 45,

46, 68, 70–71, 81–82, 88, 95, 96, 98–99, 111, 286

Albania: birth rate in, 27

Algeria: birth rate in, 27; family planning in, lack of, 204

Argentina: birth rate in, 228n; population growth in, 327; Roman Catholic Church in, 323

Asia: age structure in, 22; agriculture in, 45, 66; birth rate in, 27; epidemics in, control of, 11; family planning in, 180, 204–205

Asian Population Conference (1963), 282

Australia: birth rate in, 228n; life expectancy in, 20; UN and population problem in, 283

Austria: birth rate in, 228n

Barbados: family planning in, 205; family planning and UN, 291; UN and population problem in, 283

belief systems, 343, 345, 348, 351; in Africa, 330, 332; in Egypt, 344–355 passim, 358; and family planning, 330–34, 341–356 passim, 359; in Mexico, 343–344, 344–45, 347, 351; and sexual customs, 4, 181, 202. See also social structure

birth control and contraception, 10, 23–24, 25, 26, 29, 30, 40, 122–176, 202, 203, 205, 221, 227, 228, 237–42 passim, 260–61, 279, 303; economic incentives proposed, 223–26, 262, 263; by government-imposed methods, 123, 149, 152, 160; governmental planning and political problems, 35, 36, 124, 158–159, 174, 225, 226, 279; and Islam, 339, 340, 348, 349; and legal liability, 156–57; and